GW01238473

Copyright © 2025 by James Hugh Brennan

Published by Modernity Press, Bristol UK

All rights reserved. This book or any portion thereof may not be reproduced or used in any manner whatsoever without the express written permission of the publisher or author, except for the use of brief quotations in a book review or scholarly journal.

All references to clinical material have been heavily disguised and do not depict particular people. They are stories within stories.

Typeset in 11pt Sabon, among fifty animals.

ISBN: 978-1-5272-5502-9

MODERNITY
PRESS

TRAINS OF THOUGHT

A NATURAL HISTORY OF THE MIND

JAMES BRENNAN

To Harriet
for everything

For our children
Tom, Kate, Zoë

In memory of my niece
Eleanor Mary Durman Brennan

And for
the mentally curious

Acknowledgements

I am indebted to

Clare Moynihan, Trevor Parsons, Alice Klein, Mark Barrington, Elisabeth Whipp, Richard Gregory, Anthony and Deborah Feiler, Matthew Ellis, Hugh Herzig, Lucy Johnstone, Robert Campbell, Philip Cooper, Andrew and Christine Brennan, Virginia and Mark Waterkeyn, Shane Matthews, Luke Emrich-Mills, Ian Kane, Julie Alderson, Jonathan Evans, Ian Garbutt, James Johnston, my children Tom, Kate, and Zoë Brennan, and my singularly patient life-partner and wife Harriet Brennan.

None of these people however are to be blamed for the following pages, only me.

JHB

Bristol, 2025

Contents

Preface

The older I get the more I am mesmerised by the astonishing fact of just being alive, thinking these thoughts at this very particular moment. And when I think about that I am reminded that one day my trains of thought will stop, and that this is the same for every one of us.

Being aware of ourselves being alive requires us to have a mind, and it so happens that I have spent my whole life as a psychologist trying to understand what that really means, to have a mind. The ability to *think* is our species' most distinctive and extraordinary feature, but how do our minds actually create our individual sense of reality?

Minds are obviously reared within a biological brain, but they are required to survive within the insanely complex social world that we humans have created for ourselves. So what is this special ability that makes us *thinking* human beings? How does *meaning* come about?

Big questions like these obviously need a bit of unravelling before they can be suitably understood. The Babylonian lunar and solar calendar is one of the oldest known inventions based on systematic observation and thought. It was created nearly 4,000 years ago. In the big scheme of things, not long at all. I have come to appreciate just how recently we humans began to learn to put aside our superstitious beliefs, and base our judgements instead on plausible, evidence-based knowledge as far as it is available.

This way of thinking has probably only been around for a few thousand years and remains fallible, but it is the best we have devised and I believe that by deploying a scientific, natural history approach to thinking about the mind, we are finally able to see more clearly how we all came to be here, living our lives, and thinking our thoughts.

This book is unashamedly about the mind, how it has arisen within Nature, how we might think about it, what it is, how it works, and what this can perhaps tell us about ourselves and the way we live our lives as human beings.

That, I think, is a tale worth telling.

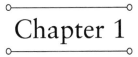

Chapter 1

Waking up

As soon as we sat down, I noticed her expensive leather boots. Well, they looked expensive to me. I didn't think I had seen them before and I imagined they were probably brand new. Today Nell was wearing an elegant cream-coloured suit with earrings and a necklace. I had met her twice before and had noticed that she was always very well turned out. Her make-up and the whole way she presented herself seemed meticulous and carefully thought about.

The referral had suggested that we were meeting because Nell could not accept that she was going to die, and would become furious whenever other people implied that this could happen. And yes, she certainly made it very clear in our first meeting that this would be the case for me too. It was a no-go area, because she was not going to die, so she was not going to talk about it. Naturally I found it interesting that she had agreed to see me.

In that first session Nell told me about the experience of her diagnosis, the sequence of events, but always with an upbeat positive manner, concluding that she was having the best-available treatment, world class, so everything was fine. She only began to cry when she started telling me how vital it was for her to be fully engaged with her life right now – seeing her family, joining her rambling group, time with her dog, her hiking, and the occasional horse riding when she could afford the time. But she did not mention her prognosis.

Nell was thirty-six years old, a doctor training in endocrinology. She had no children, a fact she said she had been thinking about a lot over the past few weeks. She wasn't sure whether not having had children was a regret or a good thing. When I encouraged her to elaborate, she began to say something but soon stopped and would say nothing more.

Despite what I now remember about Nell, the notes that I made following that first meeting reveal that I had found her 'brittle' to work with. A bit further on I wrote that a few hours after our first session I was at home having a meal with my family, when Nell came into my mind again. It felt like a slight intrusion, as if something was scratching for my attention. So, after we had eaten, I tried to think about how she had provoked this feeling in me. It occurred to me that she had left me feeling slightly wary about her, a faintly anxious feeling, as if I were about to sit a test. I wasn't sure what this was, but I felt that there was something more complicated going on than Nell 'simply' not wanting to die.

Nell had begun the second session telling me that she was cross that her medical friends had suddenly become so careful around her. She felt that other people were being sulky, when she was supposedly the ill one. She was repeatedly critical and irritated about her friends who she described as distant and quiet. Yet at the same time she indirectly acknowledged that she had told everyone that she didn't want to discuss her illness.

Whenever Nell described her friends' reactions to her, it always seemed quite plausible that they were just trying to be supportive. She described several incidents in which she appeared to be entirely unaware of the irritation she was showing towards other people. By this point it was clear that she also reacted with disdain to the very few things that I had said since we began. She just wasn't being very nice, and perhaps understandably her friends and I were all feeling a bit wary of her.

So I was in two minds. Part of me recognised something in what she was saying. People often avoid conversations they fear might find socially awkward, particularly so when a fellow doctor is ill. But I also thought it was more likely that her friends were feeling pushed away and had become careful in view of her irritability and short temper. Her bristling incisive anger often seemed as if she was trying to keep me at bay too, yet here she was again, having returned for a second session, and very much wanting to make sense of it all.

After a few minutes I tried to summarise and reflect on what she had told me, and concluded that her description made it sound like her friends might be a bit afraid of her, but that perhaps they were also afraid *for* her? Nell didn't react or say anything, and she quickly moved onto something else, so I followed her path.

Towards the end of the session she told me that until the past few days she had never really thought much about her life, let alone how long it might be. She reflected that this might seem odd, given that she was so well-educated and a doctor. I can't remember how I responded, but I remember feeling that Nell was already becoming less stuck.

In this third session it seemed that I had passed the test, because I found Nell much more pleasant and engaging to be with. Her sharp edges had melted a bit, and I felt more comfortable being with her. She had worked hard in the interval since our last session, and came with notes about what she had been thinking about. It seemed that she had begun to trust me.

So, after we discussed her very medically-dominated week and the pain from lymphoedema (swelling) in her arms, I asked her more about her childhood and upbringing. She told me that her parents were poorly educated and had been destitute for most of their lives. They had done all they could to shield the family's poverty from the judgmental eyes of others. One effect of this was that her childhood friends were forbidden from visiting Nell's home, and Nell was discouraged from visiting theirs. School trips were only allowed if they incurred no extra cost, and so on.

The family became proudly self-sufficient, and Nell and her older brother learned to make do with what they could derive from the family itself. But the family was almost totally isolated and so became inward-looking; safe, but in constant dread of shame as a result of their poverty. Her parents were miserable about their lives and one another, and Nell was anxious to keep the peace, but little was ever spoken about. No one had the vocabulary. No one attempted to speak about their lives together as a family, or suggest anything that might lead to a shared story. It was, in Nell's words, "one long dull blur".

She had somehow found her way out of this impoverished background by attending her local further education college which she loved. She became a nurse, but soon after she qualified she applied to medical school. Her courage and determination had enabled her to rise out of her deprived childhood, and these days it was mainly her loyal girlfriends who kept her going, not her family. And by 'girlfriends' she seemed to be mostly referring to her colleagues.

The pain of Nell's feelings gradually became clearer as she found the words to describe them. She tearfully said that she had only recently woken up to the fact of being alive, and of only having this one life. She was "only thirty-six years old, for fuck's sake" and now she was being told that she was going to die. Looking bitterly sad, Nell again said she was pleased that she had never had children, but I could see that her eyes were still moist. And then she quickly added that she had never felt more alive, so being dead just wasn't imaginable.

I think I responded hypothetically, that if this *were* the case, if her doctors *were* right and that she was most likely going to die from this disease, anyone in this position might naturally feel angry, sad, and perhaps scared. She stared at me fiercely and frowned, then looked away and lowered her head. By this point I was feeling that we had built up a degree of trust, but at that moment I was feeling worried that I had been too quick, too blunt, and I was regretting my clumsiness.

But then she quietly said yes, she would feel angry too. And as she said this her body shuddered slightly, as if she were physically repelled by something. She said that she would feel angry at having 'missed out' on a life that she could only now imagine herself living. I wondered what else she might be thinking about, and she responded that she could not accept the idea that her existence could be entirely extinguished at the moment of her death, that all of her thoughts would be annihilated forever. This foreverness, the *eternity* of non-existence is perhaps unthinkable, but other people had talked about similar concerns.

Her eyes had welled up again as she spoke. Rather feebly, I wondered if she had ever considered the possibility that death is no more than the oblivion of a deep sleep, an endless time when one is experiencing nothing. Yes, she could see that, but still she could not conceive of her mind, *herself*, ceasing to exist. As she continued it seemed that she could not let go of the thought of herself being aware of her non-existence. In other words, being alive in some other way.

Nell was talking as if consciousness could exist beyond the body. True old-fashioned dualism, perhaps even based on religious ideas of an afterlife, with the mind and soul as somehow separate from the body. But Nell professed to be entirely nonreligious and agnostic. A humanist in fact.

It was twenty minutes into this third session and Nell was talking about her fatal cancer. She said that simply being alive was something she had never seriously thought about. But now she found herself acutely aware of it, and was thinking about it all the time. She was both horrified and regretful at how much she had taken for granted, how much she had missed. This was her one and only life, her one chance, and it was soon to be over. It was clear to me that she was finding it a relief to be talking freely about it all. She admitted she was envious of the people around her whose lives would be going on into the future. She said she wanted to wake them up to tell them how short their lives might be. However, just a few weeks later Nell was able to see that many of the people she knew were probably also learning their own lessons from her illness.

Over the next few months she talked more deeply about her life. She came to understand that instead of embracing life's possibilities she had been brought up to do the opposite, to hide big parts of herself and what she was feeling. She had been shy about expressing herself and had grown up to become a private person, fearing shame, cool with others, and always a little hard to reach, though she did seem to have close work colleagues who liked her and enjoyed her clever jokes. These and a couple of previous work colleagues were the only friends she appeared to have.

As a child Nell had felt tested and inadequate, and in our sessions, with very little said by me, she gradually came to realise that her illness had felt like another test, and that she had inadvertently been causing the people around her (including me) to feel these same feelings. For what it is worth, the technical term for this mental strategy is projective identification.

I recorded in my notes some of the metaphors she used in our sessions and in the diary she was keeping that she would occasionally read from. She said she had never previously thought of her life as "having an expiry date" or a "full stop". On one occasion she said she felt that she had only just climbed onto a fairground ride and now she was being told she had to get off. But mostly she felt angry with herself for not having "woken up" earlier to life's possibilities. There was still so much she did not understand about just being alive, and there was "so much left to do and figure out".

In those last few months of her life Nell changed before my eyes, and although her frame diminished and her cheeks lost their colour and fulness, her outrage at the prospect of death intensified. It gave her an energy that seemed to defy her increasing frailty. She became less concerned about her clothes and appearance, she put her financial affairs in order, sought out her family to tell them what they had meant to her, and made peace with her daemons. She was intensely creative, learning to make stained glass, and clay vases that she gave to her friends. She gave me one, and I still have it.

She lacked close friends and family, but over the months I knew her she steadily became more open to allowing other people to care for her. She told me how cheered she felt by the affection and concern shown by her loyal workmates. Above all, she became more generous in expressing her joy, love and affection, and of course other people responded in kind.

It was clear quite early on that I would not be needing to tell Nell the short parable that I had sometimes found myself recounting to my patients, mostly when I felt that they had prematurely given up on their lives. It goes something like this:

A man goes to party. When he gets there, instead of taking off his coat and joining in with his friends, he leans against a wall and watches the other people singing, laughing, dancing and generally having a fun time. He becomes increasingly hot and sweaty standing there under his heavy coat. Half-way through the party the host comes up to the man. "George" they say, "why don't you take off your coat? You'd be so much more comfortable." George answers "What's the point? I'll be leaving in a couple of hours' time anyway."

Metaphorical stories are the easy bit of course, and anyway Nell was certainly no George. For her, it was *all* about shedding her overcoat, and yelling to the world that her life was not over yet, and that for as long as she was still breathing, she was furiously going to get on with what remained of her life. Nell's determination was propelled by an anger and regret at not having understood earlier what her life was all about, because now here she was, trying to make sense of it all, often with me. Her excitement for life was not some form of retreat from reality or denial, but an expression of her personal growth.

She still didn't particularly want to talk about death and it was sometimes difficult and painful for Nell to talk with me, as she reflected on her life, her experiences, her feelings and her beliefs. As with so many other people I had known, I felt in awe of her courage and moved by the transformation she was going through. She was trying hard to make sense of her life. At one point she stopped, looked up at me with wet eyes, and said "I just don't understand. How did it get to this? What are we all here for? How come I am able to think all this stuff now, but in a few months' time all this will stop? There is so much I don't understand." When I merely nodded in response, she said "You're the psychologist, you tell me!" And then she laughed, letting me off the hook. But good questions, existential questions, psychological questions.

I know that during her last few months I became someone special in her life, rather like a trusted old friend with whom she could think about these hefty questions without feeling judged. Huge scary questions that may sound daunting, but that sometimes lead to interesting and important answers. It is not my job to provide these answers, but rather to help people think about their concerns and understand them better.

Over the months of seeing Nell, and especially during our last few talks together in the hospice, I was reminded yet again that these questions have long oscillated in the background of my life too. Perhaps they are questions that everyone asks themselves in different ways at one time or another. We are here, alive in the world for this short time, and then we are lost to oblivion again. How does our experience of being alive come about? How do we create the apparent reality that makes up our moment-to-moment existence, the trains of thought that constitute our everyday mental lives?

Nell's questions were not entirely new to me. When I began working in oncology twenty-four years earlier there had been almost no clinical psychologists working in cancer in the UK's National Health Service. The oncologists, nurses and radiographers were as unfamiliar with the world of psychology as I was with oncology.

At first, my medical colleagues would refer people to me because the patient was regarded as 'difficult', or 'they cry every time they attend clinic', or 'they are too frightened to have radiotherapy', or 'the patient is in denial' about their diagnosis. When I came to meet these patients, however, I was unable to see that there was anything unusual about them, other than their lives had been turned upside down by their illness and they were trying to make sense of a lot of new experiences, scary treatments, and a whirlwind of change. And, sure, there were those with long-standing claustrophobia and other pre-existing difficulties, but most people were simply doing their best to make sense of enormous changes and uncertainty. I would have described it as a hard and unfolding personal and family transition, a tear in the fabric of normal.

However, I soon came to realise that along with the terrible distress I was listening to, I was also frequently moved by people telling me how their priorities had changed since being ill. Some patients even said they were grateful for what they had learned as a result of the illness. They talked about how their lives had actually changed for the better in some ways.

A practising clinical psychologist needs to be able to develop and draw upon plausible theoretical models for what is going on psychologically in the people they are trying to help. It was obvious that a life-threatening illness like cancer would provoke feelings of loss and anxious uncertainty, and lots of relationship issues. But I wasn't immediately sure how to think about denial. And how was it possible that so many people were gaining something positive from this catastrophic change in their lives? I started recording my thoughts.

The scientific literature available at the time was largely American and written in psychiatric mental health terms. It said that following diagnosis a third of people with cancer would develop a psychiatric disorder. This seemed entirely the wrong terminology to be using, and deeply inappropriate and unhelpful to the people I was seeing and listening to.

Lacking plausible models of how people in general adjust to change in their lives, let alone adjust to a serious illness like cancer, I soon came to the conclusion that denial was merely a rather helpful short-term defence mechanism, and usually more a problem for the professionals than the patient. And so-called 'denial' was rarely all-or-nothing.

Over the years, I listened to thousands of stories of people's lives, and the things they discovered that were important to them. They told me how the diagnosis, regardless of the prognosis, had forced them to consider their death, and consequently they learned a lot about their life. Presumably, knowing we have a limited time left makes us more inclined to use it wisely.

My patients were not only trying to come to terms with their mortality, they were often reporting that their fundamental assumptions about life had shifted as a result of their ongoing illness. It had taken a serious illness to jolt them questioning how they had been living their lives. They had suddenly woken up to the fact that this was their one and only life, and it seemed perfectly natural that they were interested in better understanding it.

This is also what this book seeks to understand. How do our minds construct the reality of our lives? How do minds adjust to change? Where do minds sit within the natural world? These perhaps sound like some of the biggest philosophical questions one could wish to ask, but they are also scientific questions, and especially psychological ones.

It has been said many times that humans are the only species that can contemplate their own death, and while that is extraordinary it can also be hard. For Nell it was a huge struggle to reconcile herself with her mortality. She was overwhelmed with having a great deal to think about, while at the same time her growing understanding was helping her to change and live in a way that she had not known before, a way that better met her needs.

So it would seem that knowing we are going to die can help us make sense of what it means to be alive, and how we wish to live our lives henceforth. While this may not be an especially original insight, perhaps if we are able to glimpse ourselves on a bigger canvas it can help us live our lives more richly. And perhaps, like Nell, it is better to ask these big questions now, before we find ourselves at the end of our lives.

Possessing a mind seems so ordinary that we more-or-less take it for granted. This is weirdly ironic, because having a mind is one of the *most* extraordinary things in Nature. Not all brains come with minds. It is in our nature, the essence of what it is like to be a human being, to have a mind with which to think. Only we, Homo sapiens, are able to make any sense of *meaning* out of our lives, because only our species is able to mentally model the world in the complex and sophisticated ways that we do.

This is not hubris. Other animals are able to represent the world in interesting and intricate ways, but there is no evidence that they worry about the future or reflect upon the past in the way that Nell was able to do, because they are unable to make complex mental representations of it. Other species get ill and die... or not. Only humans have to suffer psychologically as well. It is the price of having a mind and Nell was paying it.

What distinguishes humans from every other living creature on this planet is that human minds are able to represent the world in the form of thoughts, abstract assumptions and models. No other species can do what you are doing right now, making sense of these words. Every word is a symbol for something, and only human minds are able to represent and decipher the world using such symbols.

We only have to listen to two people having a conversation, making strange sounds at one another, noises that represent complicated ideas that mean something to both of them because they share a language. And they can both interpret each other's sound symbols, and thereby receive and understand the ideas being expressed. Thoughts are thereby conveyed from one mind to another. Something as seemingly ordinary as having a conversation is an astonishingly powerful form of social information transmission.

But that is not our only talent. Only human minds are able to draw conclusions from the past by reflecting on it, and better still they are able to imagine and model the future. Only humans can ponder their experiences and develop new assumptions on the basis of them, and then communicate their thoughts to one another using language. All this, I shall be arguing, enables each of us to construct the reality of our lives and make sense of our existence. At the same time, unlike any other species, this also freights us with moral responsibility.

I tell you the story of Nell's life, and you began to imagine her experiences and the feelings that Nell may have had. You piece together Nell's story, just as I was trying to do when she was talking to me. You try to construct an understanding of her. You may have less information than I had, but you can still conjure up her story in your mind. Perhaps you have an image of her in your mind, or you may even feel something about her. You have created a simple model of Nell in your mind. Without realising it.

And that of course is exactly what minds are especially good at doing. We construct stories out of what we hear and learn about the world, and from what we directly experience. We join together the bits and dots of what we know into a continuous story that *makes sense to us*. While listening to Nell, I was working hard to understand her experience so that I could create a plausible narrative in my mind of that experience. My formulation of her distressing situation was subtly changing as she provided me with more information, allowing me to model her thoughts, feelings, and possible options more accurately in my own mind.

My first job as a therapist is to use my meaning-making, cognitive mind to understand and reflect on the ways that my client's meaning-making, cognitive mind is making sense of what they have experienced or are still experiencing, and how that makes them feel... and also, on some level, how that makes me feel, listening to all this, and what that can tell me about what the client has been through.

There is a lot going on.

○————————○

If, like Nell, you realised that you have only one life on this Earth, a life of uncertain length and with no rewind button, you too would probably be interested in understanding how your mind works and how it came about. And not just because you are generally curious about how things work. Everything you have ever experienced, and everything you know and believe, has passed through your mind. Furthermore, the human mind, with its unrivalled capacity for thought, imagination, and reason, has crafted the incredibly complicated human society that now surrounds most of us.

But can anyone really make sense of something as fundamental as the mind? Good science depends upon people asking very specific answerable questions. The New Zealand nuclear physicist Ernest Rutherford (1871-1937) believed that "*All science is either physics or stamp collecting. That which is not measurable is not science.*" His point was that if you want to evaluate something scientifically you have to be able to measure it reliably.

Psychology is certainly not physics, but nor is it economics, and humans are neither gods nor beasts but something in between. And, anyway, if Rutherford was right then the question of how people make sense of reality, how minds work, immediately sounds far too vague and nebulous to be able to make any sensible claim on scientific credibility. It is one thing to study the relative simplicity of the physical world, and most physicists would agree that that is complicated enough. It is quite another to model the mental, let alone social world, for these contain far too many variables and changing processes to be scientifically measurable within Rutherford's tight definition.

The mind is particularly slippery to understand because although it is invisible yet also in plain sight, being something that we are using all the time. Paradoxically, things that are pervasive, ordinary, and taken-for-granted are often the hardest to discern, which is perhaps why there have been relatively few unified theories of how our minds are able to make sense and meaning out of our lived experience.

Leaving physics aside for a moment, there are a few things that have been studied that perhaps we can talk about fairly reliably. And let's be honest, even physics eventually becomes a bit metaphysical when it speculates about the 'multiverse'. As it is, we humans are starting to make sense of how we came to be here on this planet, broadly how we work biologically, and what makes our species similar to and different from other species. We are starting to understand how our brains create thoughts, feelings, and behaviour, and how we remember things, both mentally and physically. We are beginning to grasp how we react to the events of our lives, and how we construct meaning from our moment-to-moment existence and the events of our lives.

In this book I offer a *psychological* account of the extraordinary *ordinariness* of having a mind. How do our minds create our sense of ongoing reality, how does our brain create the experience of being alive and thinking? We are not yet able to explain fully how the physical world has created matter, time and space, but we are on our way to understanding how the mind enables us to make sense of the world around us. And I sometimes wonder that if Nell had seen this bigger canvass earlier, she might have led a very different life.

The Eighteenth-Century German philosopher Immanuel Kant (1724-1804) believed that any real understanding of the mind requires more than a purely scientific approach. He recognised that human minds are also rooted in culture, history and philosophy, so a broader conception of the mind is needed. He would have regarded Rutherford's science as too constraining for anyone to be able to make sense of how we think.

The Austrian-British philosopher Ludwig Wittgenstein (1889-1951) also saw that there is more to the mind than can be explained by science alone because language struggles to express the ineffable. You can admire a beautiful sunset but how can you convey what it makes you feel to someone on the other end of a telephone?

Kant and Wittgenstein perhaps believed that the mind can only be understood if its explanation is consistent with lived experience, for that too is evidence, what philosophers call phenomenology. If they are right, then we need to verify our scientific understanding of the mind by considering how it pertains to the social and cultural world around us, as well as whether it is plausibly consistent with our inner world, mindful of the notorious dangers associated with introspection.

In a similar vein, German philosopher Martin Heidegger (1889-1976) emphasised that human beings are not merely objects in the world but actively engaged with it, interpreting and giving meaning to our experiences. Human minds are uniquely aware of themselves in time, are able to project themselves into the future, and are even aware of their mortality. Once again, he argued that direct observation and logical proof would never be sufficient for understanding the nature of human existence.

So my third source of verification for my understanding of the mind has been to ask myself how well it has been corroborated by clinical observation. Are other people's accounts of their mental experience consistent with my understanding of the mind? This triangulated account therefore tries to combine academic and broadly scientific evidence with introspection, and what I have observed from working with people in psychological distress.

In the days before modern science, this sort of rational enquiry was known as natural philosophy, a part of which was natural history, the study of how species and their particular features fit within Nature as a whole. In that spirit, this is a natural history and philosophy of the mind.

What do we even mean by a mind? That seems like a good place to start. But it is not as simple as it sounds. Even the whole idea that we have minds may just be an idea that we have made up about ourselves, though of course the business of having ideas is presumably exactly what the mind is all about. But you can see why people might question whether minds even exist. Are they perhaps just another word for brains?

The American philosopher John Searle[1] has said that the mind-body problem is a bit like the stomach-digestion problem. He points

---

[1] Searle J. (1984) *Minds, Brains and Science*. Cambridge Mass, Harvard University Press

out that we don't think in terms of stomach digestion dualism, and that there are not two things going on in one's skull, but rather two different levels of description.

Minds don't exist as concrete *things*, such as rocks, cups, brains, saxophones, or indeed stomachs. 'Things' can be pinned down, examined and measured directly or indirectly with one or more of our senses. Minds are literally invisible. Yes, they exist within a living thing, the brain, and that can be examined, but the mind is not the same as the brain even though it is entirely dependent on it. The mind is to be found in the information pathways that exist within the physical brain, and the models and meanings that these pathways give rise to.

The Ancient Greeks used the word 'soul' or *psyche* to refer to mental life in general. Many years later Judeo-Christianity co-opted the word to denote something supernatural and immortal, promising that a person's sense of themselves would continue to exist in an afterlife, such as heaven or hell. Likewise, in Islam the 'ruh' refers to the spirit or divine breath of God that gives life to human beings.

These days, many people are inclined to believe that we live in a material world and that, whatever the mind is, it exists within the natural world. So that form of dualism is dead. But another form of dualism is very much alive and well. The mind and brain are quite different because, as we have said, mental phenomena are qualitatively utterly different to the physical world of *things*. Yet, while minds may be nonphysical, they still exist within the material world in the form of electro-chemical pulses in the brain, and these are entirely a product of Nature.

This is dualism, but only in the same way that hardware and software in a computer, or stomachs and digestion in a body, are fundamentally different categories of things. So while it helps to understand how the brain works, it is the infinitely varied patterns of connections and the meanings that these engender that determine what the mind is doing, not the neurons themselves.

Consequently, neuroscience may be able to explain the neural connections that underlie conscious thought, perception and memory, but it cannot understand the complexity of any one person's mental experience, or why they feel the way they do. Those involve questions of meaning. Understanding how the hardware is configured is fascinating, but brains are relatively barren vessels for whatever 'software' the user puts into them. That software is mental stimulation and 'programming' drawn from life experience, the social and relational world around each person, and the mental models that each person constructs and remembers from those experiences.

The standard analogy used to think about the mind and brain is the software-hardware distinction found in a computer. The hardware or cells of the brain (sometimes known as 'wetware') can do little without the input of content in the form of information (i.e. software) from the senses and memory.

What distinguishes human minds from the rest of Nature is not that they are actual computers, but that they are highly computational. Human minds are able to model the world, but instead of using binary data stored in memory chips, they use ideas and assumptions stored in the neural pathways of the brain. This enables them to do things that Nature has never been able to do before (such as solve problems, anticipate the future, read a book, etc.). At the same time, minds exist within brains, and brains sit within bodies that evolved, so it is essential to understand how and when modern brains came about in us humans.

However, invisibility is not the only difficulty. Life is ultimately made up of a vast number of changing moments, events, and sensations, even if we don't necessarily notice, learn from, or remember everything we experience. Our minds go on developing throughout our lives because it is *change*, in its many forms, that dictates the twists and turns of people's lives, from the micro-moments in having a shower, to the big 'life events' that alter the course of a person's life. And from change we grow and learn, for good or bad.

Minds learn from past experience in order to be able to predict, imagine and anticipate the future, a skill that defines our species. That computational feat is processed in the brain, but experienced in the mind where it becomes meaning, models and memory. Minds are literally in state of flux almost all the time, so it is vital to understand how they adjust in the face of change.

Perhaps we can start then, by agreeing that the mind is a process that occurs over time, and is embodied and bound by the brain and the lifespan of the particular person. It was that boundary that Nell could not accept, and it is why the idea of a 'life hereafter' remains so appealing. But in the natural scheme of things nothing lasts forever. In time, all experiences become memories, and when we die those memories will die with us. Memento mori indeed.

The English philosopher, William of Ockham (1287-1347) argued that it is not rational to postulate the existence of more things than are necessary to explain a phenomenon. This philosophical idea is that of *Parsimony*, whereby a simpler explanation of something, a synthesis, is preferable to a more complicated explanation, provided that it is able to provide an equally plausible and accurate account of the key facts and evidence.

Parsimony can be dry, so perhaps it is reasonable to embellish it with examples and descriptions, but parsimony is not the same as simplifying the world by omitting key relevant facts. Sometimes evidence is complicated, yet all of it may be relevant to achieving a complete picture. A court of law, for example, goes to great lengths to establish the truth, and it sometimes requires a lengthy and complex understanding of the evidence. Ockham's 'razor' is about 'shaving away' information that adds nothing of explanatory value.

Unfortunately, the mind does not have sharp edges, so it can be tricky to know how close to shave, but in the end the mind is a phenomenon within Nature, and it can be studied accordingly. It may be helpful while reading this book to remember that the mind is a *process*, not a fixed or static *thing*. But, like digestion, no less real for that. We all recognise that bodies change and develop over time, and the same holds true for our minds. It is our mental *life*.

In human society knowledge is passed on, not just in stamp collections and other records, but in conversations, ideas and theories about events and processes, knowledge that both accumulates and is lost over time. So yes, the complexity of human experience may defy ultimate scientific explanation, but even so, the principles of science can still be applied to the mind, not the least of which is making a plausible argument on the basis of reason, probability, and evidence, even if it is not up to Ernest Rutherford's standards. It's actually what psychotherapists are doing a lot of the time, trying to make coherent sense of a complex set of factors.

Science is a combination of imagination and rationality, experiment and empiricism. Any intellectually plausible explanation of our ability to think needs to be based on similarly plausible evidence from psychological, biological and social studies and inquiries. Fortunately, these subjects have been examined for centuries, and enough scientific and intellectual knowledge has accrued to be able to construct a broadly consilient and contextualised account of the mind.

Scientific enquiries start with an examination of the properties and features of the object in question, so that it can be described and measured, and compared with other things. This is the scientific method. We have already mentioned a couple of properties of the mind, that it is invisible and that it is changing and developing all the time. A third key property of the mind is that thinking occurs in the present moment. We will come back to all these properties and more in due course.

My previous book had roughly a thousand academic references, but this time I have loosened my belt a little and my arguments rest on a much wider field of evidence, yet draw wherever possible upon the broad consensus of academic opinion. My aim is to understand the mind within its wider context – what *is* this thing we call a life? Given the breadth of this landscape, I have inevitably had to simplify matters immensely, but in joining up the dots I have tried to fill in any missing ones with reason and common sense.

Each of us has an inner world, a thought world that is somehow private to ourselves. This mental life is not immediately easy to read and recognise, even by ourselves, but this inner world goes on in the background of our lives all the time if we choose to think about it. It is that quiet place where we can 'talk' to ourselves, and *from* that place that we can look out at the world beyond ourselves. This is our subjectivity, our thoughts and assumptions about ourselves living our lives in the world of other people. Our sense of our *self*, with our own thoughts and assumptions.

My thesis is to do with how each one of us constructs our sense of reality. I hope to draw your attention to some marvels of Nature as we journey through some intricate landscapes that depict the mind and brain. Our minds make us uniquely different from every other person in the world, and collectively we are entirely different from every other species that we humans have ever encountered.

I am hoping you will be able to glimpse yourself as one particular member of this one particular species on this planet, the only species with a brain and an unusually long childhood that is capable of generating a complex meaning-making mind like yours.

Minds are generated by brains, so in the next chapter, **Chapter 2,** we begin by considering how human beings evolved to have such special brains. I will show that our modern model-making minds emerged astonishingly recently within biological time and were a radical departure from all that had gone before.

We spend our lives within our bodies and these evolved to have their own demands – the emotions and instinctive drives – so in **Chapter 3** we consider these important forces. And in so far as minds exist in physical brains, it helps to have a broad understanding of how brains work and how they give rise to symbolic thought, language and ideas. **Chapter 4** examines how we store memories from the events and experiences of our lives, and how our minds draw general conclusions from experience in the form of mental models and assumptions which we then use to make sense of the world around us.

Chapter 5 describes how consciousness broadly comes about, and how each of us constructs reality. It considers how we are able to sustain a train of thought, manipulate several ideas at the same time, and sometimes come up with a new idea. In this chapter we also learn that a lot of the time we make sense of the world and operate as if on automatic pilot, freeing up our minds to think about other things.

Clearly, we can only understand the world on the basis of what we already know. Over the course of our lives we gradually learn to make sense of the world and our place within it, so **Chapter 6** describes how our minds and brains develop during our unusually long childhoods, and how they go on developing throughout our lives. In **Chapter 7** we see that, while human minds are extraordinarily adaptive, psychological flexibility has its limits. How do our minds adjust to the changing events of our lives, and at the same time resist change if it is particularly unwelcome, overwhelming, or too sudden?

Chapter 8 considers how psychological distress typically comes about and what psychological therapy can sometimes do about it. Our modern human minds have created the astonishingly complex human societies in which most of us now live, yet there remain legacies from our ancient past that continue to influence human behaviour and the way that many of us currently live. **Chapter 9** describes how these vestiges of our evolutionary past can still be observed in the way we behave with one another, and in the complex social and cultural world around us. Finally, **Chapter 10** attempts to draw some conclusions about how we might think about our minds, our short lives, and the singular wonder of being consciously alive.

Chapter 2

Genesis

Gnats
Planet of life
Behavioural Modernity
Language and symbolic thought
Working-memory

Physics is limited by materiality,
but thoughts can go anywhere.

Gnats

The Sciaridae are a family of flies, commonly known as dark-winged fungus gnats. Found in moist environments, they are known to be a pest of mushroom farms and are found in household plant pots... Currently, around 1,700 species are described, but an estimated 20,000 species are estimated to be awaiting discovery, mainly in the tropics.

Sciarid larvae are found in soil and plant litter, where they feed mainly on fungi and animal faeces. The larvae play an important role in turning forest leaf litter into soil.

Adult females lay about 200 transparent eggs (each 1 mm long) into moist soil. After one week the larvae hatch. About 90% of the larvae are female. The adults with their characteristic dancing flight do not bite. They only ingest liquids and live only long enough to mate and produce eggs. They die after about five days. [2]

Five days. I hope you are glad you are not a gnat. Small brains, short lives, and an awful diet, though presumably not to gnats. Such a brief and meaningless life, it seems barely worth a thought. Admittedly they do turn forest leaf litter into soil, and that sounds quite useful.

But while we are feeling grateful about not being a gnat, we probably might *not* want to reflect on the fact that in 100 years' time we too won't be thought about by anyone. And that, almost certainly, will remain the situation forever. Like any gnat, we are here today and gone tomorrow. Turn away if you need to, but that is just the way it is.

Watch a few old newsreels of ordinary people who lived their lives (and even got themselves into a newsreel) and they are all now dead and, with very rare exceptions, entirely forgotten. Their names might be written down here and there, and even a few recalled, as remote and ancient figures spoken about in childhood, but they are not remembered as real people and they will probably never be thought of again. The same fate awaits us all. Maybe we will leave a digital footprint when we die, provided someone is prepared to store it, but will anyone really be interested in looking at it in a few years' time? A very few people, famous figures from the past, are remembered for what they did in their famous lives, but in the big scheme of things even being very famous is not for very long.

Human history is crazily short amidst the aeons of time. And yet, rather wonderfully, none of this in any way diminishes the importance of every person's individual life. On the contrary, it makes it all the more extraordinary that every person has a consciousness that enables them to be aware of themselves living their life. Their little spell in the sunshine.

We happen to be living in a period of biological time during which a species, our species, has learned to be conscious of itself

---

2: Abridged from Wikipedia (2020)

and able to ask questions. So there it is, the big challenge: we have this one short time in which not to be a gnat.

As it happens, we are a very different species, a living *thinking* human being. We are even meta-sentient, aware of ourselves thinking, mentally conscious, so not at all like a gnat. I have to assume that you are aware of yourself being alive right now. I am also assuming that you accept that you too are living in a moment in time, this very moment as it happens. So let us agree that this awareness of ourselves being alive is our consciousness, marking time within this ever-changing moment, living in the world, in a moment when things may not be as good as they could be, but nonetheless you are here now, living and alive at this very moment. You were not given any choice in the matter, that is true. You were born without your consent, but you were born with the potential for consciousness. This consciousness is you, absorbing and making sense of these very words at this very moment. Is that not extraordinary?

Perhaps you can also sense the passage of time, when you choose to think about it. Perhaps you can even glimpse the sand in the hourglass of your particular life, slowly crumbling away second by second. But no matter how long your life turns out to be, do you also carry the awareness that this is, in all reasonable probability, your one and only life, and that it is being lived right now?

Well, good for you. Unlike a gnat, you know that the party will be ending in a few hours' time, but you have taken off your coat and have chosen to embrace the short time that you have here, being alive, thinking.

Life as a gnat is far simpler, to be sure, but nothing like as interesting. We humans are born with minds that are capable of thought, sometimes marvellous thoughts, for thoughts can range from the simple to the complex, nuanced and sophisticated. But an obvious question is: where does this ability to think come from? How is it that our species can contemplate how gnats spend their lives, let alone appreciate the beauty of a sunset, reflect on what has passed, or wonder about the future? *When* did thinking even come about?

Whatever the mind is, it emerges from within the brain and nervous system of a life-supporting body, a body that evolved. So, let us start at the very beginning and take a natural history point of view, observing the mind within its wider context. In other words, how did minds evolve in our particular species, and where do they sit within Nature at large?

Planet of Life

Human beings are just one life form on Earth, the planetary home that all species of life share. I hope that we can all agree about that. We live on this planet with over 8 billion other people, as well as all the other organisms that live here too – plants, animals, fungi, bacteria, and so on. Life.

It has been estimated that there are about eight to ten million species of life on Earth if we exclude much simpler organisms like bacteria and viruses. Among these there are those 20,000 species of gnat. It has also been estimated that over 86% of these 10 million living species have not yet been identified or described.

Of this total, only about 300,000 are plant species, the majority of which have been given names. By contrast there are thought to be 7.7 million species of animal, most of them insects, but less than 2 million animal species have so far been identified. However, what is known about these species is impressively consistent with an evolutionary account of life on this planet. Evolution describes the changes that occur among biological organisms over successive generations.

Fewer than 5 per cent of animals have backbones, the vertebrates, and of these only about 5,500 are mammals, a tiny number compared with that of all animals. We are just one member of one particular mammal species, but a species that completely permeates and dominates the planet's drier surfaces and increasingly its deep oceans. The human population of Earth reached 8 billion people in the spring of 2024, and the United Nations believes that by 2100 the world population will have largely stabilised at about 11.2 billion (though some authors believe that peak global population will occur earlier, and some later). However, despite our considerable numbers and enormous impact on the planet, an Israeli study has estimated that humans constitute merely 0.01 per cent of the world's biomass (i.e. the weight of living organisms). Plants, by contrast, represent 83 per cent.

Water is a liquid molecule and the basis of all life on Earth. That simply means that all living creatures like gnats and plants and you and me need water. Anywhere there is water you will find life trying to colonise it. Trees, for example, usually need a lot of water to survive. In fact, trees include more than 60,000 species, 25,000 of which have so far been identified. Trees have had a far greater impact on Earth than humans and, like humans, they have their own story to tell. Over aeons of time, primitive plant life slowly took root in damp rocks and rivers. Algae, lichen, and early plants like moss absorbed light energy from the sun, interacted with the minerals in the rocks they found themselves on, lived, died, and with the help of fungi rotted down to provide the nutrient base for future generations. Over time the plants became bigger and more complex, eventually resulting in plants the size of trees.

There have been many quadrillions of trees that have lived and died. Wood, coal and oil are their short and long-term by-products. Trees have been growing on Earth in one form or another for about 385 million years. By comparison, humans and chimpanzees only became separate species about 7 million years ago. So trees have always been a vital part of the human, as much as the planetary experience, and humans have always relied upon trees for food, fuel, shelter, tools and ornaments.

Wood is the trunk and branches of trees once they have been severed from a living tree or salvaged from a dead one. Wood is versatile and has vastly different properties depending on the species of tree that the wood is from. It is the knowledge of these properties that has enabled people to fashion dwellings, tools, boats, bridges, and exquisite furniture, jewellery and sculptures. Wood is roughly 50% carbon, 44% oxygen and 6% hydrogen. It is strong yet flexible and can be cut, whittled, rasped, filed, sanded, and polished. It can be joined to other wood, carved into any imaginable shape, and as any carpenter will tell we, it is warm to the touch, smells nice, and is pleasant to work with. There has been a long and natural connection between humans and wood, and humans have long exploited wood for their survival.

Wood, however, is effectively dead tree, so its natural sap soon dries out, and water, that once nourished it, is now its deadly cancerous enemy. Once wood's sap no longer repels it, water seeps into the wood's sinewy fabric, providing the conditions for fungi, bacteria and eventually plants to find a home. Within this damp micro-world these invading species feed off the wood itself. This is how wood rots and life gets recycled into earth.

Oiling and waxing wood can protect it for long periods of time, sealing it against the corrosive power of water. And if wood is kept dry and survives, over time it becomes increasingly brittle. An old violin has a beautiful resonance if it has been well made and if its wood has become seasoned through age and good care.

And so it is with us human beings. Like any tree, we are each a member of an evolved species on this planet, except that we are an animal like a gnat, not a plant like a tree. Humans are more watery than trees and are roughly 18.5% carbon, 65% oxygen and 9.5% hydrogen. We are also a mammal, an animal that has hairy skin and, among females, mammary or breast glands that provide milk for their young.

Like trees, humans have certain remarkable qualities, but first we might consider a few wonderful things that other animals can do that humans, and certainly trees, cannot, or at least things that they can do far better than humans.

For example, we can't fly (gnats can), we can't run particularly fast for our size, and we can't swim underwater for very long. We couldn't even walk as soon as we were born. Humans take about a year to get on their feet; most other animals take seconds or minutes, and rarely more than days. Our hearing is pitiful compared with many other mammals – look at a cat's ears, constantly moving about to pick up the faintest sounds. It is impossible even to begin to imagine the experience of a cat without shutting our eyes and just listening.

Our sense of smell is almost non-existent compared with bears and dogs. A bloodhound's ability to smell is a thousand times more sensitive than ours, possibly more. Moths can smell potential mates several miles away, a fact that makes one pause to consider how much smell the other moth could be generating.

Our eyesight is not bad, but we are practically blind compared with eagles whose eyes are three or four times more powerful than ours. To see as an eagle would be like looking through binoculars. What is more, we can only see the world within our own particular band of wavelengths. Bees can see ultraviolet light, and pit vipers can identify their prey by sensing its infrared radiation. We also only have two eyes, jellyfish have twenty-four. The chameleon can even use its two eyes independently of one another, so is able to look in different directions at the same time.

You might think we have a reasonably refined sense of taste, but not compared with a catfish whose entire six-inch body is covered by twenty-five times as many taste buds as we have. It is said that it would be able to detect a drop of coca cola in an Olympic sized swimming pool. One has to assume that this has never been tried.

So in many ways humans are rather mediocre within the animal kingdom, and our sporting 'world records' tell us as much about our limitations as our achievements. But what about our size as a species? Most people, if asked, tend to imagine that humans are fairly average-sized among the species. That is because it is easy to think of much bigger and much smaller creatures. Knowing that we are neither an elephant nor a mouse leads us to assume that we must be average. Later we will see how easy it is to form an assumption like this, even though it is just plain wrong. We only have to think about all those gnats and other insects, and we quickly see that most creatures are far smaller than us; humans in fact are very much on the large side.

Science has shown, with overwhelming evidence, that human beings evolved on this particular planet, Earth. Earth is the third furthest out amongst eight planets that make up our solar system and that orbit a fairly average-sized yellow dwarf star. This star, our Sun, sits roughly two thirds out from the centre of a spiral galaxy that we know as the Milky Way. On a dark clear night our eyes can plainly see the width of our galaxy. The faint haze we see, like a milky band across the sky, is made up of tens of billions of stars that make up our particular region of our spiral disk-like galaxy. Looking up at the Milky Way is one of the most genuinely awesome sights our eyes will ever see. It is hard not to be overwhelmed by the sheer enormity of what we are looking at.

It is estimated that our galaxy alone contains between 200 and 400 billion stars and about 50 billion planets, half a billion of which are likely to be located within the habitable zone of their parent star (not too hot and not too cold). That's 500,000,000 other possible worlds, a few of which just might have the right conditions to sustain life. And all those stars and planets are just within our own galaxy. The known Universe is thought to contain roughly 200 billion galaxies (two trillion in some estimates). How many stars is that, and how many potentially habitable planets? By all means do the arithmetic but, on the basis of probability, it seems very likely that some form of life will have emerged somewhere else in the Universe. And, quite possibly, thinking life.

But while it may be comforting to know that human beings are not alone, and that there may well be other intelligent life forms in the Universe, it is perhaps also worth remembering that the nearest star to our own Sun is Proxima Centauri, and that is 4.2 light years away. A light year is the distance that light travels over the course of one year. Intriguingly, Proxima Centauri has one planet just inside its habitable zone, but unfortunately it is 'tidally locked' which means that it is always facing the star on its same side, so it is very unlikely to support an atmosphere. And anyway, 4.2 light years means that if a spaceship could travel at the speed of light, it would take a little over four years to get there. The problem is that the speed of light is 186,000 miles (300,000 km) per second, or more than seven times around the equator within a second. That's 671 million miles, or over a billion kilometres per hour.

The fastest spaceship that humans have yet propelled into space is Voyager-1, launched in 1977. So far, Voyager-1 has travelled 0.0003% of one light-year in 47 years and is currently moving at 1/18,000th the speed of light. That is 62,000 kilometres or 38,500 miles per hour which, let's face it, already sounds pretty fast. At this speed it would take Voyager-1 72,000 years to reach Proxima Centauri.

And that is our nearest star, apart from the Sun. Given the distances involved, space travel to and from other habitable planets outside our solar system remains science fiction, and may well always remain so. The speed of light is a very tough barrier to get anywhere near to, even if, at the very smallest scale, quantum mechanics appears to violate it in weird and wonderful ways.

Perhaps we can occasionally catch a brief glimpse of eternity, but it quickly runs away from us. It hardly matters anyway, because the Universe isn't anything like that old, though space is truly that big. The Universe is only about 13.8 billion years old. A long time, but still finite.

Our own blue planet, the Earth, was formed roughly 4.5 billion years ago through the accretion of stellar dust particles, making it about a third the age of the Universe. No one knows how long it took for this gathering of matter to amass, but the early life of the planet, once it had formed a core and a planet-like shape, was marked by huge volcanic activity and massive collisions with other astral bodies. One of these cataclysmic collisions is thought to have caused the Earth's tilt in relation to the Sun and the formation of the Moon. Gradually, after about half a billion years, the big collisions became far less frequent, the planet cooled, and the Earth's thin surface crust began to form.

It remains an intriguing scientific mystery as to how the oceans were formed. But water somehow arrived on the planet over aeons of time, possibly from icy comets. With the arrival of water, chemical replications soon began, as molecules made random connections with one another, forming new compounds and structures that eventually became able to make copies of themselves. Replication mistakes were made occasionally and some of these mistakes led to better replicators which multiplied more effectively. Further mistakes led to further improvements, such that if the 'error' was better suited to the environment, it was more likely to survive. As the fast-expanding population of copies altered the environment, there were more selection pressures causing different copy types to do well in one area but poorly in others. In this way complexity developed. These were the earliest forms of evolution and life on Earth, roughly four billion years ago.

Of the many early forms of cell that then evolved, only one type survived to the present day through its descendants. It is believed that the Last Universal Common Ancestor of all living things, **LUCA**, lived during the early Achaean eon, about 3.5 billion years ago, or possibly a little earlier.

The great English naturalist Charles Darwin (1809-1882) imagined this very species when he poetically wrote that *"probably all the organic beings which have ever lived on this earth have descended from some one primordial form, into which life was first breathed.* " [3]

LUCA was the lifeform from which all living things today have evolved. LUCA used the same replicating method that predominates in the world today – DNA, a biological sequence of genetic information. The DNA of LUCA was presumably simple compared with that of modern species. By contrast, the human genome contains 3.2 billion base pairs, the building blocks of DNA's famous double helix. This is pure information stored in biological code (even though some of the code appears to be meaningless rubbish). With the exception of certain types of cells (notably red blood cells), every one of the approximately 100 thousand billion cells in your body (that's 100,000,000,000,000,000) has its own copy of that biological code, your DNA, or genome.

The information stored in our genes instructs proteins to combine with other proteins to make certain biological events occur at particular moments during our lifespan, provided the conditions are right. Genes influence our biological development and behaviour, but many of them are fundamentally dependent upon there being appropriate input from our environment (e.g. nutrients, stimulation etc.), and often at particularly sensitive times in our life. This dance between nature and nurture will be particularly apparent when we come to think about how children's brains and minds develop.

All life forms today – bacteria, plants, fungi, and animals (and that includes us humans) share LUCA as our one common ancestor. Since then, there has been a continuous unbroken chain of descendants branching out to every living organism that exists in the world today. In that sense, we are effectively as old as, and no older than, every other living organism on this planet, 3.5 billion years old. This branching out from ancient simpler organisms to the animals and plants that exist today can be imagined, as Darwin did, as the Evolutionary Tree of Life. Although it remains fundamentally the same tree, it has recently had to be significantly redrawn as a

---

[3]   Darwin C. (1959) *On the Origin of Species by Means of Natural Selection.* London: John Murray

result of modern genomics because some previously held assumptions were found to be wrong.

Now, so that we can better picture the timescales involved, let us imagine that LUCA existed on 1ˢᵗ January and that the present moment exists in the last moment of 31ˢᵗ December, a year later. Let us call this the LUCA Scale, a measure of those 3.5 billion years mapped onto this one year.

The LUCA Scale

LUCA (3.5bya)

In the beginning, life was microscopically small, and for nearly two billion years it remained that way. This early life existed entirely in the oceans of Earth so it is no accident that all life forms continue to depend on water today. About two and a half to three billion years ago, some early cells began using the Sun as an energy source, rather than absorbing energy from the organic molecules around them. This photosynthesis, along with water, is the basis of almost all life, converting the Sun's energy into energy that the plant is able to use. If plants could not do that, then all other life forms would die because, to put it bluntly, everything has to eat something else.

One by-product of this early explosion of photosynthesis was the release of huge quantities of oxygen into the environment. At first the oxygen simply reacted with the minerals it could easily bind with, such as iron and limestone, but once the exposed minerals had rusted and been oxidised, the oxygen began to accumulate in the atmosphere. This huge increase in oxygen led to the extinction of many early life forms, but some were resistant to it and some of these species gradually evolved the ability to use oxygen to extract more energy from the same amount of food. In time, this abundance of oxygen also led to the formation of the ozone layer in the upper atmosphere. The ozone layer protects the Earth from harmful ultraviolet radiation, without which the evolution of more complex life forms would have been impossible. Half a billion years ago stromatolites began appearing on land formed by layer upon layer of cyanobacteria, a single-cell microbe that is able to photosynthesise. These were followed by mosses and liverworts and later vascular plants which are able to capture carbon dioxide in the air. Much later ferns, pines and conifers appeared, well before other types of trees.

Single-cell creatures remained the only life form for nearly two billion years. It was a long time coming, but eventually, somehow, for this is another scientific mystery, single cell organisms evolved the capacity for sexual reproduction. Sexual reproduction was the necessary precursor to multi-cellularity, in other words creatures with more than one cell. In turn, multicellularity not only led to bigger organisms but gave rise to more specialisation and complexity within particular cells. And eventually sponges, jellyfish and coral, fish, insects, reptiles, and mammals like us.

About 600 million years ago (October 29th, over 80 per cent of the time since LUCA) the first multicellular organisms appeared in the form of sponge-like creatures. Twenty million years later (roughly two days on the LUCA scale) saw the very first animals, cnidarians, a jellyfish-like organism with nerve and muscle that enabled them to move. The first eyes also evolved at this time. Thirty million years later flatworms appeared, the first creature with a primitive brain, and ten million years after that, the acorn worm evolved to have a circulatory system, a heart, and a gill-like structure that allowed it to breathe. It was the precursor to primitive fish (10th November).

The LUCA Scale

LUCA (3.5 bya)

January								February								March								April						
S	M	T	W	T	F	S		S	M	T	W	T	F	S		S	M	T	W	T	F	S		S	M	T	W	T	F	S
						2			1	2	3	4	5	6			1	2	3	4	5	6						1	2	3
3	4	5	6	7	8	9		7	8	9	10	11	12	13		7	8	9	10	11	12	13		4	5	6	7	8	9	10
10	11	12	13	14	15	16		14	15	16	17	18	19	20		14	15	16	17	18	19	20		11	12	13	14	15	16	17
17	18	19	20	21	22	23		21	22	23	24	25	26	27		21	22	23	24	25	26	27		18	19	20	21	22	23	24
24	25	26	27	28	29	30		28								28	29	30	31					25	26	27	28	29	30	
31																														

May								June								July								August						
S	M	T	W	T	F	S		S	M	T	W	T	F	S		S	M	T	W	T	F	S		S	M	T	W	T	F	S
						1				1	2	3	4	5						1	2	3		1	2	3	4	5	6	7
2	3	4	5	6	7	8		6	7	8	9	10	11	12		4	5	6	7	8	9	10		8	9	10	11	12	13	14
9	10	11	12	13	14	15		13	14	15	16	17	18	19		11	12	13	14	15	16	17		15	16	17	18	19	20	21
16	17	18	19	20	21	22		20	21	22	23	24	25	26		18	19	20	21	22	23	24		22	23	24	25	26	27	28
23	24	25	26	27	28	29		27	28	29	30					25	26	27	28	29	30	31		29	30	31				
30	31																													

Dinosaur extinction (66mya)

September								October								November								December						
S	M	T	W	T	F	S		S	M	T	W	T	F	S		S	M	T	W	T	F	S		S	M	T	W	T	F	S
				1	2	3	4						1	2			1	2	3	4	5	6					1	2	3	4
5	6	7	8	9	10	11		3	4	5	6	7	8	9		7	8	9	10	11	12	13		5	6	7	8	9	10	11
12	13	14	15	16	17	18		10	11	12	13	14	15	16		14	15	16	17	18	19	20		12	13	14	15	16	17	18
19	20	21	22	23	24	25		17	18	19	20	21	22	23		21	22	23	24	25	26	27		19	20	21	22	23	24	25
26	27	28	29	30				24	25	26	27	28	29	30		28	29	30						26	27	28	29	30	31	
								31																						

MULTICELLULAR ORGANISMS (600mya)   **NOW**

As time passed, life evolved to become yet more complex and diverse. Some combinations of genes, or genetic errors during reproduction, were fatal and led individuals to die, while others led to functional advantages that enabled the creature to survive, flourish and pass its genes on to subsequent generations. The thing about genes is that they are neither good nor bad; they are used and reused in different circumstances, and this will alter their overall 'fitness'. Throughout these aeons, species became extinct when the physical environment changed, either as the result of natural causes or because the species was unable to compete with other species that were better adapted to the ecosystem.

Extinctions can occur suddenly or gradually over many thousands of years, but the greater the genetic diversity within a species the more likely it will survive, because its diversity gives it more options to 'choose' from as it 'tries' to adapt to changing conditions. Genetic diversity thus makes a species (or ecosystem) more resilient.

Every extinction enabled another species to thrive. It is commonly thought that 99.9% of all species that ever existed are now extinct. Mass extinctions however are rare, though it is now clear that human beings are responsible for the one that we are currently going through. Five large extinctions (excluding the current one) have been identified, including that famous one that destroyed all land-based dinosaurs 65 million years ago (25th December on the LUCA Scale) after their very long innings that had lasted 160 million years (roughly 17 days on the timeline). Currently the most popular theory is that the dinosaur extinction was caused by an asteroid, five to fifteen kilometres wide, hitting Earth and causing a massive wave of heat followed by climate cooling. In any event, this extinction is thought to have taken a matter of hours rather than years, and it killed off many mammals and other species, not just reptiles and dinosaurs. Even so, it did not destroy all dinosaurs for some of their descendants, the birds, are still with us today. Happily, our own ancestors survived and at the time they were small, nocturnal insect-eating mammals, mostly living in trees.

But back to our story. Around half a billion years ago (10th November) the first animals with backbones evolved, vertebrates in the form of fish which had cartilage rather than bone. Although the vertebrates represent merely one branch among animals on the Tree of Life, our very early ancestors evolved on that branch. A hundred million years later some fish known as tetrapods were able to manage to survive in fresh water and, a few million years after that there evolved fish that had limb-like fins with which to yank themselves around on muddy river banks. These first amphibians had both lungs and gills.

By 300 million years ago (1st December) the amphibians had evolved into reptiles, similar to modern lizards, with a relatively advanced nervous system and the ability to reproduce and lay eggs on land. They ate early insects which had first appeared on Earth a hundred million years earlier and have their own evolutionary story to tell as they branched out through the Tree of Life. A few tens of millions of years after their first appearance, reptiles split into what are regarded as the ancestors of modern reptiles and the ancestors of mammals.

True mammals appeared around 220 million years ago (9th December). Unlike reptiles, female mammals have mammary glands that produce milk. Almost no mammals lay eggs while most reptiles do. Some snakes give birth to live young, which for some people is a truly revolting thought to entertain. Reptiles abandon their offspring soon after they are hatched, while most mammals show some interest in their young. In fact, humans are unusual in sustaining a commitment to caring for their young for an exceptionally long time.

Mammals continued to differentiate into different species, and around 100 million years ago (21st December) we would have met the last common ancestor of the humans and mice that exist in the world today. Thereafter, their evolutionary line split into separate branches.

A species of mammal with the wonderful name of Purgatorius is thought to be as close as one gets to the last common ancestor of all primates. Purgatorius may have had little resemblance to modern humans, but palaeontologists believe, largely based on the fossil record of its teeth, that it was quite likely to be one of our species' key ancestors. At the very least, Purgatorius was one of the very earliest primates (or possibly a proto-primate). It was only six inches long and looked a bit like a rat. It ate insects, could run along the lower branches of trees and burrow itself into the ground. We can imagine our distant ancestor using its strong claws to tear away at the earth, but soon after this fingernails gradually replaced claws among primates, so presumably the need to dig was becoming less adaptive.

Thirty-five million years later, our ancestors were still mostly living in trees. As the Miocene era came to an end about 25 million years ago (29th December), African forests began to diminish, enabling drier, more seasonal habitats to spread – scrublands, grasslands, savannahs. One particular primate ancestor, called the Haplorrhini, diverged into two new branches. One branch, the New World monkeys, lived in land that became South America, and further evolved as the continent drifted apart from Africa. The other branch remained in Africa and again divided into Old World Monkeys and Apes, including the Great Apes, also known as Hominids.

Hominids share a common ancestor but then branched off from gibbons around 15 million years ago, from orangutans 13 million, and from gorillas 10 million years ago. Finally, about 7 million years ago the ancestors of mankind began to deviate from the ancestors of modern chimpanzees until they became separate species, which is to say that interbreeding would produce infertile offspring (like a mule) or none at all. This corresponds to about 7am on the last day of the year on the LUCA timeline. During these seven million years (the last 17 hours of the year) there have been a diversity of hominin species with several existing at the same time, most recently the Neanderthals and us humans.

Perhaps it is time to adopt a new scale, one that depicts those last remaining hours of 31st December. Let us call it the **Chimp Scale**. Imagine that the first day of the year now represents this fork on the Evolutionary Tree of Life, 7 million years ago, when our human ancestors and chimpanzees became distinct species, and the last moment of the last day of the year represents now.

The genus Homo is about 2 million years old, so according to this new scale Homo appeared on 15th September. Since then there have been several Homo incarnations and descendants: habilis, erectus, heidelbergensis, neanderthalensis, and much more recently Homo sapiens, our species, which is about 250,000 years old, appearing on 18th December of the new Chimp Scale.

The Chimp Scale

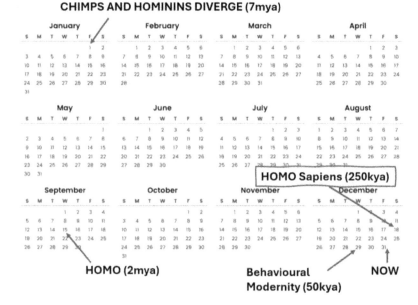

CHIMPS AND HOMININS DIVERGE (7mya)

HOMO Sapiens (250kya)

HOMO (2mya)

Behavioural Modernity (50kya)

NOW

So, as human beings, we are a species of African ape, and a close cousin to chimpanzees and bonobos. Our African origin is something that Charles Darwin proposed and which has since been confirmed by abundant fossil and genome findings. Famously, we share over 97% of our genes with chimpanzees. However, there is far more genetic variation among chimpanzees than among humans. It seems that we are an unusually homogenous species, for all our superficial differences. It has been estimated that, rather like LUCA, there is a genetic isopoint about 3,400 years ago, when the population of humans alive then were the ancestors of everyone alive today.

There is therefore no sensible biological basis for the whole idea of race. In fact, modern biologists would prefer to do away entirely with the slightly absurd concept of human 'races'. They point out that there is more genetic variation within a particular 'race' than between 'races'. Superficial physical characteristics and cultural differences may make us seem very different from one another, but they are simply that...cultural.

Our human ancestors with their front-facing stereoscopic eyes were standing on two feet some 3 to 4 million years ago, thus freeing up their hands. Bipedal walking reflects the brain's ability to constantly co-ordinate muscles and adjust the physiological functions of the body to manage the business of balancing on two legs. And we also have very special hands. From our tree-dwelling days we have hands that can sense the weight and strength of branches, and grasp objects both firmly and delicately. With a thumb that can oppose the remaining four fingers, and with fingers that can be operated individually, our hands can manipulate almost anything. In fact, the human hand has such direct neural connections to the brain that we might think of our hands as instruments of our consciousness, enabling us not only to experience touch with enormous precision but also to gesture to others in uniquely human ways. Our fingertip sensitivity is extraordinary when you really focus your attention on it. Cut a fingertip even slightly and we are reminded of the many nerve pathways that signal pain.

A precision hand is not much good however without precision eye-sight. Remember that our recent primate ancestors were clambering about in the trees of dense forests. Most mammals use their noses to read their environment; primates use their superior eyes. The evolution of three-dimensional binocular vision enabled early primates to leap from branch to branch swiftly and with accuracy. In fact, the human visual system dominates our other sensory inputs. We certainly have extraordinary hand-eye co-ordination. Notice what happens when a pen slips off someone's table and the speed with which their hand darts down to the precise spot where it is possible to catch it. Or the milliseconds it takes for a cricketer's eyes to calculate the trajectory of a ball travelling at 80 miles an hour, and their hand's ability to snatch it out of the air. That exquisite coordination is delivered by the brain.

Primates developed colour vision (distinguishing between ripe and unripe fruit) where it is absent in other mammals. In fact, the visual system is largely responsible for the relatively large brain size of higher primates and the need for better visual acuity within the ever-more complex social world. Roughly a third of the human brain is devoted to vision, the business of transforming raw photons of light into recognisable objects. We process a vast amount of information through our primary sense, vision.

Social primates have a much wider range of expressions than other mammals, and apes such as ourselves have more complex facial muscles and range of expression than monkeys. As facial expressions became more complex, so visual processing systems evolved that were better able to accurately recognise these new patterns of communication. Reading other people's facial expressions became useful for survival.

Yet despite our extraordinary advantages in sensory perception, we paradoxically don't give much attention to a lot of what our senses are experiencing from moment to moment. We will return to this important observation a little later. But for now, stop. Close your eyes for a full 10 seconds and observe what your senses are telling you.

Notice how, while your eyes are shut, you can hear things more intensely. Listen too for sounds you had not previously noticed, background sounds you had 'tuned out'. With eyes closed, sound is now your primary input. Sound can often be in the foreground, such as when we are having a conversation or listening intensely to something, but most of the time it is secondary to what we can see visually (assuming, of course, that we can). Now, shut your eyes again for another ten seconds and this time notice the intensity of the experience of sight when you reopen your eyes. Sight simply floods your brain with information.

Most of the environment that surrounds modern humans has been made by other people and it remains a largely audio-visual world. Look around again – unless you happen to be in Nature, almost everything you see has been constructed by people. We are clearly master tool-makers, and technology in its broadest sense is our trademark. The use of simple tools has been around for about 2 to 3 million years, soon after the genus Homo originated and the time when Homo habilis began developing our unusually large brain. Their hands, as already mentioned, had evolved to be skilled at manipulating objects. By 1.5 million years ago Homo had controlled fire, though some archaeological scientists dispute this, claiming the earliest solid evidence is not until Homo erectus around 400,000 years ago.

Other than Homo sapiens (modern humans), all other species of Homo are now extinct. Our most recently surviving relative, Homo neanderthalensis (the Neanderthals), died out only about 25 to 40 thousand years ago (or, on the Chimp Scale, the 29th December), a few tens of thousands of years after they and Homo sapiens had left Africa and spread into Europe and as far as China.

From all this one must deduce that our bodies, and consequently our brains, are evolutionarily primed to exploit the ecology of an African savannah. We are built for a world that existed between a million and a hundred thousand years ago. Our lives may be immersed in the complex technological world that surrounds us today but it is important not to be wholly taken in by it. Just like any other species, we have unique biological characteristics, such as drives and emotions, that evolved, and the advantages and limitations of those adaptations still shape our lives today.

So, in summary, although we have clever brains that produce minds, we are also defined by our biological inheritance. It is likewise easy to forget that we coexist with other life forms on this planet, and that we need them rather more than they need us.

When we consider that all species, including gnats, trees and ourselves, originated from LUCA, our common ancestor, we begin to see that all animals and plants are cousins in one way or another. And this also goes for species that exist in us, in as far as they live within our body. It has been estimated that there are a hundred trillion bacteria living quite happily in our small and large intestine. Even more astonishing to consider is that almost every cell in our body stores chemical energy in the form of tiny structures called mitochondria. This is how the cells of any animal are able to store energy. The mitochondria in our body's cells were once a separate species, much like a bacterium, and they carry their own separate genetic code or DNA. Everyone inherits their mitochondria from their mother. It is amazing to ponder the fact that another species effectively exists within almost all our cells.

Behavioural Modernity

It was only in the last million years that our Homo forebears became foragers, but that is long enough for our brains to be well adapted for this type of hunting and gathering. These ancestors lived in small nomadic groups of a few dozen people and obtained their food by walking long distances each day, hunting animals or gathering plants. Natural selection, generation after generation, gently fashioned the human brain, favouring brains that were good at solving the everyday challenges these ancestors faced – like hunting animals, gathering plant nutrients, finding mates, caring for young, defending against aggression, maintaining the tribe, negotiating with allies, and so on. We are descended from those humans whose brains were more effective in solving these challenges and were therefore able to leave more children.

The archaeological evidence suggests that for over a million years our ancient Homo ancestors had been using virtually the same design for their hand axes, indicating that they at least knew how to imitate one another, even if they were not imaginative enough to come up with a better design.

But then, about 50,000 years ago, the archaeological record dramatically changes (10am on 29th December on the Chimp Scale, a couple of pages back). This is the time when human creativity, and technology suddenly took off, a time when jewellery, projectile weapons, cave paintings, fish-hooks, pigments, bone tools, and, indeed, new hand axe designs, start to appear in the archaeological record. This period also coincides with a sudden rapid growth in the human population between 50,000 and 30,000 years ago.

Not quite everyone agrees that there was this sudden change in human behaviour around this time; some people believe that change occurred more continuously over a much longer period. There is evidence of burial rituals as early as 100,000 years ago. Anatomically, modern Homo sapiens dates from about 250 to 300,000 years ago, but although there were presumably innovative geniuses in much earlier times, many scientists who have studied the evidence conclude that a fundamental change in cognition occurred between 40 and 60 thousand years ago, because of the wealth of artefacts that suddenly start appearing in the archaeological record from around that time. It seems that human brains began working in entirely new ways, putting thoughts together and creating new ideas. This was Behavioural Modernity, the advent of thinking and the dawn of human civilisation.

Behavioural Modernity was an evolutionary development like no other. Archaeologists sometimes refer to it as the Great Leap Forward, or The Cognitive Revolution. Behavioural Modernity was an astonishing change within Nature: the ability of a species to symbolically model and predict the world in their brains. To think. This was the beginning of mental life.

Behavioural Modernity very likely coincided with the expansion of language, which would make sense, creating more opportunities to collaborate and cooperate with other people and achieve common goals, such as hunting together which, in turn, led to a more calorific diet. This positive feedback loop of thinking, collaboration, increased calories, population growth, and more complex language and ideas, all became part of an interactive iterative process that led to the extraordinary technological progress and understanding that humans have achieved ever since. And no, not forgetting that it has also led to the unfettered greed and consumption so common in 'developed' societies that has ultimately depleted and wounded the very planet that sustains us. If the Cognitive Revolution had not come about, climate change, habitat destruction, resource depletion, overpopulation, and many social conflicts would not have arisen, and the ecosystems of the world would likely still be intact. Well, for good or bad, Behavioural Modernity was where it all began.

A dog can read the emotional state of its owner. So yes, other animals are able to mentally represent the world and react to it on the basis of what they have learned, but with relatively trivial exceptions they appear to do so without much complex thinking or reflection. They are sentient in that their nervous system is alert and responsive, and they feel pain. Their reactions and behaviour are an expression of their genes, bodies, and instincts, and from operant and associative learning during their lives. Much of human behaviour is forged in this way too of course, but modern human minds are also entirely different.

This 'new software technique', as Richard Dawkins has referred to it, meant that suddenly humans were able to mentally represent objects that were not physically present. In time, they learned to represent ideas that are not even physical (e.g. abstract ideas such as 'beyond', 'above' etc.) This I will be arguing gave rise to human consciousness as we experience and think about it today.

Behavioural Modernity represented a fundamental shift within Nature, the capacity of a species to learn from past experience, represent it in their minds, and create new ideas and behaviour. These ideas have ultimately led to everything we know and largely take for granted in the world today, the vast complexity of human culture that surrounds us - all the customs, religions, beliefs, human-made objects (artefacts), institutions, education, medicine... indeed, almost everything we 'know' has developed during this time. These past 50,000 years contain all the civilisations and beliefs that humans have ever created for themselves. This enormous complexity is what we think of as human culture, or the social world, and we will consider this further in *Chapter 8: Cultural Storage*.

One important survival advantage of modern minds is that they are able to generalise from experience. They are able use what they have learned from their experiences to model, imagine and anticipate the future in sophisticated ways. Another critical survival advantage of having a meaning-making mind is that we humans are, within limits, capable of regulating our drives and emotions, affording us a measure of self-control. We will return to mental modelling and self-regulation throughout the rest of this book because they are both key to what makes human minds, and our species, so unique.

The true Genesis was therefore roughly 50 thousand years ago, when early humans started flexing their modern minds. It was the time when people first began to 'conceptualise', to manipulate symbols in their minds representing the world beyond, the first time a species had been able to think about the world and their place within it. With Behavioural Modernity, it was no longer only our genes that were working towards our survival and welfare (e.g. biological defences, emotional reactions etc.), it was also our minds. Suddenly, we were able to escape the present and were free to mentally play with lessons from the past and plans for the future. Cultural evolution soon began to eclipse biological evolution.

According to our Chimp Scale, Behavioural Modernity, this modern way of aggressively fashioning Nature, has only been around for the last two and a half days of the year. Extraordinarily recently. If we were to go back to the LUCA Scale, it would represent the last seven and a half minutes of the last day of the year.

But how did Behavioural Modernity come about? Why did we start thinking in these modern ways? How did our species come to make sense of the world around us in a way that was entirely unprecedented in Nature? What ultimately led to Behavioural Modernity remains another intriguing scientific mystery. Several theories have been put forward to account for this relatively sudden change in human behaviour after millions of years during which very little had changed. Was it perhaps the result of a sudden increase in brain size that caused this new and very different way of using the brain? Was it due to hunting in groups? Was it catalysed by a sudden breakthrough in tool-making technology? Better nutrition? Was it the size of the group that encouraged people to replace mutual grooming with language? Living in a larger group puts greater demands on social intelligence. Or was it the result of trade between humans that required interactions that gave rise to more and more complex verbal representation of ideas?

One convincing case, made by Matt Ridley, is that trade led individuals to specialise in making or acquiring things that they could then exchange with others. The more we do something, the better we become at making or acquiring it. The better the product, the more other people will want it. The more of it we can make or acquire, the more of that commodity we have to barter for things that we want. Exchange didn't have to be equal, it simply had to benefit both parties.

With specialisation came technological progress, and with exchange and barter came the need for better communication and more complex language. In the marketplace of barter, it was helpful if strangers could communicate and trust one another sufficiently well to trade objects. To establish trust, people need to be able to read one another's motives and intentions so that they can spot cheating. Language provided the communication method by which people could begin to exchange ideas, and human culture is ultimately built through the exchange of ideas.

This Great Leap Forward of modern minds may have been the result of trade between wary people, but it would have been strengthened by women learning to collaborate and communicate around shared child-rearing, and engaging in more complicated relationships within the tribe. In any event, consciousness ultimately emerged as a solution to the challenges of social living, enabling individuals to understand, communicate, and cooperate with one another more effectively.

Could we look at one last timeline, this time expanding those last two and a half days on the Chimp Scale, the time since Behavioural Modernity emerged, onto a full year? On this scale, 100 years is just over 17 hours.

The Behavioural Modernity Scale

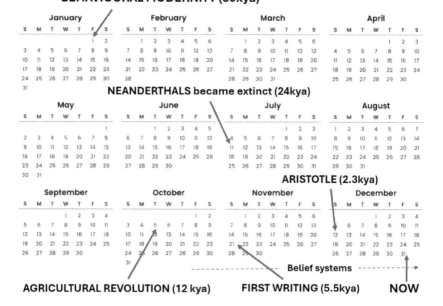

Whatever its cause, Behavioural Modernity was a revolution in cooperation and collaboration, eventually leading to the establishment of the first permanent villages in the Neolithic period, and the domestication of plants and animals (farming and herding animals) during the first 'Agricultural Revolution'. Agriculture is a fairly modern expression of our ability to model and anticipate the world, and is thought to have developed as recently as 12,000 years ago, no time at all when we consider that the earliest Egyptians were unified about 5,000 years ago, and the Christian calendar is just over 2,000 years old (16th December on the new scale).

Stable communities led to teaching and the passing down of knowledge, customs and beliefs to future generations. Human knowledge has been gradually building ever since, and exponentially since the Enlightenment of the 18th century. But on the negative side, the unfettered domestication of Nature over the past fifty years has led, among other things, to intensive farming practices and high levels of pollution. It has been estimated that 60% of the world's mammals are currently livestock, mainly cattle, pigs, and chicken, 36% are humans, and only 4% of mammals exist in the wild. That too is the result of Behavioural Modernity.

Looking at this last timeline, we can see more clearly that beliefs about the world in general, and that includes religions and systems of government are a fairly recent phenomenon. It seems likely that the many different belief systems that emerged all over the world only did so when language and conceptual thought had reached a sufficient level of complexity, corresponding to the last few months of the year at most.

Thinking

To be able to think you need three things.

First, the ability to mentally represent the world using mental symbols, so-called symbolic representations. Instead of having to point at something present to be understood we could name it with a word.

Second, the ability to maintain, or hold in mind, a train of thoughts. Symbolic thought requires a temporary store or workspace in which ideas can be 'moved around'.

Third, the ability to store what we learn in memory, so as to be able to draw on this knowledge in future situations.

Other animals can sometimes do all of these things in relatively simple ways, but only humans can think about abstract ideas like harmony, love, kindness, beauty, courage, and compassion... as well as other, less pleasant ideas.

So let us briefly look at these three critical aspects of the mind, language, working-memory, and long-term memory before exploring them more fully in subsequent chapters.

Language and symbolic thought

Some inhabitants of La Gomera in the Canary Islands communicate across valleys using el silbo, a language made up of different whistles. It may have been people imitating the sounds of Nature in a similar way, or perhaps adding emphasis to gesture and sign language in the service of trade, that gave birth to early verbal language systems. Words became symbols for objects and ideas about the world at large. The building blocks.

At any rate, what may have started as a grunt to indicate pleasure and perhaps a groan to signify displeasure has, over the 50,000 years since modern minds appeared, spawned the nearly 7,000 complex languages that exist in the world today. Sadly, about 30 per cent of them are currently endangered and it is estimated that six languages disappear every year.

There was almost certainly language before modern brains came along, but it would not have been communicating particularly complex ideas. Jonathan Turner has plausibly argued that, being visually-dominant, bipedal, and having highly flexible hands and upper bodies, early humans were able to communicate their emotions to one another through body language. Accordingly, Turner argues, gestural communication helped provide the neuroanatomical structures for the later development of verbal languages.

With verbal language, humans developed the ability to articulate a wide range of sounds that could be combined in an infinite number of ways to represent the world around them. And, critically, language allowed these verbal symbols to be communicated between people. Such symbols include words, ideas, memes, images, and yes, literal symbols like letters on a page or screen.

Perhaps the most astonishing feature of symbolic language is not that it 'contains' words that 'name' objects (nouns: tree, rock, man etc.), words that 'describe' things (adjectives: brown, hard, old etc.) and words that 'denote' actions and the 'relationship between' objects and events (verbs, conjunctions and prepositions: goes, because, from, to, etc.). What is even more amazing is that it has led to the development and use of abstract ideas, such as love, trust, courage and beauty. These do not exist in nature as things, like a tree, but simply as fuzzy ideas.

Metaphors enable people to express abstract ideas in relation to one another, *as if* they were objects or living things (e.g. a 'stormy relationship'). For example, the proto-language word for 'fire' may have been later used to describe someone's anger or passion. Look again at the first sentence in the previous paragraph – the words in inverted commas 'underline' the abstract metaphorical nature of language, one of the many features of language that the Canadian linguist and psychologist Steven Pinker has so eloquently described. When, in English, a person 'gets a handle' on a situation, the word handle is no longer describing a 'thing'. The idea of a handle is used to convey an abstract meaning.

Conceptual thought enables people to 'juggle' abstract ideas, and 'play' imaginatively with symbols, and it results in the creativity of humans compared with other animals or computers. The fact that our brain can carry, even within its billions of neural connections, the abstract idea of 'kindness' is an astonishingly clever mind-brain feat. Using analogy and metaphor, people are able to manipulate abstract images and ideas, using them as raw material for imagination and creativity in both the sciences and the arts.

But humans are not the only species capable of thinking in abstract ways. Scientists at Oxford University showed newly-hatched ducks two different objects, and they showed another group of ducks two identical objects. Later they found that, even though they had changed the objects in question, the ducks subsequently followed either two different objects, or two identical objects, depending on which they had been exposed to. This, the authors assert, show that ducks are capable of perceiving abstract relationships in the world around them. Indeed, scientists believe that this type of abstract generalisation may be common among other species. However, while this may be so, only human minds can play with several abstract ideas at once in working-memory[4] and dispatch them on a new train of thought.

Language, Pinker points out, is both combinatorial (ideas can combine with other ideas) and recursive (ideas can be embedded within other ideas). This means that although there may be a relatively finite number of words in any particular language, they can give rise to a limitless expanse of ideas and knowledge. And this of course also goes for how we think, on the assumption that language is merely the mind expressing itself. And it is true, we can think almost anything.

Whether spoken or written, language allows information and ideas to be communicated from one person to another and for knowledge to be stored and passed down from one generation to the next. In view of the importance of this remarkable feat of speaking and understanding language, it is not surprising that human brains have evolved to respond to the sound of human speech from a very young age.

Language enables this very thought from my mind to be transmitted into your mind through symbols: my ideas are turned into written letters and words and sentences, and your brain reassembles my words into coherent meanings. As Noam Chomsky has said, language is *"the core defining feature of modern humans, the source of human creativity, cultural enrichment, and complex social structure."* [5]

In the only recording Virginia Woolf made for the BBC, in 1937, she made the point that the words that make up language are not literal representations but are charged with nuanced meanings that are personally as well as culturally derived: *"Words do not live in dictionaries, they live in the mind... full of echoes, memories, associations, naturally. They've been out and about on people's lips*

---

[4] I have chosen to spell working-memory with a hyphen in the hope of making it easier for readers to distinguish this type of workspace memory from the many different forms of long-term memory. It is normally spelled without a hyphen. `

[5] **Chomsky N.** (2019) On Language and Humanity: In Conversation With Noam Chomsky. Interviewed by Amy Brand on August 12th 2019. Cambridge, MA: The MIT Press Reader

— in the houses, in the streets, in the fields, for so many centuries... *stored with other meanings, with other memories..."*

Much of what people think is mediated by language, but not everything is based on words alone. We are able to 'read between the lines', to infer *implicit* meaning from events and one another, not simply the literal and superficial facts.

Music is rightly regarded as the most abstract of all art forms. It has its own many languages and traditions, and is so diverse that people from one culture cannot always appreciate or understand the musical language of another. Even so, music is a human universal, used in every culture in the world, and has probably served as a way of bonding people together within a tribe or social grouping all the way back to antiquity – singing, drumming, and making music together.

Language has its own limitations however, as Wittgenstein pointed out. It is enormously practical, enabling the world to operate, rather than being especially good at description. For instance, we have a remarkable ability to recognize faces, but can we describe a friend's face in words that would uniquely identify them from others? Can we accurately convey the taste of steamed rice or the smell of a particular flower? Wittgenstein's point is that our minds can represent and remember ideas and experiences in ways that are beyond verbal language.

Thought is therefore not simply some internal verbal conversation because that would be too slow to account for the speed with which we are able to react intelligently to the world. Notwithstanding its limitations, language and abstract thought have liberated the human brain from evolved genetic prescriptions and the fixed action-patterns from our ancestral past. Intellectual curiosity and exploration are primary hallmarks of humanity but they are only possible because of symbolic language.

It is not only four-year-olds who are incessantly asking the question 'why'. In all verbal languages, the idea of cause-and-effect helps people structure their experience of the world. It appears to be a fundamental aspect of how we think. We are generally unable to look at the world around us without sooner or later wanting to understand what is going on.

Chimps may be able to crack open a nut using a stone, but they lack the imagination to fashion a more useful tool the way that humans can. Making a tool requires the ability to think in terms of cause and effect, and when humans see an effect, they feel compelled to understand its cause. Only humans need to understand how and why. Accident investigators go to astonishing lengths when a plane crashes in order to learn the reasons for it, so that changes can be made and crashes can be avoided in the future.

Working-memory

Language only works if the person using it is able to hold an idea in mind long enough to understand or express it. This capacity to maintain ideas in the mind is known as **working-memory**. Think of it as very temporary memory storage, or a rapidly changing workspace. Working-memory is not unique to humans for other primates certainly seem to have it, but humans make far better use of it.

The span of normal working-memory is less than a second, the present moment, and there is a limit to how much we can carry in it. And it is being constantly refreshed. Most people are able to hold about seven digits, six letters, or five words in mind. Saying a number out loud allows us to hold the sound in (the phonological loop of) working-memory until we are able to write it down.

When we hold things in working-memory it enables us to remember words from the beginning of a sentence by the time we get to the words at the end of it. That, by the way, was a 31-word sentence, though it is unlikely you can now remember the words of the sentence in the right order, so much as the general gist of the ideas. That is how working-memory works. It enables us to maintain a train of thought.

Working-memory enables us to keep ideas in mind, follow a train of thought, and manipulate ideas and images. It allows us to understand the present moment in terms of the immediate past, and provides the mental space for us to maintain our changing trains of thoughts. We sustain a train of thoughts in working memory until our attention shifts, so it is like a temporary store in which information flows into it, and information falls off the back of it. A classic example of this 'falling off the back' is what could be described as **cognitive drop-off**, such as when we lose our train of thought, or we forget what we were meaning to do or wanting to say. You walk into the other room... but you have forgotten what you came in here for.

Archaeologists believe that it was an improvement in working-memory combined with the development of language that underpinned the dawn of Behavioural Modernity, enabling humans to think about the world in sophisticated new ways. They argue that enhanced working-memory enabled ideas to be manipulated in the mind, and that all that early new technology (cave paintings, jewellery, etc.) would not have been possible without the combination of symbolic representation and a more effective working-memory.

Long-term memory

Symbols and ideas are not much use unless we are able to remember them from one situation to the next. Once again, long-term memory is certainly not unique to humans but we do seem to have a prodigious ability to retain vast amounts of information in our brains. But not all memory is alike, and in *Chapter 4* we will break apart long-term memory into its different types. More interesting than you might imagine.

The emergence of thinking minds, Behavioural Modernity, was and remains a cognitive revolution within Nature. Human minds are a form of computational biology that are able to use symbols to represent and model a world that does not necessarily exist in the present moment. This was an entirely new phenomenon, born of Nature but self-propelling beyond Nature, storing its knowledge in culture, and only limited by the natural boundary of death.

Only human minds that can maintain a train of interconnected thoughts in working-memory are able to understand the world around them, including themselves. This includes being able to work things out, create stories, and derive meaning from experiences. Only human minds worry about the future, reflect on the past, or are driven to understand what has occurred when something happens that was not expected. Only human minds are able to understand, generalise, and draw conclusions from their experiences. Moreover, only model-making minds with a capacity for language are able to lay down ideas in memory and record their conclusions for future generations, and therewith build culture.

So this was the genesis of the modern cognitive mind, just fifty thousand years ago, and when seen through this lens, we can begin to appreciate just how very recently we humans began to think in this sophisticated new way. It is so recent that we are only now starting to understand and wake up to where we exist within Nature, and what we have done, and might do, with this incredible power, opportunity, and responsibility.

⊢————————⊣

Further Reading

Baddeley, A. and Hitch, G. (1974) Working memory. In The *Psychology of Learning and Motivation* (Bower, G.A., ed.), pp. 47–89, Academic Press

Brand A. (2019) On language and humanity: In conversation with Noam Chomsky. *MIT Press Reader*, August 12th. https://thereader.mitpress.mit.edu/noam-chomsky-interview/

Capra F. (1996) *The Web of Life – A new synthesis of mind and matter*. London: Flamingo (Harper)

Carruthers P. (2013) Evolution of working memory. *Proceedings of the National Academy of Sciences*, 110-S2, 10371-10378

Csíkszentmihályi M, Csíkszentmihályi I. (1988) *Optimal Experience: Psychological Studies of Flow in Consciousness.* Cambridge: Cambridge University Press

Darwin C. (1859) *On the Origin of Species by Means of Natural Selection*. London: John Murray

Dawkins R. (1976) *The Selfish Gene*. Oxford: Oxford University Press

Dawkins R. (2004) *The Ancestor's Tale: A pilgrimage to the dawn of life*. London: Weidenfield and Nicolson

Donald M. (1995) The neurobiology of human consciousness: An evolutionary approach. *Neuropsychologia*, 33, 1087-102.

Donald M. (1998) Hominid enculturation and cognitive evolution. In Renfrew C, Scarre C. (Eds.) Cognition *and Material Culture: The Archaeology of Symbolic Storage.* Cambridge: McDonald Institute for Archaeological Research

Donald M. (2010) The exographic revolution: neuropsychological sequelae. In Malafouris L, Renfrew C. (Eds.) *The Cognitive Life of Things – Recasting the boundaries of the mind*. Cambridge: McDonald Institute for Archaeological Research

Dunbar R. (1997) *Grooming, Gossip and the Evolution of Language*. Cambridge, MA: Harvard University Press.

Gerland P, Raftery A, Ševčíková H, Li N, Gu D, *et al.* (2014). World population stabilization unlikely this century. *Science,* 346, 234-237 doi:10.1126/science.1257469

Gibson K. (2007) Putting it all together: a constructionist approach to the evolution of human mental capacities. In: Mellars P, Boyle K, Bar-Yosef O, Stringer C. (Eds.) *Re-thinking the Human Revolution*. Cambridge: McDonald Institute of Archaeological Research

Hinde R. (1998) Mind and artefact: a dialectical perspective. In Renfrew C, Scarre C. (Eds.) *Cognition and Material Culture: The Archaeology of Symbolic Storage*. Cambridge: McDonald Institute for Archaeological Research

Lowe E. (1998) Personal experience and belief: the significance of external symbolic storage for the emergence of modern human cognition. In Renfrew C, Scarre C. (Eds.) *Cognition and Material Culture: The Archaeology of Symbolic Storage*. Cambridge: McDonald Institute for Archaeological Research

Mellars P. (2007) Introduction. In: Mellars P, Boyle K, Bar-Yosef O, Stringer C. (Eds.) *Re-thinking the Human Revolution*. Cambridge: McDonald Institute of Archaeological Research

Mithen S. (2007) Music and the origin of modern humans. In: Mellars P, Boyle K, Bar-Yosef O, Stringer C. (Eds.) *Re-thinking the Human Revolution*. Cambridge: McDonald Institute of Archaeological Research

Pinker S. (1994) *The Language Instinct: How the Mind Creates Language*. London: Penguin

Ridley M. (2010) *The Rational Optimist*. London: The Fourth Estate

Rutherford, A. (2020) *How to Argue with a Racist*. London: Weidenfeld & Nicolson

Turner J. (2000) *On the Origin of Human Emotions: A Sociological Inquiry into the Evolution of Human Affect*. Stanford: Stanford University Press

Wilson EO. (1975) *Sociobiology: The New Synthesis*. Cambridge: Harvard University Press

Wilson EO. (1984) *Biophilia*. Cambridge: Harvard University Press

Wilson EO. (1998) *Consilience*. London: Abacus, Little Brown and Co

Wynn T, Coolidge FL (2007) Did a small but significant enhancement of working memory capacity power the evolution of modern thinking? In: Mellars P, Boyle K, Bar-Yosef O, Stringer C. (Eds.) *Re-thinking the Human Revolution*. Cambridge: McDonald Institute of Archaeological Research

Yinon M, Phillips R, Milo R. (2018)The biomass distribution on Earth. *Proceedings of the National Academy of Sciences*, 115 (25) 6506-6511, https://doi.org/10.1073/pnas.1711842115

Zimmer C. (2001) *Evolution: The Triumph of an Idea*. New York: Harper Collins

Chapter 3

Bodies and Brains

Rats and dogs

When I was a recently-qualified and much younger version of myself, I was living in a one-bedroom flat in central London. It was a damp and dingy apartment on the ground floor of a pebbledash Victorian terrace, but it was the first home I had owned and of course I loved it. Best of all, it had a small overgrown garden at the back and along the side. I enjoyed the challenge of turning this neglected plot of turf and rubble into a beautiful garden (or so it seemed to me). So that first summer I put many hours into it and soon began to relish my time there.

One summer evening I was sitting in the garden with my girlfriend at that time, showing off my progress. Liz had brought along Bob, her playful Jack Russell, a small terrier bred for its springy white hair and hunting aggression. Bob and I had become friends. As Liz and I chatted away, drink in hand, enjoying a warm London evening, a rat suddenly dashed across the grass, and disappeared under a wooden fence into the neighbour's garden. Instantly, our friendly playful dog turned into a fierce snarling predator. Bob tore after the rat, smashing his head into the fence where the rat had escaped. He began digging furiously at the grass but could not dislodge the hard ground. Bob leapt back and forwards, continuing his savage barking, now jumping into the air in a vain attempt to scale the wall. He barked, snarled, prowled and yapped, taking momentary breaks before resuming his ferocious assault. His muscles were tense and he was growling with fury.

We did our best to calm him down but for the next hour Bob was shaking, almost vibrating with visceral excitement, snarling at us too if we got too near. His instinctive drive as a hunting predator was not only alive and well, it was suddenly violently active. Liz and I had never seen Bob so fired up and in such a frenzied state. But from this I learned that animals can change their emotional state very quickly. What had happened to this otherwise gentle domesticated creature? How had the rat suddenly turned Bob into this wild, raging animal?

Around this time, I met a man who was referred to me with claustrophobia and panic attacks. The first time we met he asked that the door to my consulting room be left wide open. The poor chap was overwhelmed with fear, and this is what he told me.

On his car journey back from work each day he would get as far as the Blackwall Tunnel and then have a panic attack. It was clear from his description that they were indeed panic attacks. His thoughts and emotions were intensifying one another in a feedback loop to the point where he felt utterly out of control.

The Blackwall Tunnel is actually two tunnels, both nearly a mile long, that run underneath the River Thames in east London. The tunnel was well-known at the time for its traffic slows-downs and hold-ups during rush-hour. Over the course of a few months these traffic jams caused the man more and more anxiety to the point where he was feeling panicky every time he entered the tunnel, regardless of whether the traffic was slow-moving or not. If nothing else, his panic attacks were potentially dangerous for him and other drivers. In fact, it had become so bad that his fear had generalised to all enclosed spaces, including, it seemed, my consulting room.

Somehow, he was still managing to complete his journey through the tunnel, but every time he approached it his body would shake with fear until he was on the other side of the tunnel, when he knew that he would shortly be with his wife and children and finally safe in the security of his home.

I noted that his first panic attack had occurred on his way home, and he confirmed that all his early panic attacks had occurred in this same direction of travel. I asked about his home life, but this seemed supportive and largely happy. And then I asked him more about his work which he had said was stressful. But it soon emerged that he was being bullied at work by a nasty vindictive boss who persecuted him on a daily basis. He said that his boss was only interested in results and showed him no respect. It seemed that he was being regularly humiliated by his boss, often in front of other people. (Much later he contacted a lawyer.)

What we soon worked out was that on his way home in the car he would mentally relive the events of his day, particularly when the traffic was once again, irritatingly, stopped in the tunnel. He would become enraged as he thought about the ways his boss had humiliated him earlier in the day. At this point my patient would often notice his heart thumping and his arms shaking, and he interpreted his body's reactions to mean that something was wrong, he was out of control, perhaps he was seriously ill or even 'going mad'. It was terrifying. These thoughts only made his panic worse until his thoughts and emotions escalated into a full-blown panic attack.

But he was not really experiencing fear at all, so much as intense anger and injustice towards his aggressive boss, anger so strong that it led to the same bodily reactions as fear (muscle tension, erratic breathing, increased pulse rate, and so on), and this intense physiological and emotional arousal had become associated with the Blackwall tunnel. The Blackwall tunnel became the threat and an apparent source of danger. His emotions were energising him to resolve a situation that was making him angry, but he was misreading what his emotions were telling him. The conclusions he was drawing from his distress were misplaced. Once we came to understand this, we agreed that he perhaps needed to relearn how to regulate his emotional reactions and consider how best to address the cause of it.

So the lesson I learned is that the way we interpret our emotions can influence the meaning we give to the events that happen in our lives. The assumptions we make are often informed by the emotions we feel at the time, and those assumptions subsequently shape the memories we make. Although they can sometimes overwhelm us, as they clearly had Bob, a lot of the time we don't even take note of the emotions we are feeling. But our emotions and drives are there within us all the time, influencing our judgments, our goals and motivations, and our reactions to other people. Emotions orientate the mind to threat and survival, but they are also intrinsic to our relationships with other people and the memories we form.

Human brains

We tend to take it for granted that we humans are fundamentally different from rats, dogs, gnats, bats, or any other species. For one thing, as we have seen, we happen to be a type of ape and are able to stand up on two legs rather than four. It is far more normal for mammals to walk on four legs, but apes like humans use their front legs as arms and hands.

Get a length of thin wire, or a hunk of clay or something like it, and try to make a *free-standing* figure with roughly the same proportions as a human being. You quickly realise how hard it is to create one, particularly a figure that can stand up and balance on its own two feet. The ability to balance on two legs takes a special kind of brain. When we stand on one leg, the muscular adjustments required for balance become more obvious, but even on one leg the brain does a wonderful job in managing all the micro-adjustments required. Bipedalism is highly efficient, enabling humans to walk very long distances. So much so that, for example, the San people of the Kalahari Desert are able to hunt other animals simply by outwalking and exhausting them.

We also happen to have particularly amazing hands. Match the fingertips of both your hands and very lightly rub your corresponding fingertips together. Close your eyes and visualise the nerve impulses almost instantly shooting up your arms to your brain as you feel those many sensations from your fingertips. Information up both arms too. But are you feeling the sensations at the same time or is your attention shifting from one hand to the other? The main point to grasp is that we have extremely fine fingertip sensitivity, allowing us to hold fragile objects and even read braille if we need to. Our thumbs can press against any of our long fingers, a physical ability that provides us with exquisitely delicate digital agility. That last phrase is worth saying aloud, if for no other reason than to demonstrate the equally extraordinary muscular agility of our larynx, tongue, mouth and lungs to articulate a wide range of sounds enabling us to speak and sing. And speaking of sound, most musical instruments are played with the hands. That exceptional physical skill and dexterity also takes a special kind of brain.

Above all, you can understand these words. No other species can understand complex symbolic language. Combine that two-legged, free-handed dexterity, and now add our species-unique ability to think, to reason, to imagine, and to communicate abstract ideas using language. This extraordinary combination allows us to negotiate the astonishingly complex world that human beings have fashioned for themselves, and it enables us to regulate our immediate urges and emotions to everyone's mutual advantage. Now that takes an incredibly special brain and an unusually long childhood.

No one has ever seen their own brain with their own eyes, or held it in their hands, but most people can accept the idea that they have a brain in their heads and that, housed within it and more generally their body, is their unique mind. Ourselves. So how does that come about? How does a brain work such that it is able to produce minds like ours? To properly untangle that story, we need to understand what brains are made from, and roughly how they work.

It used to be thought that Homo sapiens simply had bigger brains. But it turns out to be not that simple at all. The actual or even relative size of the human brain is no longer considered as important as it was just a few years ago. Neanderthals, for example, had larger brains than Homo sapiens. Not just that, sperm whales have brains five times the weight of human brains but have not shown themselves to be particularly creative as a species. Shrews, which incidentally have hands fairly similar to our own, have the largest brains of all mammals in proportion to their body size, but they are not known for being especially shrewd.

In fact, over the past 30,000 years the human brain has actually shrunk in size and is now roughly 1.5kg (just over 3 lbs). That 1.5kg nonetheless contains so many billions of neurons that there is an almost infinitely large number of possible connections. And within those many connections is you.

So it's not about size, it's more about what can be done with it. And there are many things that human brains can do that other species cannot. Reading a book is merely one of them.

Neurons and neural pathways

Our body contains a *nervous system* that comprises the **brain** and the many nerve fibres that extend from the brain to the far reaches of the body, known as the *peripheral* nervous system. Short and sometimes long 'nerves', or **neurons,** enable information from the senses (sight, hearing, touch, taste, and smell) and pain receptors to travel quickly from the outer extremities of our body back to our brain with split-second speed. For example, when we feel a pain in our toe, the signal reaches our brains via the peripheral nervous system. When we walk, the motor cortex controls movements by sending signals from the brain to the muscles. Sweating, digestion, and heart rate regulation are also part of the peripheral nervous system.

Housed behind our eyes and between our ears, our brain (and spinal chord), also known as the *central* nervous system (CNS), is the most densely packed region of the nervous system. It floats in a fluid that is held within the bony globe of our skull, which helps protect it. The brain is spongy living organic matter that, among other things, processes raw information from our senses about the internal and external world. It receives signals from the body, but it also sends messages out along nerve fibres back to the rest of the body, enabling our muscles to respond.

Our brain is continuously noting and responding to information coming to it from the external world delivered via our senses (our eyes and ear predominantly), from the internal environment of the body, and from our stored memories and associations that are unique to each person. This is a constantly changing informational world, so it makes sense that the neurons of the brain are firing almost continuously. A typical neuron fires 5 - 50 times every second. The brain uses up 20% of our body's oxygen consumption, yet it weighs only 2% of our total body weight. The reason is that the electrochemical nerve impulses that make up the brain's information transmission system guzzle a lot of our body's energy. No wonder we get tired after concentrated mental effort.

The nervous system of any animal is primarily made up of nerve fibres (neurons) that communicate with one another in these constant bursts of electrochemical energy. Neurons are able to influence other neurons (as well as muscle cells and chemical-secreting endocrine cells). This enables networks of interconnecting neurons to form pathways that transmit and store information. And that of course is exactly what the brain is: an information processing and storage system.

A neuron has three parts: the cell body, or **soma**, at one end, with **dendrites** that branch out from the soma in a profusion of tiny filaments (as many as ten thousand). And finally a single **axon** which, in the human nervous system, can be as long as a metre (such as the sciatic nerve), or as short as a millimetre or less (as in the brain). The axon from one neuron can stimulate one of the many dendrites of another neuron which can then transmit the signal down its own axon to the next neuron. And so on. The place where the axon of one neuron makes an electrochemical connection with another neuron is called a **synapse.**

For example, when we move our bodies, Purkinje cells in our cerebellum (a crucial part of the brain at the back of the skull) enable us co-ordinate and balance our movements. These neurons frequently have thousands of dendrites on a treelike structure that allows them to receive a large amount of synaptic input very quickly. Their function is to inhibit other neurons, and that helps us to refine our body's movements and maintain our balance.

The human brain has roughly 86 billion neurons, and every one of them potentially has many thousands of synaptic connections to other neurons. It is estimated that a mature adult brain contains between 100 and 500 trillion synapses. The number of different possible pathways within this vast network of neural connections is, for all practical purposes, infinite. And then some.

So information storage is not a problem, and this is just as well because this where our minds are located and where our memories are stored. Children's brains are creating and pruning back new synapses all the time, something we will consider more in *Chapter 6*.

The very thing you are thinking right now, the feelings you are getting from your body, the sounds you can hear, what you are looking at, whatever your senses are detecting, all of it is the result of a number of cascading networks of neurons in your brain, firing unceasingly. These networks of connected neurons are known as **neural pathways**. Just one neural pathway may be made up of many thousands of synapses between individual neurons. A neural pathway therefore connects one part of the nervous system with another part. Our minds exist within these many neural pathways.

Once a pattern of neurons have operated together for a bit they are more likely to work together in the future when something similar happens, in the same way that the more often we have a certain thought or experience, or we practise something, the more likely we will remember it. Donald Hebb's famous maxim, '*Neurons that fire together, wire together*', says it nicely. The neurons within a neural pathway physically change through a process known as long-term potentiation.

The more a neural pathway is used, the more efficient its synapses become at transmitting information between the neurons involved. Rather like a path that we have cleared in thick undergrowth, it is far easier to use it the next time we need to go from A to B. Similarly, the neural pathway carries a greater potential to fire again because the pathway has been potentiated. In this way, neural pathways are being created, altered or strengthened continuously. This is how our brain is able to create memories and make meaning.

However, to make things just a little more complicated, a single neuron may be involved in multiple neural networks. Because neurons have so many connections with one another, a neural impulse can activate pathways that have less direct or less relevant associations with the original mental event. This can introduce 'noise' in the system, contributing to why we don't always remember things perfectly. On the plus side, however, this 'noise' can also lead to imaginative leaps of thought, creative 'errors,' and novel associations. It does seem that confusion and chaos can sometimes lead to creative insights.

Thinking requires the ability to represent the world using mental symbols that are stored in memory. The mind is the process by which our computational brains analyse and organise information from the senses and from existing memory. We impose our own order on what we perceive, and sometimes use this information to a guide our future behaviour. So in this very real sense the brain operates as an information processing and storage system. Computers are also information processing and storage systems but they use binary data and work in an entirely different way. However, both are *computational* in that they both use a temporary memory or storage area in which computations take place, RAM (random access memory) in the case of computers, and working-memory in the case of brains.

The human brain has more-or-less the same structure as that of other mammals but the relatively large area of our brain that is most recently evolved is known as the neocortex ('new brain'). The neocortex is also sometimes referred to as 'grey matter' and exists in the outer folds of the brain, a layer of brain that is far larger than in other animals, and it is this area of the brain that is more 'plastic', or capable of physically changing in response to the creation, or pruning (for lack of use), of neural pathways. The older areas beneath the neocortex are less amenable to this **neuroplasticity**.

Neuroplasticity is the brain's ability throughout life to reorganize and adapt by forming new neural connections. This flexibility enables learning, memory formation, and recovery from injuries like strokes or trauma.

An intriguing, now famous, demonstration of how memory can alter the physical structure of the brain was made by neuroscientist Eleanor Maguire of University College London. She discovered that London taxi drivers, having learned 'The Knowledge' of London streets, had more grey matter in their posterior hippocampi than non-taxi drivers of a similar age, education and intelligence. The result of more potentiated neural pathways.

The *most* recently evolved parts of the brain are at the front of our the brain, behind the eyes. This frontal cortex is also strikingly larger than that of other species. The neocortex (the outer layer of the brain) plays a crucial role in memory, attention, thought, language and consciousness, while the frontal cortex is associated with planning, reasoning, abstract thought, impulse control, and working-memory. All these brain functions are crucial to supporting a conscious mind and all are connected to one another.

In recent decades there have been huge advances in the neurosciences which hold great promise in precision medicine, stem cell therapy, and non-invasive brain stimulation. But although neuroscience may eventually be able to describe the broad anatomy of mental processes, it will probably always be limited by the sheer complexity of individual minds and the fact that the *content* of thought is as unique as each person. For example, the idea of 'Edinburgh' is not located in the same place in everyone's brain, if it exists at all. It is an idea with a unique register of meaning for each individual person. For some people, it carries a very personal meaning with many associations, for others it is merely a name on a map, and for some people it is simply a new word. It seems fanciful therefore to imagine that one day there will be computers capable of recording and mimicking this overwhelming complexity.

Individual thought will probably always remain private, even if we can read its neural correlates and emotional signatures. Neuroscience may even be able to say what bits of the brain are involved, down to the patterns of neurons that we use to associate and internally represent the world, but its content will essentially be unique to each person and, for all practical purposes, indecipherable.

Neuroscience may help in understanding brain injury and brain disorders, but for all its wonders, it can tell us very little about how life is lived, how to speak to an adolescent child who is confused about who they are, nor what to say when your partner suddenly becomes ill. These are the domain of the mind.

Bodies

It is not my brain alone that takes me from here to there. My brain does not eat, it is not able to touch something on its own, or even move. These things occur in the body and nervous system. If we are to make any sense of what is involved in how we think, we must acknowledge the physical and embodied nature of being a person, because in this regard we are much like any other animal.

Behavioural Modernity may have been the dawn of thinking, but in the big scheme of things that is the recent past. Our modern minds exist within an evolved nervous system and body, and the body has its own drives and emotions, its own ways of functioning. The rest of this chapter is therefore an overview of how brains, drives and emotions work together.

Much of what we do with our bodies is so practised, effortless, and fluid that it has become habitual, and consequently largely invisible. Our bodies inform our conscious thinking minds when it is time to eat, sleep, and drink, when we need to pee and shit, when we want sex, and when we are damaged or sick. Our embodied drives direct our motives, and our attention is inevitably drawn to what our needs and emotions are signalling, whether or not this breaks into the conscious mind.

The nervous system stores what we have learned from our experience of life, but this so-called long-term memory is not just a vast repository of consciously remembered thoughts in the central nervous system of the brain, it is also remembered by the body and the peripheral nervous system. So-called muscle memory, or know-how knowledge, is often held within the habitual procedures of the body. Walking downstairs, playing the piano, opening a door, laying a row of bricks, dancing a pirouette, all entail the body remembering what to do. The neural pathways become such well-worn grooves that we no longer need to think about what we are doing. Our bodies appear to do it for us. Practice enables the nervous system to store incredible detail in the body, with the result that people can sometimes perform as gracefully as a bird in flight. Think dancers, football players, musicians, athletes, and so on.

At this precise moment, your brain, while mentally considering these words, is simultaneously coordinating your body, regulating and stimulating your organs and muscles, and working alongside the hormone system to keep your entire body functioning in harmony. With any luck your stomach is digesting food. Your muscles may be supporting your body, perhaps just keeping yourself sufficiently upright so as to be able to read this page. Most of the time our organs (kidneys, gut, liver, lungs, heart, and so on) go on working without us giving them a moment's thought.

Even our breathing is automatically regulated by the nervous system, though like our muscles this is something we can control. Well... to a point. It is very difficult to hold your breath until you faint. With every breath we take, oxygen molecules are drawn into the lungs and absorbed through its tiny capillaries, and with every outbreath carbon dioxide is released. Our heart pumps that oxygenated blood throughout our body, and most importantly to our brain. Our organs chug away automatically, unless for some reason they malfunction, and all of them are linked to the nervous system in one way or another. When there is malfunction or injury, pain receptors send messages to the brain enabling us to become aware of the problem. Other receptors scream at us to breathe again. Nausea encourages us to vomit.

Just like every other animal, we have special adaptations, biological drives and built-in tendencies to behave in one way rather than another. Our brain evolved within a body that was unwittingly structured over the course of millions of years of evolution, in order to survive within an ecosystem that existed until quite recently. These 'hard-wired' primitive biological imperatives are most clearly expressed in our **drives** and **emotions**, so it is helpful to understand a bit about them. They too are a big part of how we think and behave, and ultimately how each of us creates our own sense of reality.

Drives and emotions

It is not only dogs that instinctively chase after rats, and not only rats that run for their lives. All mammals have biological drives and emotions. These instincts motivate them to take action in the interests of their survival and the survival of their genes. And this is true for us humans too.

How would you react if your child was being threatened or hungry, or your mother attacked, or if someone were trying to steal your property? What would you feel if you were entirely defenceless and surrounded by hungry wolves? Imagine yourself alone in a rowing boat at night in the middle of the ocean.

You may answer that these are not situations you would ever find yourself in, and that may well be true, but they *could* happen and it is probably quite easy for you to visualise them. You can understand and imagine the intense thoughts, drives and emotions that these situations would almost inevitably evoke in you. We are able to mentally model a situation, recognise our own imagined feelings, and even our emotional bodily reactions.

Drives and emotions are the big biological backdrop to how we think, and also the most recognizable link that we have with our evolutionary origins. They are the instinctive failsafe programs of physical and behavioural activity that provide us with biological protection, much like our immune system.[6] Importantly, they rarely

---

NOTE 6: The distinction between drives and emotions is subtle. 'Drive' is another way of saying need. Drives tend to be persistent and induce motivation towards a goal, or towards the satisfaction of a particular need. They tend towards pleasure, survival and safety, and away from pain, discomfort and death. When people's drives are satisfied they feel pleasure, gratification and fulfilment. When people's needs are not being met they generally feel distress.

Emotions on the other hand tend to be more reactive to the events we experience, providing us with a physiological, behavioural and cognitive response that is in the best interests of our survival. When something happens that we were not expecting, our emotions are activated. This may happen when our drives are not being satisfied. For example, our need for safety provokes distress when it is threatened, and our need to drink evokes the distress of thirst and the pleasure of rehydration when it is quenched.

involve much thinking (although thinking, talking and writing can help us regulate these impulses).

Drives and emotions evolved. They cause us to respond and behave in particular ways. They are our genes expressing themselves through proteins to form complex structures of brain function, operating as genetically-programmed brain modules. These work by causing physiological reactions to stimuli in the environment. However, our hearts are not pounding because we are afraid, we are afraid because our hearts are pounding. We *feel* our emotions by recognising the physiological responses our bodies are making to what is going on in our lives.

Emotions can be short-lived, as when we are momentarily afraid and surprised by something, and they can be enduring, such as when we mourn the loss of someone we loved. The evolutionary biologist Richard Dawkins has described our drives and needs as *archaeo-purposes*, and the many personal goals and plans we make during the course of our lives as *neo-purposes*. Archaeo-purposes inevitably influence neo-purposes, so it is helpful to understand these drives. For good or bad, emotions and drives permeate the mind and give everyone's lived experience a sense of colour, direction, and texture.

Drives

As is true for any other animal, our drives arouse us in order to satisfy them. Hunger, thirst, self-protection, care and connection with others, lust, pleasure and comfort, and the avoidance of pain... all these drives are there to motivate us to behave in certain ways

---

Drives induce emotions but sometimes it is the other way round. For example, fear (an emotion) can induce the drive towards the protection of others, while loss (emotion) can lead to a lack of appetite (drive). Sexual lust (drive) can provide pleasure (emotion), and lack of shelter and security (need) often leads to fear. Injustice evinces anger and seeks justice and sometimes retribution. The need to protect one's young leads to many emotions particularly aggression and anger.

Both drives and emotions are constantly influencing behaviour and either can take a hold of someone in a flash. But emotions also leave an imprint on a person's memories and beliefs about the world. For example, people may 'carry' their pain and hurt from one relationship to another, and envy and jealousy can slowly poison a person's life goals.

and not others. All of them are in the service of the universal, powerful, overarching, and lifelong drive to survive.

Our goals and values are rarely consciously held, though of course, with a little reflection, most of us can generate a plausible description of what they might be. They may be based on the biological drives (archaeo-purposes) discussed here, but they will also include goals and values (neo-purposes) that have been internalised from the prevailing culture we happen to have lived in, things like career ambition, acquiring wealth, doing good for the community, and so on.

Humans are an unusually social species, so naturally social connection is a powerful drive. The social sciences are replete with evidence for the vital importance of social relationships ('social support') for a person's emotional wellbeing, health, and mortality risk. Connection with other people is essential to a person's survival, and is often central to what they regard as meaningful in their lives.

One recognisable and nearly universal drive can be seen in the powerful instinctive feelings of love, protection and care that parents feel towards their young. This need to nurture and safeguard offspring is a typical mammalian drive because as parents we have a genetic investment in our children. If you have ever deeply loved someone (mother, father, child, partner, or friend) you will know about how powerful these relationships are in your life. Communication and relationships with other people are so essential to survival that people start learning about them from the moment they are born. Having an intimate, caring relationship with someone leads our neurons to become bathed in the warm glow of the hormone oxytocin. People generally enjoy and crave these sorts of connections with one another.

But when this drive for social contact is frustrated or unsatisfied, it can result in the psychological pain of loneliness, dejection and a lowering of self-worth. Loneliness is a horrible emotion, partly because the person feels excluded, and partly because it undermines their confidence in being with other people, the very thing that is most likely to improve the situation.

Uniquely among species, humans are prepared to care for others outside their own family. In fact, humans are uncommonly altruistic and caring towards people they have never even met, and citizens are prepared (albeit often reluctantly) to contribute to things that benefit everyone, not just themselves. Taxes pay for common social infrastructure like roads, railways, schools and hospitals, while charities raise huge sums of money for the benefit of refugees, victims of famine and so on. These altruistic acts reflect the fact that *reciprocal altruism* (people caring for one another) evolved in our distant human ancestors. Early humans learned that it was in their survival interests to help one another on the assumption that, by doing so, others would do the same for them in the future should the need arise.

Overlapping with this need for connection is sex. Sex is a powerful drive because, second only to personal survival and the survival of one's genes (children), procreating the species is the primary genetic imperative. It is especially potent because it offers deeply biological pleasures, so much so that it can easily become a central motivation for people, particularly during their fertile years.

But it is also a dangerous drive because some people, almost always men, are unable to regulate it, and end up inflicting truly terrible suffering on other people, mostly women. Sexual violence is a genuine danger and no wonder sex has long been a taboo subject.

Nonetheless, sexual behaviour is an expression of this natural animal drive, even if it is not expressed in quite the same way in everyone. A person's sexual preference is to do with which sex, if any, they find sexually arousing: men, women, both, or neither. It is also contextual in that it can change, depending on the context that people find themselves in, and how they may be feeling at the time.

Although sexual arousal is very much a bodily drive, well beyond thought, thoughts alone can lead to delirious sexual fantasies which themselves can arouse the body's physical lust. Only human minds are capable of mentally representing the world with such intense fantasy and imagination, and when imagination is not enough there is always pornography to help.

Pornography is mostly used as fantasy material with which to masturbate, and the so-called 'porn industry' is a response to this very real drive within people, especially men, to fantasize about having sex with other people. More money is spent on pornography in the United States than on all the performing arts combined and it has been estimated that thirty per cent of internet traffic involves sex websites. Or so it has been reported. Sexual release is what people seek and, as such, fantasy and masturbation are entirely natural and harmless, provided no one is being exploited. However, pornography can present a distorted view of human sexuality that can lead people to have similarly distorted expectations.

Studies suggest that 95% of men and 75% of women regularly masturbate. Religious people masturbate and have sex as much as non-religious people, though intriguingly in one study older religious people used more pornography than non-religious people. The main problem tends to be guilt. People all over the world 'beat themselves up' over their sexuality, mainly due to having absorbed social taboos about sex from their local culture, particularly of course religion.

Beyond the purely physical aspects of sexual arousal, a sexual relationship with someone can be one of the rare times when we glimpse the possibility of transcending the existential divide that separates each of us from another person's mind. A sexual communion with someone else is an ecstatic pleasure and there is a lot to recommend sex whenever it is available, but of course only with the uncoerced consent of all those involved, and of course respectful of the laws on child protection and the responsibility we have for any vulnerable person, relative to our power in the world. Sex, it hardly needs to be said, feels just great when it feels right for all parties involved, and when there is mutual pleasure and fulfilment.

Men's sexuality is generally more promiscuous than that of women because it evolved to be so. It is more likely that a man's genes will survive if he can impregnate as many women as possible, whereas it is more likely a woman's genes will survive if she can find the best possible (genetically endowed) male to mate with, particularly if he is likely to stick around and invest in their offspring. But, as an aside, let us remember that although sex is a core drive within both sexes, it is not as imperative as the need for intimate bonds that will ensure the individual person's survival. In other words, we must stay alive first, before we are able to have sex.

Yes, sex is a natural drive, much like eating, and a drive that humans share with almost all animals (though sexual monogamy is rare among other species). As creatures we have a pretty strong sex drive, much like our evolutionary cousin the chimpanzee, though perhaps not as much as our other cousin, the bonobo.

Whether we are a man or a woman, lust is a strong drive that often motivates our behaviour and, because we are human, our fantasy life. Other animals don't have sex because they want to have offspring, they are instinctively motivated by a desire for sex because it is in their genes to do so. Only humans know that sex can produce babies, but for most of the time that's not why we do it. We do it because our bodies evolved for it to feel good.

Our sexuality is uniquely our own. It is influenced by beliefs and expectations that have been shaped by our cultural and religious background as much as by our personal experiences. We may define our sexuality and sexual satisfaction by how often we have sex with someone else, by how often we have sex of any kind, or we may see it in terms of physical and emotional intimacy with others, or even our own feelings of attractiveness to other people.

The sexual drive, incidentally, finds expression in many forms, notably homosexuality, sexual attraction to someone of one's own sex. And why not? Other primates do. Why would anyone deny someone a personal preference that is as harmless as preferring cheese to chocolate, or both, or neither? But, unfortunately, archaic religious beliefs ensure that the social conditions for most lesbian women, gay men, bisexuals and transgender people the world over remain chronically stressful, and they continue to suffer cruel persecution and discrimination.

We are each unique in terms of who and what we find sexually exciting, and how much importance we place on our sexuality. If you like sucking big toes and I happen to like having my big toe sucked then we have the potential for a mutually satisfying sexual relationship. Everyone has the potential to be sexual, but it is not only nuns and priests who choose not to be sexually active. Sexuality is an important part of some people's overall identity, but not everyone.

Are you a greedy, dishonest, or violent person? One only has to consult The News to be immediately confronted by Nature's 'red claw and tooth', both in the way that human beings have killed or destroyed the lives of most other species on the planet, and in the way we continue to be so harsh and adversarial with one another. Cruelty and violence are still hideously evident among modern humans, even if violence on average has been reducing in recent centuries. It is probably there within you and me too, given the right conditions.

Wars, conflict, murder, cruelty, abuse, and brutality often stem from a fundamental mammalian drive: the desire for dominance and power. This drive may have originated from the basic need for survival, but in modern humans it is also manifested in competitive sports, capitalism, military aggression, career ambition, wealth acquisition, and even gossip. But independent of actual violence, there are many other morally reprehensible aspects of our drive for dominance and self-interest: dishonesty, scamming, stealing, cheating, abusing, meanness, manipulation, exploitation…

Give someone a little bit of power over other people, no matter how menial their role may be, and you can be damn sure they will use that power to the limit. People often strive for, and appear to enjoy achieving a more dominant position in the social pecking order, seeking power and influence over land, resources, and other people. It is about winning status, control, fame and resources. Money, of course, is the universal currency of this drive for power, but this resource-seeking drive has of course also led to shameful levels of inequality. Yet, at the same time, we humans are the one species that is able to restrain our self-interest so that it is not disproportionately or unfairly derived at the expense of other people or other species.

So, trundling beneath our conscious experience of life are our *drives* that biologically orientate our behaviour towards one thing over another. When our eyes linger a few milliseconds longer on someone we find attractive, and we take a second glance, our lust drive has been activated and may need restraining. We simply can't just rape someone because we find them sexually attractive. When we see a slab of chocolate cake and yet we also don't want to get fat, we feel the conflict of having to resist the temptation to eat it. When we see an opportunity to acquire power through dominance, money or influence we may well want to grab it with both hands, but we may also wish to temper our greed in the interests of other considerations. Fortunately, our minds can sometimes regulate our drives, and that is more than can be said for dogs like Bob.

And that is the thing about drives, they often need regulating, and self-regulation isn't easy, or always enough. As any parent will tell you, one of life's early challenges is learning to regulate and control one's drives, something that can continue to be a challenge well into adulthood. Little wonder that religious and secular laws have long tried to rein in some of our drives. Three of Christianity's Seven Deadly Sins were basic drives – greed, gluttony and lust. And every legal system in the world prohibits violence and stealing.

Emotions

But what of emotions? Our emotions are clearly also a vital part of being alive, affecting us almost all the time. So, what are they? When people describe an act as emotional they are often implying a temporary loss of rational self-restraint: 'uncontrollable rage', 'passionate love', 'blind panic', as if a primitive impulse has been unleashed, no longer tempered by reason or thought.

The classical approach to emotions is that they *are* more primitive in the sense that they evolved much earlier than modern conscious thought, well before primates developed the neocortex, the layer directly beneath our skull and the part of the brain that enables us to think. The emotional areas of the brain are found in deeper structures nearer its centre.

Remember that within the timescale of evolutionary history humans have only been thinking in modern ways very recently, equivalent to the last seven and a half minutes of the year using the LUCA timescale. Our emotions are much older and more physiologically rooted within us. Some paleobiologists have suggested that emotions evolved when mammals became nocturnal about 180 million years ago, about 12th December.

During this Jurassic period, as dinosaurs and other reptiles slept, smell was the dominant sense among the night dwelling mammals. The odour-detecting parts of the brain gradually formed the basis of what is known as the limbic system in the modern brain. The **limbic system** is a group of brain structures just beneath the outer neocortex, nearer the centre of our brain. Although many other parts of the brain are active when an emotion occurs, the limbic system is central to emotional processing. Similar structures are found in the brains of other animals and they too are involved in emotion. The limbic system supports several other essential functions including long-term memory, behaviour, and it continues to be critical to smell.

You have probably noticed that your memory for smell has a rather special quality. This is not surprising when we consider that memory for smell was once far more important to us as a species, as it still is for most other mammals. A particular smell can evoke a person, a time, or a feeling in a way that is well beyond words, similar to the way that a painting can ineffably convey something that a photograph cannot – impossible to articulate in words and probably unique to each person. It turns out that emotions and smells are inextricably tagged onto memories. Like ink absorbed by paper, they seep into its fabric, becoming an inseparable part of them. Our bodies and nervous system remember for us.

Some researchers these days maintain that we have only a generic form of emotional arousal. That may be so, but our culture and history have developed many different terms for what we feel. In 1872 Charles Darwin published *The Expression of Emotion in Man and Animals*. In it he noted that people seem to have five basic emotions from which all others are derived: Fear, Anger, Joy, Sadness and Disgust. But it was not until the 1970s that Paul Ekman's cross-cultural research confirmed that, with very slight variations, the facial expression of these basic emotions appears to be universal among people, regardless of their culture, age, 'race' or gender. Ekman added a sixth emotion – Surprise! – though some people have reasonably argued that surprise originates in the fear response.

Darwin's five basic emotions have held up remarkably well over the past 150 years, even though it is now widely agreed that the expression of emotion varies depending on the context we are in, much of which is social, and that we interpret our emotional state partly on the basis of our past experience. The ups and downs of life are determined by the extent to which events activate emotions, usually because our drives have been frustrated or satisfied. Are you disappointed by a missed opportunity (sadness), grieving for a loss (sadness), hopeless about the future (sadness), delighted by a promotion (joy), frustrated by the situation you find yourself in (anger), feeling a sense of injustice (anger), embarrassed or humiliated by something you have done (self-disgust), worried about next week (fear), or just plain happy to see me again (joy)?

If we are not careful, and even if we are, our emotions can sometimes overwhelm us. They can cause the most unbearable suffering – grief, shame, remorse, guilt, despair and excruciating fear – but also sometimes ecstatic joy, hilarity and happiness. But unlike drives, emotions are largely self-regulating. In other words, emotions are tiring to sustain, so over time they tend to lessen in intensity as our brain habituates, or gets used to whatever is causing the emotion (provided we don't avoid it, which of course people often do). In the case of grief, for example, time really is the great healer.

If we wake in the night and hear the sound of breaking glass, we may well describe the feelings in our body as fear, thinking that someone is trying to break into our house. But if we interpret the same sound as the neighbour's cat knocking over the milk bottles again, we might well turn over and fall back to sleep. Similarly, if we count to ten when we are enraged by something it gives our thinking minds a chance to catch up, assess, regulate our emotion, and decide what we might wish to do next. In both these examples, how we think about the situation we are in will alter how we experience the emotions we feel.

Thinking can also keep emotions aroused, or even escalate them as happens in a panic attack, but there are also mental methods of regulating our emotions. We can focus our attention on something else (distraction), change the way we think of the situation that is causing the emotion (reframing), and we can change or suppress our emotional responses (such as learning to physically relax when confronted by a threat, or soothing a state of vigilance). But above all, emotion signals to us to do something to change the situation that is giving rise to the emotion. So, for example, if we are worrying about an upcoming exam, we may be able to reduce our fears by studying hard.

As if that were not complicated enough, when we experience an emotion caused by a change in the environment (a threat, a loss, something disgusting, or something good happens) we might reasonably think that the emotion we are feeling has been caused by what our thinking mind has concluded about what we have experienced. Well, it can be like this, as we have just seen, but research has shown that people label their emotions in response to the context and what their bodies are doing, and only later do they mentally interpret what has changed in the environment.

The American neuroscientist Joseph LeDoux makes the important distinction between the fear we experience and the biological threat-detection circuits in the brain. He argues that the experience of fear is something that only animals with consciousness can feel, because they have learned to recognise and label the situation they are in as dangerous, and recognize their internal states and behavioural responses to threat. Brains per se do not generate the experience of fear; it is something that people construct from past experience and from reading their body's physiological responses.

And this does appear to be true. Faced with something unexpected and intensely threatening (a very loud unexpected noise, a traumatic event) we don't stop to *think* about it. We freeze for a split second while our **amygdala**, an almond-shaped structure in the emotional limbic part of our brain, activates our body to escape. It sets off a chain reaction of neural and chemical signals, hormone secretions and other physiological changes throughout the body that cause our behaviour to change. Only later do we piece together intellectually what has happened, try to determine if the threat is still present, and decide what to do next and whether we need to remain vigilant. Emotions evolved to maximise the survival of the animal and, as such, they are automatic, non-conscious, and much faster than reason when reacting to the environment. The body simply takes over and assumes control, and the mind often struggles to catch up.

One consequence of this is that people often behaviourally react to their emotional state without even being consciously aware of it. Brain studies have shown that a person's amygdala is activated even when the person concerned is unaware that they have been presented with a fear-provoking stimulus.

Have you ever felt angry and irritable when in fact you were anxious and worried about something? Or the reverse? Have you ever felt sad and tearful when you were simply tired and perhaps emotionally and physically depleted? Remember the Blackwall Tunnel story? Fear and anger are so closely linked that they can easily cover for one another. As Shakespeare's Charmian says to Cleopatra, "*In time we hate that which we often fear*". Emotions, and bodies more generally, communicate information, so it helps if we can read that information accurately. We should probably therefore pay less attention to what we fear and more to what is actually dangerous.

It seems that we humans share at least some of our emotional states with other animals, threat-detection for example, but we obviously have a far larger repertoire that includes the more complicated and varied *social emotions* of love, jealousy, pride, contempt, shame, envy, and so on. These secondary, social emotions are thought to involve one or more basic emotions (guilt, for example, combines anger and self-disgust, while remorse adds in a dose of sadness). Social emotions always involve particular thoughts and social contexts. In collectivist cultures like Italy, for example, there are strong cultural expectations that everyone will be connected. Loneliness can therefore be a bigger problem there in the context of such strong social expectations. However, embedded in all these complicated social emotions is at least one of 'the five basic emotions' – Fear, Anger, Sadness, Joy, and Disgust.

Some social emotions, such as pride and shame, are also seemingly universal. In a study at the Beijing Olympics in 2008, the body postures of athletes after having won or lost were filmed. Notably, in this study 53 of the 140 judo competitors were blind, 12 of them from birth, yet their emotional behaviours were easily recognised and 'read' by people studying only their facial and postural responses. Some social emotions can even be seen in other social species. Primates, in particular, are believed to show signs of embarrassment, compassion, envy and injustice.

Two of Darwin's five basic emotions, Joy and Sadness, are effectively opposites, the two poles of our mood. Joy is an emotion served by the satisfaction of drives, but also the sensual pleasure of enjoying something, such as a hot bath or a massage. Dolphins, incidentally, appear to surf waves for the sheer joy of it. Pleasure can be naughty of course, but it can also be innocent and pure, such as when we are achieving something, reading a child a bedtime story, doing something well, listening to music, dancing, or indeed surfing. The nucleus accumbens in the limbic system is thought to be an important reward centre in the brain which is activated when we feel Joy. But because Joy doesn't propel us to do or avoid anything in particular, it can sometimes be harder to recognise within ourselves. This may be why people often say that they only became aware that they had been happy when looking back on their lives (e.g. a holiday), rather than noticing their joy while they were experiencing it.

There are so many forms of pleasure, and we humans are very imaginative in creating and satisfying them. Eating and sex may be the most obvious and simple pleasures, but scratching an itch can feel nice in the moment, and there is even joy to be had in mere contentment.

When things are going *really* well, people are sometimes able to enjoy a feeling of 'being in flow'. This is perhaps more easily recognised as a physical phenomenon, such as when one is running, cycling or rowing. **Flow** is a state of joyful consciousness identified by a Transylvanian psychologist with the formidable name of Mihaly Csíkszentmihályi. It describes a state-of-being in which one's mind and body are being stretched to their optimal efficiency. Csíkszentmihályi believes that people are happiest when they are in a state of flow, absorbed, 'in the groove', engaged in the present moment, in a slightly suspended state of consciousness, running with the grace of a gazelle, feeling one's body swimming through dense water, and so on.

At the opposite end of this continuum is Sadness. Sadness is the emotional response to loss. It may seem hard at first to see what possible evolutionary advantage Sadness could offer. The psychological anguish of losing someone we dearly love is about as painful as it gets, and on the face of it, crying, pining, and withdrawal do not sound like behaviours that would have been useful and adaptive to our ancient ancestors.

Sadness must have had some helpful purpose or it would have been naturally deselected from the species, and it turns out that Sadness does serve a useful function. The loss of something or someone important changes the survival odds, and as a result life now may be more dangerous or uncertain than it was before. So, with that in mind, sadness increases the chances of survival by encouraging the unfortunate lost person to cry and call out for their care-givers, thus increasing the probability of being found (albeit sometimes by predators). It is no accident that babies are particularly talented in this regard.

At the same time there is an obvious advantage in withdrawing to a place of safety when we have lost a person who previously provided safety. By temporarily withdrawing, the sad person gives themselves a chance to ruminate about the loss, lick their wounds, reassess their safety within the world, take stock of their remaining resources, and consider possible changes they may wish to make if they are to survive in the world with all its new uncertainties. Withdrawal gives the person some breathing space in which to catch up, a chance for the mind to recalibrate its assumptions and mental models about the world before venturing out into it again. Problems arise when people become stuck in their sadness and find it ever harder to re-engage with the changed world around them. They feel unable to invest in the future, and their withdrawal leads to a loss of hope, energy and confidence.

After Joy and Sadness, come Fear and Anger, another natural pairing though for quite different reasons. They are emotions that we very obviously share with other animals, producing almost identical behavioural and physiological reactions within the body. If escape is not an option, then Anger, hostility and ultimately aggression become the next best thing. So Anger and Fear are two sides of the same coin – fight or flight, and as we have seen, they often flagrantly substitute for one another.

What happens when we clap our hands around birds? They immediately fly away. What happens when we walk up to sheep? They too run away. The same is essentially true of people. When we are frightened by something sudden or unexpected, such as a loud explosion or something threatening or unfamiliar, our first instinct is to freeze, and then it is to escape and run away, and subsequently avoid the threat. We resort to anger and hostility when we feel (our needs are) threatened and escape is not an option.

So what happens in our body when we are frightened, when we feel fear? Our breathing rate increases from that first gasp, immediately allowing our lungs to oxygenate more blood. The hormone cortisol is secreted into the bloodstream, altering the metabolic configuration of the body. Our heart beats faster to pump more blood through our arteries to our muscles, supplying them with the oxygen necessary to release their stored energy. We will need these muscles to flee. Meanwhile the blood supply to our digestive system is reduced. We don't need to be wasting energy on digesting food if we are running for our life. And at the same time our muscles become immediately tense as we bolt away from the sabre-toothed cat that has emerged from behind a tree (or whatever threat we care to imagine). Anything unexpected is coded first as a potential threat because this maximises survival. A fear of the unknown is therefore adaptive.

The problem for us humans is that we only have to *think* about something scary and our brain engages all these physiological changes. As soon as we imagine what we fear, our brain stimulates an emotional reaction in our body as if we were actually being confronted by the threat right now. Our amygdala triggers our body to become an athletic animal, ready to sprint to safety. So, although the events we fear are not actually happening in that moment, our brain arouses our body to behave as if they were. It is a common human affliction.

Worry *per se* can be highly adaptive, but it can also cause tortuous mental misery. Worry is obviously a big asset to survival if, by anticipating and mentally modelling the future, we are able to manage the threat more effectively by preparing for it or taking evasive action (e.g. studying for that exam). Worrying about something energises not just the body to attend to a threat, but also the mind. Problems can occur though when people become stuck in their worrying or make unhelpful assumptions about the future based on a biased way of thinking. Such biases include catastrophising about the future, using all-or-nothing thinking, and confusing possibilities with probabilities. Before long, the person's own thinking becomes a tyranny for them.

There are also some things that our brain innately knows can be a danger to us, so these things automatically activate our emotions so that we can avoid them. For example, as we have said, people instinctively fear the sudden or unknown because doing so aids survival. We naturally fear standing on the edge of a precipice for this too could potentially be dangerous, and the brain already knows it (though babies only develop depth perception when they are about five months old). Many more people fear snakes and spiders than fear rabbits and sheep. Our brain is evolutionarily prepared ('hardwired') to be afraid of spiders and snakes because they too could be dangerous. But not rabbits.

Only Disgust stands on its own without a natural partner. Although disgust continues to prompt us to avoid things that are potentially hazardous (slimy putrid food, disease, mutilated flesh etc.), it is more commonly experienced as part of a social emotion.

Remorse, shame, embarrassment and humiliation are forms of self-disgust; contempt and hatred are more about finding others repugnant or beyond the pale. Racism, taboo, fashion, and bigotry often involve a strong element of disgust, even if many other emotions and assumptions are at play.

Our emotions help us survive by causing the body to react to something in the environment, such as a bus hurtling towards us, but sometimes they bias our interpretation of what is currently happening due to their association with previous experiences. If you have ever been trapped in a lift for a few hours, there is a good chance that you were more wary and vigilant the next time you entered one. Emotions become tagged onto memories, and memory is the subject of the next chapter.

Our drives act like motivational catalysts, while our emotions provide us with an essential source of information, particularly when the environment in some way threatens to disrupt our needs and goals, or those of our kin. Together they can propel or withhold our energies, and inhibit or potentiate our actions. Some scientists even think of emotions as being a lot like the five senses, providing us with another way of perceiving the world around us. This idea is not as farfetched as it may seem at first. Emotions and drives are as important to mental life as language is to thought, so much so that is it often hard to disentangle them from what we are thinking. This is probably why we use catch-all words like 'feelings'.

Feelings

In the English language the word *feeling* is used in so many ways that it is in danger of tying us up in knots. We can describe our 'feelings' about people; for example, how warmly we 'feel' towards someone as an indication of how much we like them. We also react to other people on the basis of incoherent assumptions that we describe as our 'feelings' about them ("She feels condescending").

We can use 'feelings' when we are signifying an emotion ('I feel angry', 'I feel afraid', 'I feel sorry'). We invoke the word 'feelings' when we are referring to the overall emotional or physical state of ourselves or others ('How are you feeling?'), or a more specific state

('My shoulders feel tense'). "I feel for you" is an attempt to convey empathy for another person's thoughts and emotions. We sometimes use the word to describe the glow that comes from pleasure, or intense engagement with an experience: the enjoyment of a bath, interest in a problem, the excitement of achievement in sport, the ecstasy of sex, a state of depletion and exhaustion, an attraction to someone, eating with relish, being in love. Here our drives, emotions and thoughts are all at play, but the word 'feelings' is often used to describe the experience.

Finally, the word 'feeling' is often used to acknowledge and convey the fact that we believe something without quite knowing the reason why. 'I feel that it's going to rain tomorrow', 'I feel that you're not being completely honest with me'. Here, 'feeling' refers to a more intuitive type of knowledge.

Such 'gut feelings' reflect a biologically-derived tendency to reach conclusions without conscious reason. The world is a complicated place so we depend on our immediate 'gut feelings', our intuitive grasp of the situation, to make quick decisions. Subtle physiological changes in the body, associated with particular emotions, have become tagged onto the memories of previous experiences and this informs the present moment. Although we don't consciously remember the associations we have formed, some things 'just don't feel right', and some just do.

Something feels intuitively right because it tallies with previous life experience, as we draw on conscious and unconscious associations and assumptions, involving both thought and emotion (and context). We will have more to say about unconscious knowledge later, but for now let us regard *'feelings'* as a combination of thoughts and emotions, often represented as our hunches, beliefs, and assumptions – the heuristics of everyday life.

The Portuguese-American neuroscientist Antonio Damasio has argued that feelings are based on a recognition of physiological and brains states that we have learned from past experience. Accordingly, feelings are assumptions tinged with emotion. They can be a recognition of our body state, highly nuanced, and deeply buried in places that are intuitively known but impossible to capture in words. Other feelings, however, can be identified, expressed, and discussed.

Our drives and emotions are blended with the complexity of thought to produce the rich emotional texture of our life, and this is often expressed as our 'feelings'. They subtly animate, focus, and give direction to our mental activity, but again they also need restraint and regulation if we are to co-exist with other people and live a contented life.

Self-regulation

British psychologist Paul Gilbert has proposed that people have three drive-emotion systems that regulate how people feel, and that ideally they should all be in balance. First there is a *self-protection* system (primarily located in the amygdala and mediated to some extent by the hormone cortisol) which detects threat quickly and provokes emotions such as anger, fear or disgust which then motivate us to take action to avoid the threat in question.

Second there is what he calls the *resource-seeking* system which motivates people to acquire things such as food, sex, friendship, money, status etc. because these things provide us with pleasure and positive emotions like joy. However, this system can get out of control when someone feels they cannot get enough of something (money, fame, power) or when they overindulge in what they can obtain (food, sex). For example, humans did not evolve in an environment anything like some parts of the world today where there is an almost limitless supply of cheap high-calorie food without the need for regular physical exercise to obtain it.

People with persistently low mood (depression) often lack the resource-seeking motivation that this drive provides, and therefore have fewer opportunities to experience pleasure. People can feel beaten down and beaten up by the events of their lives, but withdrawal, as already mentioned, can easily become self-defeating and self-fulfilling. For example, if we feel hopeless in general we may be less motivated to go out into the world (make new friends, achieve things etc.) and, in time, we will end up having fewer things to look forward to and fewer things to achieve. Resource-seeking, moreover, is often limited by the social conditions of one's life – the hopelessness of deprivation and unemployment, for example.

Finally, Gilbert points to a third emotion-regulation system. This one is to do with care-giving and care-seeking, what he calls the *soothing and contentment* system. This system is underpinned by endorphins (a form of naturally produced opioid) that are associated with a feeling of calm, and the hormone oxytocin which promotes bonding between animals (and, as we will see, our mother with us). This system leads us towards a sense of belonging, comfort, connectedness, safety, and contentment. It also underlies our capacity for compassion and our drive for connection with one another.

But unless these three systems are in balance, there can be problems. If either the self-protection system or the resource-seeking system becomes dominant and ends up regulating feeling and thinking, then compassion goes by the wayside. In fact, Gilbert argues that modern industrialised society emphasises and overstimulates us with the incentive and self-protection systems to the detriment of the soothing and contentment system. This is perhaps why people in richer nations are often less content or happy with their lives than people in poorer countries.

Fortunately, with a bit of practice, our clever modern brains can override and regulate the animal drives within us, but equally they can craftily work out how to satisfy them. We are not rats or dogs but human beings that can exercise an impressive degree of restraint and control over our immediate impulses and our emotions.

Over the course of your childhood, as your brain matured, your parents hopefully taught you to tame your emotions and drives, and in time you learned to defer or even deny your immediate gratification. Even so, self-control or self-regulation requires conscious effort, and the research so far suggests that self-control is tiring to sustain, a bit like exercising a muscle.

This is not at all how other animals behave in the wild. Like human children, other animals (such as Bob) are feeble at holding back their impulses and needs. In fact, this difficulty with 'impulse control' seems to be a common problem in specific areas for people in prison. As we shall see, *self-regulation* involves both brain development and learning. Teaching children to regulate their drives and emotions is thus one of the key responsibilities of parenthood, and indeed human society depends upon it.

Typically, by the time we reach adulthood, we do not shoot our boss when we have been refused a pay rise, we do not molest people in the street whom we find sexually attractive, and we do not take things that belong to other people simply because we want them. Moreover, we have learned to feel confident enough to venture from the safety of our home, so that we can absorb useful knowledge from new experiences in the wider world.

Over the course of our childhood, we ideally learned to regulate our emotions and control our behaviour, at least to some extent, and we learned to censor what we think rather than always blurting everything out. And, all being well, we also learned how to engage in trusting, even intimate, relationships with other people. These other people in turn helped us to temper our emotions and drives. If we had not learned some self-restraint over our voracious greed for pleasure and self-interest, we might well be dead, in prison, or in hospital.

We live in a world where 'civilised behaviour' requires us to tolerate other people's behaviour as much as possible, whilst regulating our own. Human societies have worked out that it is in everyone's interest to live by laws that restrain people's impulses and delineate where the agreed boundaries of behaviour lie. Everyone seeks a life where needs are sufficiently met and emotions are appropriately self-regulated. But it is primarily in childhood that we are taught how to self-regulate our impulses and learn to manage and tolerate the complexities of coexisting with other human beings, until we feel ready to take charge over our own lives. This is one of the main reasons that human childhood takes so long.

By the time they reach adulthood, children have learned a great deal from the people and the culture they have been brought up in, and they will use what they have learned to make sense of the world around them and survive within it. All this learning is stored in the brain and nervous system as memory, though, as we shall see, not all memory is consciously remembered. However, everything we experience in life is understood on the basis of knowledge we have already acquired and stored in memory. Without memory it would be impossible to experience consciousness, and without consciousness we would not be able to make sense of our lives. So in the next chapter we will consider how memory is organised, and in the following chapter we will think about how consciousness subsequently comes about. These two processes are fundamental to how we each construct a sense of reality.

Further Reading

Barrett L. (2017) *How Emotions Are Made: The Secret Life of the Brain.* London: Macmillan

Csíkszentmihályi M, Csíkszentmihályi I. (1988) *Optimal Experience: Psychological Studies of Flow in Consciousness.* Cambridge: Cambridge University Press

Darwin C. (1872) *The Expression of the Emotions in Man and Animals.* London: John Murray

Davis M, Whalen P. (2001) The amygdala: vigilance and emotion. *Molecular Psychiatry*, 6, 13-34

Damasio, A. (2012) *Self Comes to Mind: Constructing the Conscious Brain.* London: Vintage

Donald M. (1995) The neurobiology of human consciousness: An evolutionary approach. *Neuropsychologia*, 33, 1087-102.

Edelman G, Gally J and Baars B (2011) Biology of consciousness. *Frontiers in Psychology.* 2(4). doi: 10.3389/fpsyg.2011.00004

Ekman P, Friesen W. (1971). Constants across cultures in the face and emotion. *Journal of Personality and Social Psychology*, 17, 124–29 doi:10.1037/h0030377

Frijda N. (1988) The laws of emotion. *American Psychologist*, **43**, 349-358

Frith C. (2011) What brain plasticity reveals about the nature of consciousness: commentary. *Frontiers in Psychology*, 2: http://dx.doi.org/10.3389/fpsyg.2011.00087

Gibson K. (2007) Putting it all together: a constructionist approach to the evolution of human mental capacities. In: Mellars P, Boyle K, Bar-Yosef O, Stringer C. (Eds.) *Rethinking the Human Revolution*. Cambridge: McDonald Institute of Archaeological Research

Gilbert P. (2009) *The Compassionate Mind*. London: Constable and Robinson.

Gregory R. (l966). *Eye and Brain: The Psychology of Seeing*. London: Weidenfeld and Nicolson.

Hinde R. (1998) Mind and artefact: a dialectical perspective. In Renfrew C, Scarre C. (Eds.) *Cognition and Material Culture: The Archaeology of Symbolic Storage*. Cambridge: McDonald Institute for Archaeological Research

James W. (1890) *The Principles of Psychology*, Cosimo Classics, p.609

Kuo B-C. (2016) Selection history modulates working memory capacity. *Frontiers in Psychology*, 7: doi: 10.3389/fpsyg.2016.01564

LeDoux J. (2013) The slippery slope of fear. *Trends in Cognitive Science*, 17, 155-156. doi.org/10.1016/j.tics.2013.02.004

Lehrer J. (2009). The frontal cortex, porn and mirror neurons. *ScienceBlogs*. http://scienceblogs.com/cortex/2009/08/24/porn-and-mirror-neurons/

Logan C, Jelbert S, Breen A, Gray R, Taylor A. (2014) Modifications to the Aesop's Fable paradigm change New Caledonian crow performances. *PLoS ONE*, 9(7), doi: 10.1371/journal.pone.0103049

Luo J, Yu R. (2015) Follow the heart or the head? The interactive influence model of emotion and cognition.

Frontiers in Psychology, 6:
http://dx.doi.org/10.3389/fpsyg.2015.00573

Pinker S. (1994) *The Language Instinct: How the Mind Creates Language.* London: Penguin

Plotkin H. (1997) *Evolution in Mind – An introduction to evolutionary psychology.* London: Penguin

Chapter 4

Memory and Mental Models

The structure of memory
Explicit conscious memory
Implicit unconscious memory
Making stories
Mental models and assumptions
Memory retrieval

"The stream of thought flows on; but most of its segments fall into the bottomless abyss of oblivion. Of some, no memory survives the instant of their passage. Of others, it is confined to a few moments, hours, or days. Others, again, leave vestiges which are indestructible, and by means of which they may be recalled as long as life endures."

William James (1890), *The Principles of Psychology, Vol.1*

What is your earliest memory? Whatever you think it is, your earliest memory probably exists as an inchoate mess of associations and images from some experience you had when you were very, very young. While some part of your mind has a memory trace for it, you cannot consciously recall the experience, let alone describe it in words. But even though you may not actually know your earliest memory, why did you remember that particular memory you first thought of? Is it perhaps a memory that you have thought about before?

A chapter about memory may sound unpromisingly dry, particularly after a chapter about brains and bodies, but memory is a crucial ingredient in how we make sense of reality and our lives. If you have travelled together with me this far, I am confident that you will find memory far more interesting than you may think.

Each of us has personal memories, such as our earliest memory, that we may or may not be able to express in words. Our inner world involves many such stories and images from our past and they are collectively known as our *autobiographical memory*. But it is only one form of memory.

It is self-evident that everything we think, feel and experience can only be understood by us on the basis of what we already know about the world. Our senses on their own provide us with a constant babble of information, a cacophony of raw data, but our brains and minds manage to bind it all together into coherent information that means something to us. We discard the noise and pick out the important information on the basis of what we already know about the world.

We only know that the apple in front of us is an apple because we have a memory for what an apple looks like, the name for it, that it can be eaten, and even a memory of what it tastes like. It is much harder to understand and adjust to something new. A mobile phone is a meaningless lump of shiny magic to someone who has spent their entire life in the Amazon rainforest and never seen such a thing before. As we will come to see in *Chapter 5 – Trains of Thought*, our long-term memory of what we have experienced is vital to how we make sense of the present moment.

We might start by remembering that Behavioural Modernity, roughly 50,000 years ago, was when our ancestors first began thinking in modern ways. From then until now, this ability to mentally simulate the world has led to its utter transformation. As we have said, in order to be able to think in this modern way, our ancient ancestors required three essential ingredients: they needed to be able to represent the world in their minds in symbols (tree, hill, woman, child, fire, etc), they needed to be able to hold these symbolic representations in their minds long enough in order to be able to do something useful with them (such as interpret and produce language, generate models of the past and future, contemplate the past, predict the future, etc.). And above all, they needed to be able to remember these symbols and models so that they could draw upon them later. The functional importance of memory is not so much to remember the past as to be able to use it to understand the present and anticipate the future.

Cultural memory storage, by contrast, is the product of what people in general have thought about, made, recorded and preserved since the advent of Behavioural Modernity, the ideas and material things that have been retained in one way or another within human societies. Cultural memory storage is expressed in the complexity of the social world around us – the cultural symbols, beliefs, institutions, religions, ideas and customs, etc., as well as the material culture of objects, technology, artefacts and buildings. Our individual lives exist within this much wider eco-system. The social world is thus vastly more complex than individual personal lives, which are complicated enough, but we will consider a few aspects of it in *Chapter 9 – Cultural Storage.*

But before we delve into memory, let us quickly review what we have established so far. We have seen that brains evolved over millions of years, enabling animals to process information in ways that help them survive. The information comes from the outside world and from the animal's body itself, and this is used to maintain the animal's physiological systems and aid their survival. Each animal has drives and emotions that guide their behaviour in the interests of survival, and human beings are no exception.

Brains are information processing systems and are therefore nothing without the input of information. That information occurs from moment to moment throughout our lives, and the memories we form on the basis of that information (what we have experienced) are stored in potentiated neural pathways, tagged with emotional associations. All our experiences are processed within the physical neurons of the brain and nervous system, and the mind is therefore ultimately 'embodied' in that we exist within bodies and brains that enable us to act upon the world.

However, as we have seen, the human brain has an amazing additional feature that emerged quite recently in our evolutionary past, the ability to construct a symbolic mental model of things outside itself, and even including itself. By learning from new experiences and other people, the mind is able to grow its knowledge base and make more sophisticated plans for the future, such as creating ingenious technology, starting a business, creating a work of art, and so on.

But perhaps equally remarkable, if less obvious, is the mind's ability to quickly absorb new experiences and rapidly turn them into routine, taken-for-granted assumptions, to the point where they are rarely thought about again. This too is a function of memory and something we need to understand.

For example, at what point did you learn that cats like to be stroked, that milk comes from cows, that windows allow light to enter a building, and so on? You may not have been explicitly taught these things but nonetheless your mind carries these implicit assumptions, and they are stored in memory and taken for granted. From earliest childhood we learned most of what we now assume to be true by watching and listening to other people. All through our youth and beyond, we soaked up and reproduced other people's behaviour without realising it. We followed our parents' instruction and advice, we copied a brother's or sister's behaviour, and we learned from schoolmates and friends.

In other words, we learned by osmosis, absorbing ideas and behaviours from the intricate social and cultural world of the people we have encountered in the community and society in which we happen to have lived. But much of the time we were not aware of what we were learning, or *that* we were learning. This is how the mind works.

That is the intriguing thing about human memory. It is not always clear what we have learned, or the conclusions we have reached. Our memory is often invisible to us. This is known as the unconscious mind.

The structure of memory

What were you doing yesterday morning? Did anything special happen? How would you even know if something special *had* happened? To know that something is 'special' requires us to already know something about the normal state-of-affairs. And that knowledge is stored in memory.

A person's mind and brain contain a record of their experience in the form of personal memories, knowledge, skills and assumptions. All these very different types of memory are stored in neural pathways. However, these memory imprints are often a low-resolution record of past experience, and not all of them are accurate or well-remembered. It helps if we can separate out the different types of memory we store and how they affect what we think.

The Structure of Memory

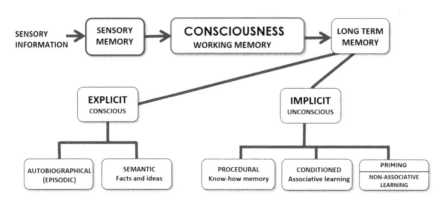

Diagrams like this can be a bit daunting for some people. So if you are someone who would normally shy away, please give this one a chance. It may look a bit complicated at first, but I will walk you through it and you will see that the structure of memory is far more intriguing than you may have thought. It may even lead you to think about your own memory in a different way. And why wouldn't you want to know about how your memory works? Our memory is self-evidently a vital part of who we are and how we think.

So... starting from the top left, *Information* enters our senses and we vividly store what we experience for a split second, almost like an afterglow, or sensory perception afterburn. Just stare at something, close your eyes and immediately notice how the image very quickly fades. That is *sensory memory,* which passes quickly into *working-memory* where the information is registered, and then discarded or worked upon.

At any one time, we are receiving more information than we can take in so we need to be able to select what we are going to focus our attention on and what we are going to ignore. We do this by developing a state of readiness which psychologists call the perceptual set which helps us anticipate what is coming so we can attend to that and discard information that does not seem relevant.

Working-memory, as we have already mentioned, is essentially a temporary store of very recent and present experience, a transitory cache that occurs in the present moment and is able to retain images and thoughts from the last few seconds. When you try to hold that phone number in your mind as you search for your phone, you are holding it in working-memory. In the next chapter we will see that consciousness occurs in working-memory, the same place that we make sense of information and manipulate it.

Being able to consciously maintain ideas in working-memory enables us to hold a conversation with someone else, because we are able to remember what they have just said and what, as a result, we intend to say. When we fail to maintain this, such as a switch in our attention to some new focus, our trains of thought change track and working-memory is now used to process this new thought, and this in turn sometimes results in cognitive drop-off, a failure to remember what we were thinking about.

British psychologist Alan Baddeley has outlined a model of working-memory that accounts for both the temporary storage systems involved (visuo-spatial sketchpad, phonological loop and episodic buffer) and the control system which is known as the central executive. Readers may wish to explore this further but for our purposes it is enough merely to understand the general function of working-memory.

Long-term memory (*see diagram*)is where our brains and bodies set down experience so that we can draw upon that knowledge later. The encoding of all *long-term memory* begins life in working-memory. Once an experience is processed in working-memory, the information moves to the hippocampus where it is given emotional context and from there it may be stored in long-term memory. Let us simply call long-term memory 'memory' from now on, on the understanding that working-memory is something quite different.

Memory can be sensibly divided into two parallel branches: *Explicit memory* and *Implicit memory*. **Explicit memory** refers to those memories that we can talk about (which is why it is sometimes known in psychology as 'declarative memory'). *Implicit memory* refers to memories that we struggle to articulate because they are hidden from our conscious minds, and are therefore **unconscious** memories. So this division between explicit and implicit memory is effectively the long-recognised distinction between the conscious and the unconscious mind.

Explicit conscious memory

Explicit Memory (*see diagram*) is about the things we are conscious of knowing. It can also be usefully divided into two parts.

Autobiographical memory

Most of what we think about as our memories falls into the category of **Autobiographical memory**, the memories we have of what has happened to us during our lives, the events and episodes that we can recall and even perhaps describe. Psychologists also refer to this as *episodic memory*.

Semantic memory

The other branch of explicit memory, **Semantic memory**, refers to the facts and ideas that we have picked up from the world around us. These include cultural knowledge, often acquired through formal education. You either know what the capital of France is, or you don't, but if you do it is freely recalled. Now, try *not* to think of what 7 and 4 add up to. You may have found it hard to stop the answer popping into your head because it is so well learned within your explicit semantic memory. We have a capacious store of such information, especially if we have been educated and curious about the world, and have been able to access information about it.

However, it is probably a little more complicated than that. How does a ticket inspector remember which passengers on their train have already paid for a ticket? It seems that working-memory has particularly good access to face recognition and recent events, even if those memories are never fully consolidated into long-term memory.

Implicit unconscious memory

So far, this rendering of memory probably seems quite straightforward, because explicit memory is the kind of memory we are all familiar with. Now let us look at ***Implicit Memory***.

Sigmund Freud (1856-1939) popularised the idea of the 'unconscious'. He described the important insight that not all memory and lived experience is known to us. In other words, we know a lot more than we think we know. Unconscious or implicit memory is a vast repository of memories based on past experience, but ones that are not readily accessible to conscious thought.

These days, modern cognitive scientists refer to the unconscious as *implicit memory* and it is no longer such a controversial idea that people possess knowledge about which they are largely unaware. Therapists have long understood that people's experiences are often shaped by their implicit memories, such as deeply hidden feelings, and that with time and effort they can sometimes be brought into conscious awareness.

Incidentally, perhaps the converse of the unconscious mind is being aware that one is aware. This is known as meta-awareness. We are a species that can make sense of itself being alive. The dying David Bowie (1947-2016), in one of his last songs, poignantly described *meta-meta*-awareness: "*the moment you know you know you know"*. It turns out that the unconscious has been there all along, only now people of science are allowed to talk about it again.

Implicit (unconscious) memory has been divided into four areas but we are only going to consider two of them in any detail.

Conditioned memory

Conditioned memory refers to the things we learn as a result of association. The behaviour of all animals is shaped by the rewards and punishments that follow their behaviour. You are simply more likely to do something again if a reward follows, and less likely to do it if nothing happens or something negative follows. For example, many experiments have shown that you are particularly likely to keep on doing something if you don't quite know when a reward will occur. Gambling is the obvious example. In this respect we are not entirely unlike pigeons, as we shall see.

Although our actions are constantly being fashioned by subsequent rewards, lack of rewards, and penalties (known as *operant* conditioning), we can also be affected, like any animal, by the emotional and physical associations that our behaviour has with things in the environment. This is known as *classical* conditioning and again is often established without our awareness. The Russian psychologist Ivan Pavlov (1849-1936) is best remembered for his experiments with dogs. He showed that by pairing the sound of a bell with giving the dog some food, he could induce the dog to salivate merely in response to hearing the bell. This is also conditioned memory.

Operant and classical conditioning are powerful forms of learning for all animals, and that includes humans. We compulsively check our phones in response to a notification. The sight of the refrigerator door can make some people salivate. Certain smells or pieces of music can evoke indescribable feelings and associations reinforced by the past. Sexual fetishes (e.g. caressing rubber) are born from conditioned memories, even if the individual cannot recall when the original association occurred.

People inadvertently develop conditioned responses, but some memories have phobic consequences. Until I was a teenager, I was inexplicably fearful around Alsatian, or German Shepherd, dogs (which, perhaps sensing my fear, would always growl), until my mother told me that I had once been attacked by an Alsatian when I was three years old, a memory for which I have no conscious recollection.

Conditioned memory is responsible for many fear-based psychological difficulties. Some people refuse to leave their homes because they associate the outside world with danger. One of my very earliest patients with agoraphobia had not left the house for over two years when I first met her in her home. Unusually, she was able to remember clearly that her fears started after being startled by a car backfiring as she was passing it. She had become embarrassed that other people had seen her understandably frightened response, and thereafter she avoided going out. She had associated going outside with feeling humiliated and embarrassed.

The son of one of my patients who had died some years before, phoned me from the north of England to say that he was having panicky feelings every time he drove south to visit his daughter. He said that each time it was a relaxing drive until he came across road signs for Bristol, the city in which his mother had died three years earlier. Even though he was not travelling to Bristol, the road signs alone had become associated with the anguish he had felt when he used to visit her in the hospital where she was being treated. Again, this type of learning often occurs almost entirely beneath conscious awareness. He had not predicted that he would react with such anxiety, and he had certainly not noticed himself learning this association. So we arranged for him to visit the hospital again, so that he could develop more benign associations with it and the city where his mother had died.

Procedural or know-how memory

Imagine yourself cooking a particular dish that you have never made before. You are following someone else's recipe, such as a cookbook or a video, and you have to concentrate on getting things right. Performing the many steps involved this first time may be tricky and demanding and requires your conscious attention.

But if you like that recipe and cook it several times, before long you won't be looking at the recipe at all because you will have remembered all the steps involved. And after years of making that recipe over and over again, you will be able to do it without giving it a moment's thought. You can be singing along with the radio or talking to one of your children, yet you move from step to step without much conscious awareness of what you are doing. Your mind and body have made the making of the dish automatic. You have turned it into a series of actions that take minimal attention. This is known as **Procedural** or **know-how memory.**

Driving a car is the standard example. Once again, a new driver initially has to apply a lot of conscious attention towards changing gears at the same time as steering, but soon the many skills involved in driving become so automatic that neural pathways work together fluently to deliver the behaviour without conscious thought, allowing the driver to relax and even talk to their passenger.

Tying your shoelaces, riding a bike, dancing a Highland Fling, and laying a row of bricks accurately, are all examples of procedural memory. Simply put, the more you do something the more the neural pathways involved become strengthened (remember that neurons that fire together, wire together). What was once conscious and explicit becomes implicit and unconscious. We develop know-how. With habit, routines, and repetition, much of what we learn soon recedes into procedural memory, knowledge that we simply take for granted. This, as we shall see, is both a good and a bad thing.

Learning any new skill essentially involves the same process. At first it is laborious and tiring because we are having to be deliberate and use conscious and explicit memory, but with practice it becomes automatic, requiring less and less concentration or attention. Procedural memory is how children learn to walk. Repetition leads to automation as specific patterns of neural pathways become potentiated, eventually becoming well-worn grooves of thought.

Playing the piano is another good example. The more you practise, the more your brain and nervous system develop new neural pathways that fire more quickly (and with fewer mistakes). Such know-how, or embodied knowledge, underlies the skills and expertise of athletes, dancers, musicians, artists, stone masons and so on – genetic endowment combined with physical practice and persistence.

Finally, there are two remaining areas of implicit memory that I will only briefly mention because, although they both wield a strong influence over our behaviour, they are not as central to our story of the mind.

Priming

Priming is a form of learning in which you are more likely to think of something in one context rather than another. Recently-thought-about ideas are more readily available to consciousness than less-recently-thought-about ideas. Rather like perceptual set, people construct the world on the basis of what they expect, and pay attention to some things more than others as a result of prior experience.

For example, if you have spent the morning thinking about which car to buy, you are more likely to interpret the sound of an alarm as being a car alarm than a house alarm. If I tell you I am going to the beach today and a few minutes later ask you to guess the two missing letters in the word s_ _d, there's a good chance you will have thought of the word 'sand'. If someone points out a particular tree in flower, you may subsequently find yourself noticing that same species of tree in other places. Such priming is fairly short-lived, but it is likely to unconsciously influence our perceptions. One of my patients once mentioned how seeing a white feather always reminded her of her late father. Later that week it seemed as if I had noticed several white feathers at different times since she told me about them. Perhaps this will happen to you, now that I have mentioned it.

Non-associative learning

Non-associative learning is equally interesting, despite its dreary name. Once again, non-associative learning comes in two flavours, but this time they are almost the inverse of one another. *Habituation* is when a stimulus occurs continuously or repeatedly without any apparent effect, with the result that the brain no longer responds to it. For example, wherever you are at this very moment, close your eyes for a few seconds and think about what you can actually hear. How many sounds can you hear that you were not consciously aware of until I asked you to notice them? Your brain had tuned these sounds out. You had habituated to them.

This phenomenon was noted by one of the fathers of modern psychology, William James (1842-1910), who wrote "*We do not notice the ticking of the clock, the noise of the city streets, or the roaring of the brook near the house; and even the din of a foundry or factory will not mingle with the thoughts of its workers, if they have been there long enough."* [7]

There is a more general meaning of habituation which is when things that were once new recede into background and become taken-for-granted, such as when thoughts and behaviours become habitual.

The counterpoint to habituation is **Sensitisation,** whereby we become *more* sensitive to, and *more* aware of a particular stimulus. Imagine you had woken up and noticed a humming sound coming from the wall. If you are lucky you will soon habituate to the noise, think about something else, and fall back to sleep. Your brain habituates to the sound to the point where you no longer notice it. On the other hand, you might feel annoyed by the sound and your annoyance focuses more attention on it, to the point where night after night it becomes all you can hear and think about. That is an example of sensitisation.

In summary, memory is stored in the brain within neural pathways that have become primed or potentiated by experience. These neural pathways are therefore more readily activated when similar events occur again, whether or not the memory is explicit (known to us) or implicit (unconsciously known). Studies have shown that story, place and emotion are strongly featured in our strongest personal autobiographical memories, and they are very often coloured by emotional associations (such as those road signs to Bristol, or the Blackwall Tunnel).

The brain stores long term memories by maintaining stable changes in the synaptic connections within neural pathways, pathways that have been strengthened by previous neural firings.

Note 7: William James (1890), *The Principles of Psychology, Vol.1*, p.455

Particular neural pathways become associated with particular thoughts or physical tasks to the point where they become the spontaneously preferred option. In other words, once something has become habitual (a mental or physical habit), the brain tends to follow its well-trodden neural pathways. This enables people to do and think things more automatically, releasing their mental resources to respond to other priorities. What was once consciously learned becomes implicit, background, taken-for-granted knowledge. We will talk more about automatic thinking in the next chapter, but first let us look at how we develop more abstract memories and record the lessons of what we have learned.

Making stories

For most of our lives we lay down long-term memories without being aware we are doing it. But there are times, particularly when we are young and needing to learn about the world, when fixing or pinning down long-term memories requires effort and concentration, particularly if we want to be sure that our memories will be there later when we need them, such as a school exam. Repetition is one common method of 'fixing' the neural pathways involved, but it is far easier if what is being remembered has some form of meaning. A related mnemonic technique is story-telling, embedding information within a narrative. This book, for example, began with the story of Nell and has been trying to tell a story of the mind.

Story-telling has a long history. Before the advent of written language just over 5000 years ago it was the only method of retaining human history. Stories were passed down from one generation to the next in the form of poems, chants, songs, and dances, depicting gods, creation myths, and explanations for the natural world. Story-tellers became revered as both entertainers and spiritual guides. This oral tradition of cultural storage went on for many millennia, and inevitably many stories have been lost.

Turning experiences into stories aids memory storage by embedding small ideas or events within a larger framework. By chunking information together, and placing particular memories in particular imagined places, it becomes easier to recall the information later because one only has to remember the skeleton of the story for the details surrounding it to 'reappear' in memory. It remains a useful mnemonic technique for those wishing to retain a large body of knowledge. In 2015, a blindfolded 21-year-old, Rajveer Meena, managed to recall Pi to 70,000 decimal places. The Hindu newspaper reported that he achieved this extraordinary feat by "sequencing the numbers into an episode or transforming them into an object".

Our autobiographical memory is also largely structured around stories. What do people talk about when they meet? They tell stories about what they have done, what they have seen, or what they have heard. The memories we hold about ourselves and what has happened in our lives are stored and communicated as simplified stories.

Reading and listening to stories is much the same. Human minds are adept at filling in the details of stories they have only heard in outline, and quickly constructing a plausible narrative. Remember Nell? With just a few elements to seed our thoughts, we are able to imagine what is happening and where the story is likely to go next. An engaging story, such as a novel, is one that plays with and defies those expectations. We fill in the blanks of stories that we hear with our own assumptions, and don't always notice new information when it has become available because we tend to perceive what we expect to be there.

The stories we make help to structure our experiences, and it is these stories that we will remember. We don't encode detailed objective reality into memory, so much as our assumptions about what has happened. The story we remember will be based on any particularly intense ('memorable') moments in the experience, and especially how it ended. We see what we expect to be there, and even when things turn out differently, we end up constructing a story that, as much as possible, maintains continuity and coherence with what we previously understood about the world.

It is therefore not surprising that two people can experience the same event but come away from it with adamantly divergent interpretations about what happened, based upon the different life experiences that they each brought to it. They saw the world through eyes that were coloured by different assumptions, and they ended up constructing different models and stories of what they had seen. This is what makes each mind unique, and the testimony of eyewitnesses so problematic.

This human need to make stories from experience goes on to the very end of our lives. In dementia, the mind struggles to make new neural pathways or retrieve old ones. Part of the tragedy of dementia is having to watch the sufferer continue to construct stories from their fragmented memory store by filling in the blanks as plausibly as they can, a feature of the condition known as confabulation. As long-term memory becomes more and more fragmented, there is a hollowing out of the individual's personhood. The person we know fades before our eyes, even while their emotions stay intact.

Story-telling is a universal human activity which not only infuses the culture around us (news stories, literature, folklore, theatre, films etc.), but is central to how individual people make sense of their lives. Telling the story of what has happened to us helps us clarify our thoughts and feelings, and sometimes even reveals the assumptions and mental models that we have been unwittingly using.

Mental models and assumptions

Earlier today I learned that John did not pay Mary the money he owed her. This very simple story contains information that has implications that are not explicitly expressed by the words alone. The new information may subtly alter my assumptions about John in all sorts of ways. Perhaps it will change my assumption that John is honest, but it may also confirm my assumption that Mary is far too trusting for her own good. In other words, what we store in memory is a reflection of the changing assumptions and mental models of the world that we have developed over the course of our lives.

Our minds, after all, work to ensure that our memory record of what we experience offers generalisations that may be useful in similar situations in the future. In our evolutionary past we didn't need to remember the details of what happened to us so much as the general lessons that could be gleaned from them. In making stories about our experiences therefore, we not only code into memory the broad outline of what has happened to us, we are also working out and recording the lessons that we have learned and the conclusions we have reached.

In 1871 Charles Darwin published *The Descent of Man* and wrote that *"Man cannot avoid looking both backwards and forwards, and comparing past impressions."* Typically, he was right, although he did not go on to mention that people compare past impressions so as to be able to construct more effective mental models with which to anticipate the future.

This is the essence of Behavioural Modernity, the capacity to symbolically model the world in our minds so that we can use it to intelligently predict the future. It is plainly in the interests of our survival as we go through life to be able to recalibrate our mental models so that in future they do a better job in helping us negotiate the world. So Darwin was definitely on the right track.

Whether we are a primary school child or a theoretical mathematician, our minds are model-making machines. At the core of what makes our minds human is this ability to *represent* and *model* the world around us. Because human brains can symbolically represent the world, primarily through language, they are able to form **assumptions** and **mental models** that describe and represent the world in abstract generalised ways, rather than simply recording the superficial details.

So, you may be asking, what is a mental model or assumption?

A mental model is a framework of ideas that represents an object or other idea(s). Once a model has been formed it soon becomes an assumption in its own right. For example, a glass is a vessel used for conveying liquid to one's mouth. When you think of a glass your mind doesn't have to think of a particular glass, so much as the idea, or model, of a glass and its function. Several ideas and assumptions are carried by the idea of a glass. A glass is usually made of glass, hence its name, but not always, and it can have many shapes and designs. But when someone says 'I was holding a glass' you get the general idea of what they mean. That's what models do, they generalise to become abstract hypotheses, or propositions, about reality. A generalisation. An assumption. And we are using them all the time.

In our minds we can carry the idea of a glass, a chair, a hand, a tree, and so on. These words are symbolic representations of the world that are held in long-term explicit memory, enabling us to recognise and understand these objects when we come across them. We also carry the idea that one thing may have a relationship with another thing, and this relationship can be described by other types of symbols or ideas, such as verbs and prepositions.

A glass, a chair, a hand, and a tree are things which may or may not have a relationship with one another, but we can quickly construct a story or model of how these different ideas might relate to one another. We can imagine a boy sitting on a chair under a tree with a glass in his hand. As you think and imagine this, the image is held in your mind as a model or proposition. It doesn't exist, except in your mind as a train of thought or image while you are thinking about it in working-memory (whether or not it is subsequently stored in long-term memory). This is a mental model, a configuration of ideas. Some models are fairly concrete, like a glass, and some are abstract, like the idea of kindness or integrity.

The assumptions that make up our mental life are just what they sound like, propositions or proposals about the world that are represented as symbols in our mind. In cognitive psychology these are known as *propositional representations*, while psychoanalysts tend to use the term *symbolic representations*. Everything we know about the world is made up of these representations, assumptions, or models about the world and other people, and of course they include ideas about ourselves.

We are introduced to someone new. We hear about the other person's situation in life, their background, job and personal life. We notice the way they are reacting and responding to us, the words they choose to use, their accent, their smile. Our assessment of them depends on a whole number of associations and changing cultural currents of which we are intuitively aware but not always able to articulate. But it is these assumptions and mental models that enable us to think.

Although humans are particularly sophisticated in their ability to model the world, other animals are intelligent within their own particular ecosystem. Octopuses use coconut shells as camouflage and appear to be able to plan ahead in a limited way. Spiders, crabs, sea urchins, birds and many mammals have been observed to use tools, but none of them are able to teach what they have learned (except through simple mimicry), or store that knowledge for future generations. Only human minds can do that. And only humans have the dexterity for making things, using a mind that is able to model the world in complex ways, work out cause and effect, and imagine a different possible future. For all their reputed intelligence, dolphins cannot make things that other dolphins can use.

Crows' brains are large relative to body size, with a highly developed nidopallium caudolaterale, analogous to primates' prefrontal cortex. New Caledonian crows craft tools like hooked sticks to extract insects, showing problem-solving and foresight. In Japan, carrion crows drop nuts near traffic lights, let cars crack them, and retrieve the food safely when the lights change—an observed case of causal reasoning and pattern recognition.

Yes, other animals experience the world and learn from it, and some animals appear to be able to model the world in very prescribed practical ways. But one only has to look at the reckless creativity of the world around us so see that, for all our shortcomings, we humans are uniquely able to mentally model the world in remarkably complex and interesting ways.

Over the past century there have been many names in psychology for more-or-less this same idea, and it is no accident that current Artificial Intelligence is largely based on large language and concept models. The general idea of models and assumptions as mental representations is associated with some of the most celebrated psychologists in history. Here are some of the terms they used.

Symbolic representations	1920s	Sigmund Freud, Melanie Klein
Mental models	1940s	Kenneth Craik, (↓Philip Johnson-Laird)
Cognitive maps		
Mental maps	1950s	Edward Tolman, (↓Antonio Damasio)
Construct systems	1960s	George Kelly
Internal working models		John Bowlby
The Assumptive World	1970s	Colin Murray Parkes,
Schema/core beliefs	1980s	Aaron Beck, Albert Ellis (↑Jean Piaget)
Core assumptions		Michael Horowitz, Ronnie Janoff-Bulman
Schematic models	1990s	Michael Power and Tim Dalgleish
Cognitive models		
Propositional representations	2000	Cognitive neurosciences

I will be using the terms **mental model** and **assumption** to convey the same notion. In as far as a model is a representation of a thing or a structure of ideas, it is also itself an assumption, so these terms will be used interchangeably, depending on the context. Mental models enable our minds to symbolically represent the phenomenological world we experience, our particular reality, and that includes stories we have constructed about the past, and ideas we have about the future.

From earliest childhood each one of us has been doing exactly what Darwin suggested – drawing conclusions from what we have experienced. We have been constructing and altering our mental models about the world, as *we* understand it: where things exist in the physical world, how things work, what we think and feel about our family, the people we know, the things we do, what we have learned from the cultural world that we happen to have lived in, how we expect other people to behave, and so on. Our mind represents all this in models and assumptions, all the stuff we consciously know, and all the stuff we know but don't know we know.

The Assumptive World

Ever since we were a baby our conception of 'reality' has been changing and growing because our models of the world have become ever more refined and sophisticated. And yes, all these models and associations of thought are coded in the neural pathways that constitute memory, thanks to the astronomical number of possible connections between those 86 billion neurons. Just try for a moment to imagine all those billions of neural networks firing away throughout the many folds of your brain at this very moment, and literally all the time. All those gazillions of tiny, almost instant bio-electrical impulses and synaptic connections. It is within our brain's huge networks of potentiated neurons that we store something of what we have perceived, understood and remembered from the world around us throughout our lives. The fact that this is happening in our minds is really just as awesome as staring up at the Milky Way!

We should therefore perhaps develop the previous diagram of the structure of memory to include the assumptions and mental models that we hold (*The Assumptive World* diagram).

The Assumptive World

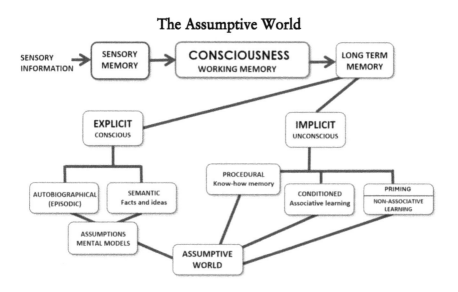

The totality of the assumptions and models and other forms of memory that we hold about the world at large, including assumptions about ourselves and others, is known as the **assumptive world**. It is the aggregate of the different types of long term memory in the diagram. The assumptive world includes thoughts and ideas held within both conscious and unconscious memory, all our individual habits of thought and behaviour. It is the repository for all the assumptions and mental models that we hold about the lifeworld, and all the intuitive, mental, and physical routines we have developed to make life simpler. Our individual assumptive world reflects our unique personality. As we will soon see, this personal assumptive world enables us to make sense of moment-to-moment experience in our own unique way.

Memory retrieval

My earliest memory is of my mother walking into my bedroom one morning when I was four years old. She was speaking to me as she walked across the room and drew open the curtains. I can still see the sunlight on the windowpanes, the light pouring through the glass onto her kind face, her red lipstick, her still youthful complexion and her 1950s haircut. I remember being aware of her over there, and me being over here, sitting up in my bed, looking at her. I was suddenly aware of my separateness from her.

I like to imagine that this is when I first became properly conscious, but actually it is more likely that I am just reconstructing a fossilised memory that has become so overlaid from the various retellings to myself that it has become barnacled with associations with what I was feeling at the time of those many recollections. In other words, this current version of my memory of that morning all those years ago, while still vivid, is one of many.

There are other tricky things about memory. Memories become distorted in the process of remembering and retelling. When we recall a memory, we are forced to reconstruct something that was coded in the past, but we can only create this reconstruction (re-representing the past) from the perspective of the moment we are in now, so that means that what we remember is inevitably coloured by the context we are in now and what we are currently doing and emotionally feeling, not to mention all the other times we have remembered the same thing and all those other contexts. The 9/11 memory study demonstrated this. Similarly, covid-19 memories have become distorted by time. Memories and stories become embellished or simplified, and there are many other ways in which memories can become distorted and hard to access. Diaries are an attempt to swim against the currents of time.

On the whole, however, long-term memory is fairly robust and seems to decay little over time, even if the details become distorted and more fuzzy. Retrieving memories, however, is another matter. People 'forget' memories when the synaptic connections within the neural pathways that make a memory become weakened through lack of use, or when a new neural network uses some of the same pathways as the old memory, causing interference to the pre-existing network. Memories can also be hard to retrieve if they were poorly coded into memory in the first place, perhaps through lack of rehearsal and repetition, or perhaps because we were distracted or very emotional at the time.

We are more likely to remember times of momentous global events like 9/11, Kennedy's death, or the first Moon landing, or when we first learned about something catastrophic. We tend to remember the gist of what happened, what we saw, what we thought, and what was happening. However, autobiographical memories shift and change over time, especially it seems when it comes to remembering what we felt at the time. The reason we think we remember certain events vividly is because we have refreshed our memory of the event by rethinking and retelling it. But in the telling there is drift. So that cherished earliest memory may well have become part of your own personal folklore.

Mostly we remember *where* we were. Place seems to be a particularly strong factor in memory when shocking or very unexpected events take place. A year after 9/11 people remained consistent about where they had been. However, more than a third of the detailed memories that people provided a week after the 9/11 attack in New York City had changed over the course of the first year.

Antonio Damasio believes that there are areas of the brain that represent the world, image-making regions that interpret information coming from the senses, particularly visual and auditory ones. These image-making regions of the brain represent what you experience before storing it as a memory. When that memory is later recalled, the same image-making regions are used again, only this time re-representing or projecting the memory in working-memory.

So, as our mind draws up the representational models of the taste of steamed rice onto what Damasio calls the projection areas of working-memory, we almost get to re-experience the taste and smell. Our brain is firing up all its associated neural pathways, its millions of synaptic branches that echo off one another, resonating with our past experiences of warm rice. If we have never tasted or smelled hot steamed rice, then we can only imagine it, but that too is based on other associations and mental models, and these too are represented in neural pathways in our brain.

When you haven't seen someone for a long time it can be difficult to remember them well. After ten or twenty years without contact, your memory for this person you had once known well, perhaps even intimately, becomes fossilised and reduced to an abstract ill-defined idea. But if I were to show you a very short film clip of that person, or ask you to listen to an audio recording of them, it would likely cause you to feel a deep sense of recognition as those projection areas in your brain light up and cause many subtle memories to come flooding back into consciousness, evoking some indescribable quality of what it is like to be with them.

This also goes to show that there is a big difference between free recall memory (simply trying to remember something) and recognition memory (remembering it when you see, hear, smell, taste, or feel it). Free recall is not as easy as recognition memory because in our evolutionary past there was little survival advantage in our brains being able to recall a high level of detail, most of which was unnecessary, but it was helpful to recognise landmarks and other features of the natural environment so that you could find your way around and find your way home.

See for yourself. After a day-long walk in varied countryside it would probably be difficult to tell a stranger how to follow the route you had taken because you will have forgotten the details. But if you did the same walk the next day, or even a month later, you would be surprised by how many of the details you would recall as soon as you saw them.

So it turns out that the details and texture of what we experience are coded in implicit memory but largely 'forgotten' in our conscious memory. What *is* remembered is perhaps a rough image, an assumption or a simplified story. But when witnessed again, we experience that oh-yes feeling as we recognise the subtle details of what we thought we had forgotten. This immediately engenders a more embodied visual memory, quite different from a simple abstract idea. Perhaps this is how ticket inspectors are able to recall which passengers have already paid their fares, using face recognition memory.

Similarly, we can usually recognise what is required of us from one situation to the next because each moment is similar to a situation we have been in before, even if we cannot freely recall the previous situation. So it is worth remembering that the importance of memory is not to be able to remember the past accurately so much as to recognise things in the present and be able to anticipate the future.

Most of the time we are not even trying to remember anything. We are simply responding to the familiar world around us. Moment-to-moment experience feels coherent and continuous because it tallies with what we already know (from memory) about what reality should look like and feel like. These assumptions and models are mostly implicit and unconscious but, as we are about to see in the next chapter, our assumptive world is vital to helping us make sense of reality. They inform our consciousness about what is happening in the present moment, along with expectations about the future, and they help maintain that sense of continuity and coherence.

◆———————◆

Further Reading

Baddeley A, Hitch G. (1974) Working memory. In The *Psychology of Learning and Motivation* (Bower G., Ed.), pp. 47–89, Academic Press

Baddeley A, Wilson B (2002). Prose recall and amnesia: implications for the structure of working memory. *Neuropsychologia*, 40, 1737–43. doi:10.1016/S0028-3932(01)00146-4

Carruthers P. (2013) Evolution of working memory. *Proceedings of the National Academy of Sciences*, 110, 10371-10378

Chen I. (2011) How Accurate Are Memories of 9/11? *Scientific American*, Sept 6th issue, www.scientificamerican.com/article/911-memory-accuracy

Craik K. (1967) *The Nature of Explanation*. Cambridge: Cambridge University Press

Darwin C. (1871) *The Descent of Man, and Selection in Relation to Sex*. London: John Murray

De Timary P, Heenen-Wolff S, Philippot P. (2011) The question of "representation" in the psychoanalytical and cognitive-behavioral approaches. Some theoretical aspects and therapy considerations. *Frontiers in Psychology*, 2: http://dx.doi.org/10.3389/fpsyg.2011.00071

Ericsson K, Kintsch W. (1995) Long-term working memory. *Psychological Review*, 102, 211-245

Horowitz M. (1976) *Stress Response Syndromes*. New York: Jason Aronson

Janoff-Bulman R. (1992) *Shattered Assumptions: Towards a New Psychology of Trauma*. New York: The Free Press

Logie R. (2023) Strategies, debates, and adversarial collaboration in working memory: The 51st Bartlett Lecture. *Quarterly Journal of Experimental Psychology*, 76, 2431-2460

Parkes CM. (1971) Psycho-social transitions: a field for study. *Social Science and Medicine*, 5, 101-115

Pinker S. (1997) *How the Mind Works*. New York: W.W. Norton

Power M, Dalgleish T. (1997) *Cognition and Emotion: From Order to Disorder*. Hove, East Sussex: Psychology Press

Rimé B. (2009) Emotion elicits the social sharing of emotion: Theory and empirical review. *Emotion Review*, 1, 60-85.

Squire L, Zola S. (1996) Structure and function of declarative and nondeclarative memory systems. *Proceedings of the National Academy of Sciences*, 93, 13515-13522

Turner JH (2000) *On the Origin of Human Emotions: A Sociological Inquiry into the Evolution of Human Affect*. Stanford: Stanford University Press

Ungerleider LG. (1995) Functional brain imaging studies of cortical mechanisms for memory. *Science*, **270**, 769-775

Woollett K, Maguire EA (2011) Acquiring "the Knowledge" of London's Layout Drives Structural Brain Changes. *Current Biology*, 21, 2109-2114. doi: 10.1126/science.270.5237.769

Wynn T, Coolidge FL (2007) Did a small but significant enhancement of working memory capacity power the evolution of modern thinking? In: Mellars P, Boyle K, Bar-Yosef O, Stringer C. (Eds.) *Re-thinking the Human Revolution*. Cambridge: McDonald Institute of Archaeological Research

Chapter 5

Trains of Thought

In the last three chapters we set the stage for how we might understand the mind, and how we each make sense of reality. We saw that although the mind is invisible, it exists within the neural pathways of a brain, and a nervous system that spreads throughout the body. We learned that at the heart of the cognitive revolution that drove Behavioural Modernity was the relatively sudden ability of humans to model the world in their minds, in working-memory, using symbols such as, importantly, language. We saw that our model-making minds exist within brains and bodies that evolved and come with their innate drives and emotions. We are thus as much our bodies as our minds.

I have tried to show that a central purpose of brains, and ultimately minds, is to move information about, while storing some of it in memory that may be helpful in the future. We learn facts and ideas from other people, draw conclusions, and make generalisations based on our experiences. We store this knowledge in memory as mental models and assumptions. Our memory storage is both known and unknown, conscious and unconscious, explicit and implicit, and we have called the aggregate of all the knowledge that we have acquired in our lives thus far 'the assumptive world'.

In this chapter we will see how long-term memory (the assumptive world) enables us to make sense of moment-to-moment experience.

Consciousness and the present moment

It is perfectly reasonable to ask if we can ever really be objective about something so entirely subjective as consciousness. Like the mind in general, consciousness is not a material *thing*. It is a mental and ultimately neural process, an electrochemical series of events embodied within something that *is* materially real, the brain and nervous system. Like digestion and stomachs.

Our drives and emotions may be the animal dynamos that engage our attention and behavioural responses, but we also have this special sense that enables us to *experience* our lives. How is it possible that you can be aware of yourself understanding and taking in these words right now? It is as if we have an inner sense of ourselves, almost like a voice within our head, thinking thoughts and having feelings in reaction to what we think and sense within ourselves and the world outside us.

Our minds, when called upon, seem able to provide an almost constant commentary on what is going on. Our self-talk, our reflective thinking and the stories we tell ourselves, may not be a sequence of words and sentences, though clearly ideas and language come into it a lot, but can also involve patterns of images based on memories. This ostensible commentary helps us create the stories and memories of our lives. It is how we remember things one day to the next, how we make plans for the future, and how we acquire an understanding of the past. Rather important then.

Although this is not ostensibly a book about consciousness, it is hardly a subject we can ignore. Daunting as that may sound, we will take a pragmatic psychological perspective and try to join up a few dots. However, before we do that, and without wishing to complicate matters further, we need to clarify the two meanings of the word consciousness, even though both of them exist entirely within the neural pathways of the nervous system.

One meaning of consciousness signifies that our nervous system is fully functional and alert to the world around us. We are not asleep or in a coma, too heavily drunk or otherwise intoxicated, and we are physiologically responding to the environment we find ourselves in. All animals share this form of consciousness, so let's leave it at that and say no more about it. There are of course many *states* of consciousness so there is much more to be said about this meaning of consciousness, but that is not what we are considering here.

The second meaning of consciousness relates to the fact that we have minds that can experience themselves making sense of the moment they are in. Our human minds have a sense of themselves, consciousness, even if it is just the personal narrative that we each construct for ourselves. No other known life form has a brain that can do quite that, neither bats, nor cats, nor rats, nor gnats. We are able to think in abstract ideas, they cannot, other than in very limited ways. Evolution has unintentionally fashioned a species whose nervous system can generate not just sentience but thought and self-awareness.

But maybe it is not quite that simple. Yes, the nerve endings in our eyes, ears, noses, mouths, and on our skin, where our senses meet the world, send signals along neurons to our brain, but at what point do we *feel* the experience? Who is doing the feeling? How do physical neurons in the senses, nervous system and brain become *felt* experience – the recognition of your mother's voice, the taste of jam, the quality of redness, the feeling of cloth? Are such 'qualia' perhaps merely a form of neural pattern-recognition in so far as we have heard, tasted, seen, or felt the experience (or something similar) before?

This does seem like a hard problem: how does phenomenological experience emerge from neurons, and how can the enormous complexity of what we experience be represented in our neural pathways? How does the living biological matter that is our brain become the conscious lived experience of our lives, and how is it that only human minds appear to be capable of achieving this self-conscious, existential, phenomenological self-awareness? This question was famously posed by the neuroscientist David Chalmers:

"It is widely agreed that experience arises from a physical basis, but we have no good explanation of why and how it so arises. Why should physical processing give rise to a rich inner life at all? It seems objectively unreasonable that it should, and yet it does." [8]

It is indeed weird and extraordinary that we have consciousness but perhaps there is a partial explanation. This second meaning of consciousness is this awareness of ourselves being alive, with a mind that can feel. Homo sapiens has evolved a mind that can think *for* itself, and think *about* itself. This is central to what a mind is, a computational operating system that is capable of self-reflection, fresh ideas and intentions – action derived from thought. Subjectivity.

We have a mind and brain that can hold a train of thought in working-memory long enough to record, manipulate, remember and communicate ideas and plans, and even create new ones. Above all, we have a consciousness that anchors time by distinguishing between past and future. It acts as the bridge between our memories of the past and our thoughts about the future. Consciousness occurs only in the present moment, a fact that British neuroscientist Richard Gregory (1923-2010) was keen to note. It allows us to be aware of ourselves in this very moment, you in your time and me in mine.

---

[8] Chalmers D. (1995). Facing up to the problem of consciousness. *Journal of Consciousness Studies*, 2, 200–219, p.

Trains of thought

Consciousness emerges as a result of working-memory constantly processing information brought to it from two sources: **our senses** (eyes, ears, nose, mouth, skin, and the body more generally), and our long-term **memory**. From these two sources of information our mind creates mental representations of the world, sequences of images, thoughts, and visceral experience, the very trains of thought that make up our moment-to-moment experience of reality. All this information is integrated by the brain, enabling us to model and derive meaning from our experiences and react with appropriate behaviour. The complexity of the integration required of the mind and brain is truly bewildering.

Consciousness is the very act of thinking, reacting to, and generating representations. It can only ever exist in the present moment because working-memory is a temporary memory store, a constantly changing constellation of thoughts and images. And it *is* almost always changing. Moments of consciousness are constantly receding into the past as working-memory attends to the next sensory experience or thought. This appears to be a basic property of the mind. We may be able to *think* about the past or anticipate the future, but consciousness emanates from, and is locked within, the present moment, and that moment is always changing.

By existing only in the present moment, consciousness provides us with a helpful partition between the past and the future.[9] It is hard to imagine how thinking would work without this nifty separation; the future and the past would be indistinguishable. We can reflect on the past but the future is ultimately the mental model we construct in the moment when we consider it. Consciousness is like a continuously breaking wave of awareness, the stream of thoughts in working-memory... happening in the present moment.

This quality of consciousness, sitting astride the gap between the past and the future, was poetically noted by the American psychologist William James in 1890: *"In short, the practically cognized present is no knife-edge, but a saddle-back, with a certain breadth of its own on which we sit perched, and from which we*

Note 9: Richard Gregory, personal communication

look in two directions into time." He was essentially talking about working-memory.

Your ever-changing mind is you, a *consciousness* of yourself in this moment right now, with a past behind you and, with any luck, a future in front of you. Only that moment has gone and now this is now... and now... and now... always. Human consciousness requires a subject, a someone, an 'I' that is able to mentally experience what there is to experience. It requires a mind that can think in sophisticated ways. A mind capable of subjectivity requires the ability to construct representations or models of the world, models that even include the person doing the thinking.

Other animals can form relatively simple mental models of the world, even abstract ones, but none of their models includes a model of themselves experiencing their lives. They react in the present moment using their working-memory to interpret information from their senses, but they are not constructing sophisticated models from their experiences, nor drawing on complex abstract conclusions from their past. As Daniel Dennett (1942-2024) said, other organisms' ability to respond appropriately to the environment is a form of "rudimentary intentionality", but it is not the "reflective loop" that is consciousness.

At every moment, our brain is processing information coming to it from the senses. The incoming information is compared with expectations and assumptions streaming in from the assumptive world (memory), enabling us to recognise and understand, or not, the information we perceive. At the very heart of the mind is its capacity to construct an ongoing series of thoughts, trains of thought, until the chain of ideas is broken and our attention switches to something else.

And our attention switches a lot. Observe your own thinking and you will quickly notice that it flits about from one image or train of thought to another. This too is an important feature of consciousness. Dip your toe into what William James described as the 'stream of consciousness' and you will notice that your mind is constantly altering its attention from one area of interest and intention to another.

A train of thought is a sequence of ideas, one idea leading to another. Trains of thought are often short-lived, such as noticing the kettle is boiling, briefly turning our attention to that, making an instantaneous plan for using the boiled water to make some tea for example, and then switching our attention to another train of thought, such as perhaps taking note of the fact that we will need to buy more tea, or reverting back to what we were thinking about before, and so on. Again, if you observe your own thinking you will quickly recognise that this is how we think; we string together ideas and images in real time, in working-memory.

Our minds are constantly constructing models of the current moment, making sense of it and planning accordingly, and sometimes we are able to sustain a particular train of thought over a longer period of time by concentrating our attention on it. Working, reading, watching or playing a sport or game, watching a movie, and so on.

Admittedly it is not easy, perhaps even ill-advised, to observe yourself falling asleep, but if you do try you may notice that as you drift off into sleep your thoughts become less intelligible and continuous. It becomes harder to maintain a coherent train of thoughts. Instead, our thoughts fragment into non-sequiturs and vague images until we sink into unconscious oblivion.

Constructing reality

Consciousness is therefore essentially our working-memory manipulating information derived from both our senses in the present moment, and an expectation and understanding based on the past. Our stored memories are drawn from the social and cultural environment in which we happen to have lived our lives, and they constitute our unique assumptive world. Our mind contains billions of emotionally-tagged memories and associations that we may or may not consciously remember. Add to this all the assumptions we have formed about the world, about other people, and about ourselves.

The complexity of all this information quickly becomes a gargantuan computational jigsaw puzzle but, astonishingly, our brain draws together all those neural pathways, all those trillions of synaptic connections, and provides us with a continuous and coherent sense of what is happening in the present moment.

The mind is probably able to achieve this through what is known as generative modelling, associated with the work of Karl Friston among others. In simple terms, generative modelling, or 'predictive coding' as it is also known, imposes order on what we experience by using immediate feedback from our senses and our existing knowledge to fill in the gaps of what we perceive and what we remember. It uses the context to generate moment-to-moment predictions that are subsequently updated on the basis of immediate feedback. Perception is a comparison between these predictions about incoming sensory information, and actual sensory input. It should be no surprise therefore that generative modelling is widely used in Artificial Intelligence.

Switching attention

Astonishing as consciousness is, the explanation for how it works is conceptually relatively straightforward, even if the brain science underpinning it is not. And perhaps it is not as 'objectively unreasonable' as Chalmers suggests. One plausible explanation is that consciousness is the mind's ability to observe itself working, and to mark continuously the moment of now.

We are aware of our consciousness when we choose to take note of it. It is what our senses and thoughts are offering us about the ongoing but ever-changing moments of our lives whenever we pay attention to them. We are able to observe our own trains of thought, and our own changing focus of attention. In other words, we can observe ourselves thinking. Consciousness is this awareness of our own thoughts and experience at the moment they are happening, and, critically, as we have said, it enables the mind to distinguish between the past and the future.

We recognise patterns of information from moment to moment, based on our memory of the past – other people, where we live, objects we use, and so on. Consequently, reality feels coherent, continuous, and plausible, joined-up. But the moment is always passing, ticking away throughout our lives, and the future is always sliding past us. As events change, so consciousness marks the unfolding present moment.

Just as we are able to think about objects outside ourselves, we can have thoughts about our own mental experiences and be an observer to our own thinking, with our own commentary. All of this is accomplished through the trillions of neural connections that enable the brain to perceive, represent, remember, recall, and think (not to mention the fact that nervous system is simultaneously maintaining the many functions of the body).

It is this ability to hold a train of thought in working-memory that enables us to come up with new thoughts, new ideas, new intentions. The existential thread that runs throughout the span of our individual lives is a continuous sequence of switching thoughts, one train of thought following another as we react to the world and ourselves. Our trains of thought are broken up, not least by sleep, but we each do our best to construct a sense of continuity and coherence with one moment following the last in ways that are broadly predictable.

The assumptive world, all our background implicit and explicit knowledge, is therefore vital to our ongoing experience of consciousness. The world *seems* continuous and plausible because our brain is able to bind together all the different inputs from our senses, thoughts, emotions, drives, memories and fantasies, into coherent trains of thought. Our minds are constantly resolving any anomalies in the stream of new information in order to make sense of it, and at the same time discarding, simplifying, chunking and storing it away in memory.

A solar eclipse must have been a terrifying experience for our ancient ancestors because they had no stored knowledge with which to make sense of the Sun suddenly growing dark during the day. Consciousness only *seems* relatively continuous, and appears to make sense, because our moment-to-moment experience is reasonably consistent with the taken-for-granted assumptions that we have developed since we were born.

Our past therefore frames how we experience every new moment because our minds try to fit the present moment into these pre-existing assumptions. Even dreams appear to tell a story that feels relatively coherent at the time, because our minds are used to linking trains of thought into stories. As we will see in a later chapter on therapy, psychological trauma effectively lacks this continuity and coherence, and has a disconnected dreamlike quality.

So how does consciousness fit into the model of memory that we described in *Chapter 4*? If we reconsider the diagram of how information flows into different forms of memory, we can now include the influence of the assumptive world (the dotted line) on how our consciousness constructs reality from moment to moment in working-memory (*see diagram*).

Memory and Consciousness

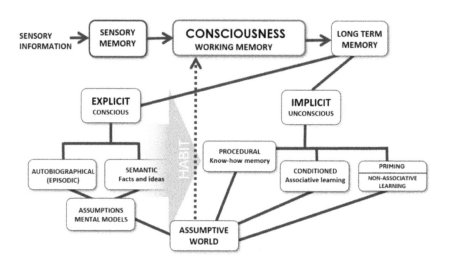

In summary, working-memory is constantly processing information brought to it from two sources: the senses (eyes, ears, nose, mouth, skin, and the body more generally), and memory (assumptive world), as the mind attempts to create representations of the world in the present moment (*see diagram*). All this information is integrated by the brain, enabling us to make sense and derive meaning from our experiences, and react with appropriate behaviour.

Consciousness is being constantly fed with assumptions, associations and expectations from the assumptive world that enable it to evaluate new information. But as ideas and models are repeated and become familiar, they are increasingly taken for granted and become part of unconscious procedural memory.

We experience our consciousness as a series of changing trains of thought as our attention shifts from one thing to the next.

Sometimes we are able to sustain our attention for a while, such as when we read a book, but even then our attention is constantly being altered and redirected by the author. So the mind is rarely still and has clearly evolved to be an active, inquisitive and creative information processing system. And all that meaning and knowledge needs time to be absorbed.

We seem to value the time we spend fantasising, working things out, ruminating, daydreaming, and imagining. It can feel good to sit in a quiet place, free from distractions, close your eyes, and simply think. Contemplation and reflection are not only quintessentially human, they are positively helpful if the mind is to grow and develop, because reflexivity is an essential form of self-regulation and development.

So it can often be helpful to train our minds to be calm and still, practices such as meditation and mindfulness, spending time in the present rather than the past or future. These practices are not merely pleasant, they can enable us observe our frenetic thinking and sometimes let it go. Being still allows us to give our rabid minds a rest and, at the same time, being mindful about what we are doing enables us to notice the details of moment-to-moment experience, the trains of thought passing through our minds and working-memory, the continuous stream of consciousness.

People need time for reflection if they are to learn and self-regulate, and this is helped if we are able to calm down our physiology and our minds. The social conditions of people's lives can often make this difficult to achieve, but wherever it is found, quiet time to think can be restorative.

So-called **qualia**, the subjective qualitative sensation of something, only occurs when we focus our controlled attention on something ineffable, such as the taste of wine, the redness of a rose, the smell of honey, the sound of birds. The sensory experience enters working-memory and that is where our intense awareness of the taste, colour, smell, touch and sound takes place. The qualitative feeling of redness, or the tangy acidity of wine is caused by an observation and recognition (or non-recognition) of a similar mind-body state from the past. Like any other information, we try to find patterns in the sensory information we experience and compare it with patterns of understanding from past experience, even if words fail us. But the rich qualia-like sensory recognition quickly fades as we switch attention onto something else, or in the case of colour we close our eyes.

In as far as we are aware of our mind thinking and switching attention, we can become aware of ourselves anchored to the present moment, experiencing our moment-to-moment trains of thought. It is in this subjective awareness that consciousness emerges. There is no unified Self behind this subjectivity; it is more likely that we merely have the illusion of a consistent self because we have autobiographical memory. Over the course of our lives, we unconsciously construct a more-or-less coherent story of our life that helps us account for experiences that belong to the same 'me' – our own life story, our own assumptive world. This gives us a sense of perspective, *our* perspective and subjectivity.

This central requirement of symbolic language and memory combined with an expanded working-memory makes it hard to imagine any other creature experiencing this type of consciousness. They just do not have minds that are capable of it. Animal brains tell them to feed, shit, procreate, and how to react to threat in order to survive. They experience pain and react to it, and they have drives and emotions that are adapted to their particular ecological niche, but they do not wonder or contemplate. They respond to the world around them, but they do not think about it. They may have the intelligence to solve simple practical problems but they lack the imagination to take it further. They may have body clocks, as many species do, but they have no sense of time in the way we do.

For a tiny creature that only lives a few days, gnats actually fly rather well within their little biospheres. They can see the world and are born with their own danger-recognition systems, but they don't *feel* fear. They react to threat with biological responses associated with threat-detection, but they do not *think* about the threat or experience worrying fearful thoughts. They are certainly not aware that they are shortly to die. We have the good fortune of knowing that we are.

British neuroscientist Anil Seth maintains that there are different levels of consciousness and that it is far from being an all-or-nothing phenomenon. Other animals are sentient in the sense that their moment-to-moment experience of sensory stimuli is coloured by associated emotions, often derived from past experience, but their thoughts are locked within the present moment and they are not troubled by concerns to do with the past or future. Cows may ruminate, but only when it comes to their digestion. Humans can thought-travel.

It follows from this that pre-verbal children, likewise, do not experience consciousness in the same sense that adults do. That is not as strange as it may first sound. When a child learns to understand and speak a structured language, it liberates them from the present moment and their immediate perceptions, and gradually opens the door to abstract thought. When children learn to talk they are soon talking to themselves, and this external expression of their developing consciousness becomes gradually internalised until it turns into private thoughts and musings. Consequently, talking to yourself, or to anyone else, can be revealing because it helps you to become conscious of what you are thinking and feeling, and sometimes what you need to do. By talking, you get to hear what you think. Psychological therapy facilitates and makes use of this effect, and that is the subject of a later chapter.

To go one stage further, it is even hard to imagine that children develop full consciousness until they have learned to mentalise or imagine other people's perspectives, and begin to experience themselves as separate from the people around them. We will think more about this in the next chapter as we track the way that children mentally develop into adults.

Human consciousness therefore seems to be a *function* of the processes and contents of the brain, but it is not a *mechanism* of the brain. You could say that it is an emergent property of the brain's ability to mentally represent and model the world, including itself. As digestion is to the stomach. Consciousness is simply the moving window of working-memory as it passes through time. For those seeking a more exotic explanation of consciousness, such as quantum mechanics, this may seem disappointingly pedestrian, but this computational account of consciousness seems the most plausible and parsimonious one for now.

A rather harder problem, even than consciousness, is the puzzle of 'who is doing the talking' inside your mind. Who is doing the directing, as it were? Where is that part of you? What part of your brain is choosing what to think, or say, or do next? There is clearly no other person in your brain, no homunculus. So where is that sense of intentionality located? How are your priorities determined in the face of all those needs, goals, emotions, thoughts and wishes that call out for your attention? Where can that self-directing part of you be found in the brain? These are all good questions.

But first...

Thinking, fantasy, and imagination

A species that can manipulate symbols in working-memory and generate a new idea is also one that can imagine a state of affairs by which to improve its lot, anticipate a threat, or simply make a hopeful plan. That species is able to be adaptive and creative because it can imagine the world existing in a different state. It is able to string together trains of thought and assumptions into a story or idea. And being able to fantasise and imagine is one the most fun things about being alive.

Human imagination and reason are together responsible for our ingenuity, our scientific and technological knowledge, the arts, humanities, and the social institutions that make up the fabric of modern life. Our choices and decisions may not always be wise, but the human capacity for imagination and creativity is unmatched, because only our species can think and string ideas together in the way we do. In fact, all our thoughts about the future can only ever be a fantasy or plan, the product of putting together different assumptions in working-memory and coming up with an image or train of thought that represents a model of the future.

Imagination involves trying out different models, images and assumptions in working-memory, without being restricted to habitual trains of thought. Instead of sticking to conventional pathways, imagination allows us to play with novel combinations of ideas that, in turn, lead us to create new ones. Our trains of thought in working-memory can be informed by images, ideas and assumptions from both conscious and unconscious memory, but they may well be inchoate or incomplete.

There is a space between sleep and wakefulness where all sorts of thoughts and images can pass through our minds if we allow them to. As we drift in and out of a state of hypnagogia, we can notice thoughts and images constantly popping up from our assumptive world, but like dreams they do not always make rational sense.

One of the most extraordinary things about being a person is being able to fantasise about anything we wish to. But what is even better is that we can be stimulated by the imagined ideas of other people: writers, actors, musicians, dancers, and other talented and brave artists. The Arts are all about people modelling and reflecting the world, and expressing their imagined representations of it with the rest of us. In fact, artists routinely make use of the incoherent offerings from *their* unconscious and allow themselves to follow their trains of thought to see where it takes them. Their fantasies may lead nowhere, but sometimes, through skill and hard work, they lead to creative masterpieces. Scientists similarly pursue intuitive hunches and trains of intellectual thought of course, but they must then subject their insights to the rigors of scientific scrutiny and methodology.

But while imagination and intelligence are arguably our greatest assets as a species, such thoughts can also be the source of great psychological misery. Many people become stirred up by what they imagine could happen in the future, rather than what is likely to happen, or indeed what is actually happening in the present moment. We explore this further in *Chapter 8: Therapy*.

Minds are generating new assumptions and modifying old ones all the time. We interpret what is happening from moment-to-moment and fit it into a coherent, continuous sense of conscious reality. Problems only arise when we take our thoughts too seriously and end up being ruled by them, rather than regarding them as mere propositions or assumptions. So if you believe that people are inherently dangerous, or you feel you are not safe in the Blackwall Tunnel, or you sense that germs are everywhere and that you might inadvertently cause an epidemic, or if you believe that you are fundamentally an awful person, or you feel hopeless, and so on...then your imaginative trains of thought can lead you to *feel* emotional distress.

Automatic and controlled minds

When I walk to my local shops, I am not actively thinking about what I am doing, where the pavement is, or where the crossings are. And I know where the shops are because I have walked there many times before. But I have no memory of having learned all these things. We saw in the last chapter that moment-to-moment experience can be coded into long-term memory without our conscious awareness. This simply means that we learn things that we subsequently take for granted, but do not necessarily know that we have learned them.

When people say they are conscious of something, they usually mean that they are focusing their attention on it, actively thinking about it in the present moment. As I walk to the shop, my mind is thinking about other things, so I am not fully conscious of what I am doing. In fact, a lot of the time we are in a similar state of nonconsciousness because we are not actively thinking about what we are doing. For all our clever minds, we humans vastly overestimate the extent to which we are consciously in control of our behaviour. Instead, we do things on 'automatic pilot', like walking to the local shops.

Routines and habits cause people to become less and less conscious of their actions or thought processes, freeing them to think about other things. A huge amount of what we each 'know' about the world is 'assumed'. Our habitual trains of thought become unconscious, taken for granted, procedural memory, and almost invisible (see *Memory and Consciousness* diagram).

So there are effectively two different ways of thinking: **automatic thinking**, of which we are rarely conscious, and **controlled thinking,** which is when we give something our conscious attention or concentration. The prefrontal cortex, the bit of brain just behind the forehead, becomes active when we (and even babies) are acquiring a new skill that requires controlled thinking. But once the skill or idea has been learned, this part of the brain goes quieter. It seems that the prefrontal cortex is vital to controlled thinking, such as when we are concentrating, giving mental attention to something, or learning something new. But this part of the brain becomes less important once a skill or thought has been learned and has become automatic and taken for granted (i.e. procedural memory).

Automatic thinking is fast and information can be processed in parallel. An experienced driver is able to drive a car, eat a banana, and listen to a radio show at the same time. Controlled conscious thinking, by contrast, can only focus on one thing at a time and is relatively slow. In computer and memory science jargon, this is known as serial processing, using just one channel of communication at a time. We cannot read a book and talk at the same time, unless we happen to be reading from the book out loud. We cannot simultaneously sing a song and write a sentence. Hearing is largely automatic because it is one of our senses, but listening requires conscious effort. Similarly, there is only one channel of conscious thought.

Habits and routines, however, allow our actions to flow like well-practised neural melodies. These habits of thought and behaviour become part of our unique personality and individuality. They may well start as thin as a spider's web, but in time can grow into cables.

As long as the activity is familiar, such as having a shower or preparing food, it proceeds in a way that is roughly consistent with the overall plan or model that we have formed. With everything running smoothly, it allows our conscious controlled mind to turn its attention to other more interesting and important things. The automatic mind, drawing mostly on its implicit knowledge base, gives us the sense of coherence and continuity that we all like to feel. The controlled mind only kicks in when the automatic mind doesn't know what to do, or something unexpected happens.

Automatic thinking: the habitual, routine, and taken-for-granted

People don't get up in the morning and consciously think to themselves "I will have a shower, and then go to work." It is something they simply do as a matter of habit. And when we do have a shower, we go through the many actions involved without thinking too much about what we are doing. In fact, the next time you take a shower, go to bed, or brush your teeth, you might notice the many tiny steps involved in doing these things, and just how many of them you do in exactly the same way, day after day without noticing. One step seeming to provoke the next.

Most of what happens in life is stuff that we have done before and repeatedly experienced in the past (bathing, eating, going to work, being at work, walking to the shops, and many other familiar routines). The obvious is strangely invisible, so the things we do on automatic pilot are hard to notice. Accordingly, I invite you to be a little more introspective over the next few days, and try to notice the things you simply take for granted or do automatically.

Routines and habits of thought and behaviour are a function of the same *procedural memory* that we encountered in *Chapter 4*, information and behaviour that has become *assumed*. Once the controlled mind has decided on a plan ('I'll have a shower'), the automatic mind is able to run through a program of behaviour, a mental model involving a number of steps that is nonetheless so familiar that we don't have to think about it consciously much at all. We are simply using well-worn neural pathways, with each action prompting the next. Consequently, most of the time we construct our sense of reality by drawing on this repository of unconscious implicit assumptions (feelings, hunches, habits of thought and action, etc.), as we *intuitively* respond to the challenges and demands of everyday life.

When you have an intuition, make a snap decision based on a 'gut feeling', or have woken up with an insight into a problem you had been grappling with the night before, it is your unconscious automatic mind that has been doing the work. Even when dreaming, our automatic mind continues to weave images from our memories into vaguely plausible stories. However, our controlled mind is nowhere to be seen, so in our dreams we have no control over events. You can't read in a dream.

Controlled thinking and attention

The pioneering Swiss child psychologist Jean Piaget (1896-1980) remarked that *"Intelligence is what you use when you don't know what to do."* Controlled conscious attention leaps into action if the automatic thinking part of our mind gets into trouble, or if we are deliberately concentrating on something.

For example, we use controlled thinking to create a plan (like that shower). Once put into action, controlled thinking monitors our progress, but unless the plan involves something novel or unfamiliar (the soap slips out of our hand), requiring our momentary attention and concentration (we bend down to pick it up), the automatic mind will do a pretty good job at executing the plan. However, when automatic thinking is unable to progress the plan, or 'doesn't know what to do', controlled thinking is enlisted to help. Once activated, controlled thinking constructs models of the problem in working-memory, and applies analytical reasoning so that, if necessary, it can create and execute a new plan in order to address and resolve the problem. In this way, mental models are updated. Of course this happens so fast that we don't notice ourselves switching between automatic and controlled processing.

Unlike automatic thinking, controlled thinking is relatively slow and takes effort. As everyone knows, concentration is tiring, so people are paid good money for applying their controlled thinking, knowledge and experience in the service of someone else's aims. By contrast, repetitive routinized tasks are generally less well rewarded. One might think of controlled thinking as the real brainchild of Behavioural Modernity.

Our automatic unconscious mind continuously monitors what is going on inside and outside our mind. From this cacophony of stimuli, the automatic mind recognises patterns from the past and provides us with a constant stream of impressions, predictions, intuitions, intentions, emotions and feelings. It is drawing on the assumptive world and memory associations from the past that relate in some way to the current context, and generates a narrative stream of possible plausible meanings along with any emotional connotations. All this goes on beneath our level of awareness, yet it underpins the way we think and feel by helping us to maintain a sense of mental coherence and continuity.

Controlled thinking involves working-memory and, as we have said, is taxing and tiring. Too many demands on the system, commonly known as stress, can sometimes threaten to overwhelm it (traumatic stress), so people naturally reduce the complexity of the demands they face by developing habits and routines that allow procedures to become automated, and thereby less taxing to perform. People often use other strategies to diminish stressful overstimulation, such as simplifying the world, avoiding unwelcome information, or by using counter-productive solutions such as excessive alcohol and drug use.

So, in summary, our minds contain many taken-for-granted assumptions about the world, but we are mostly unaware of them. We use these learned models and assumptions to recognise common patterns within our current moment-to-moment experience. These memory associations enter working-memory and help to inform consciousness. Much of the time we use automatic thinking to react to moment-to-moment experience, relying upon implicit memory (habits and taken-for-granted assumptions). But when this is not sufficient, we apply conscious controlled thinking and focus our concentration on what we are doing. Intelligence (controlled thinking), as Piaget said, is what you use when your automatic thinking doesn't know what to do.

As far as possible, minds try to make sense of new information in terms of what is already known, modelling it on the basis of past assumptions, but, if necessary, new assumptions may need to be formed. It is this cognitive flexibility that makes our human brains so special and so fundamentally different from other species. Unfortunately, however, this mental gift is far from being entirely reliable.

Habits, distortion and bias

Minds are fallible in a number of ways. Automatic thinking is brilliant at reducing complexity and creating a feeling of continuity and coherence in our moment-to-moment existence, but this does not mean that its conclusions are always right. It may be capable of constructing a good story of what is going on, but it is also prone to jumping to conclusions and taking things for granted.

You are at a party, and you strike up a conversation with someone you've never met before. Your automatic thinking kicks in, rapidly processing various cues like their body language, tone of voice, their choice of words, what they are saying, etc., to form an initial impression of them.

As the conversation progresses, your mind constructs a narrative or model about who this person is, based on the limited information available. Maybe they mention they work in a certain profession or share a particular interest, and your mind starts filling in the gaps, creating a more coherent story about their personality, background, and beliefs.

However, because your mind is fallible, it's also prone to jumping to conclusions based on stereotypes or assumptions. You might assume they have certain characteristics or beliefs simply because of their profession or a passing comment they made.

Later in the conversation, you might realize that your initial impression was off base. Perhaps they reveal something unexpected about themselves that contradicts the narrative you had constructed in your mind. This highlights how automatic thinking, while efficient at processing information and creating a plausible sense of coherence, can also lead to misunderstandings or inaccuracies if not tempered with controlled thinking and open-mindedness.

So automatic thinking can both streamline social interactions by quickly forming impressions, but also potentially lead to misunderstandings or misjudgements if we are not careful to question our assumptions and remain open to new information.

There are many ways in which we can distort what we perceive. For example, the mind tends to value what is happening now over what may happen in the future. So it is easy to overeat if you don't think about the consequences of what you are doing while you are doing it. The frontal lobes are only *so* effective at resisting temptation.

We use circular reasoning, such as you must obey the law because it would be illegal not to. What we first experience distorts our perception of what we subsequently experience, a type of priming. Eyewitness accounts are highly influenced by context and the person's prior experiences. We overvalue coincidences and anecdotal evidence over reliable evidence or reasoned judgment. If someone tosses a coin five times and it come up heads every time, they are inclined to think that the sixth toss is more likely to come up tails. We focus on one feature of something and ignore other perhaps more important features. We assume that if we like someone, everything about them is likely to be good (known as 'the Halo Effect', though it can work in a negative direction too).

The Israeli-American psychologist Daniel Kahneman (1934-2024) described many other such mental biases in sophisticated detail. It seems that human minds frequently process information in less than purely rational ways. One reason for this is because our implicit knowledge (the assumptive world) automatically biases what we perceive and choose to consider. Once we have a belief about something, we are inclined to go on assuming it is true, regardless of whether we have any current evidence to support it. 400 years ago, Francis Bacon (1561-1626) recognised this when he said *"Man prefers to believe what he prefers to be true."* In fact, entrenched opinion often comes well-armed. It is an example of what cognitive psychologists call *top-down processing* – our expectations shape what we perceive. *Bottom-up processing* is when our senses manage to override our mental expectations.

Top-down processing is particularly evident in the way we see the world. Look at the image to the right. Can you see a white square? Our neural pathways are so used to seeing one object sitting on top of another object that we are inclined to 'see' a white square where there are only black circles with quadrants cut out. In other words, we unconsciously add the missing lines to form the square.

Now look at this triangular image.

Did you read 'Paris in the Spring'? Most people do when they first encounter this. In fact, even when people look at it a second or third time, they often still see 'Paris in the Spring.' At first glance, our brain disposes of what it does not expect to see. To read it accurately requires us to read it consciously, line by line, using a tiny bit of controlled thinking. So in the first illusion we add information that is not there, and in the second we subtract information that we don't expect to be there.

Top-down processing is endemic in people's assumptions and attitudes. People who hold strong beliefs are generally convinced that their assumptions have been repeatedly confirmed by their experiences. Consequently, people blindly follow their leaders and maintain their beliefs because their expectations filter and fashion what they 'see' and remember, a phenomenon known in psychology as 'illusory correlation'. They even maintain their stereotypes despite being shown contrary evidence.

A few decades ago, most men in the UK believed that women were bad drivers compared with them, and intriguingly many women agreed that this was probably true. The actual evidence was clearly to the contrary. However, when asked, these men were able to remember numerous incidents where they observed women driving badly, entirely dismissing the greater number of times when they had seen a man driving badly. They were not lying. On the contrary, they would have sworn by their experiences.

A lot of this could be simply put down to social prejudice towards women, but it was also a function of how people give more weight to information that confirms their expectations than to information that defies them. As Hamlet says to Rosencrantz, "*For there is nothing either good or bad, but thinking makes it so*". Those male drivers remembered the things that they expected to see, not the things they didn't. The result was that their original assumption appeared to be consistently confirmed and was therefore strengthened. Such stereotyping is all about making life simpler, and biases like this enable people to maintain the integrity and consistency of their mental models.

Intentionality

Earlier we mentioned that there is a question that is even more perplexing than consciousness: who is doing the directing within the mind? How does our consciousness choose where to direct our attention?

Well, when you think about it, where we allocate our attention is mostly determined by our existing priorities, the things we have been thinking about and doing. These are based on the mental processes that are currently active, such as cognitive goals (neo-purposes), assumptions, and trains of thought, but also our drives and emotions. These contextual inputs produce the prevailing, albeit switching, plans and intentions of moment-to-moment consciousness.

As we have seen, human minds are able to flit about like music, quickly switching from one concern to the next, much like the switching attention of any mammal in the wild. Just try to notice how your eyes switch from one image to the next. Most experiences are predictable and routine, but sometimes they are not. We are constantly redirecting our attentional gaze to novelty, the unexpected, a memory, or imagining something new; fascinated one moment, disengaged the next. Selective attention drags relevant information from our senses and our assumptive world into working-memory to be worked on.

Our conscious experience is created by our controlled mind switching its attention from one thing to the next, even if much of the time we do things automatically with little conscious thought. Sometimes our thoughts are still and calm, and sometimes they are flitting and switching like a murmuration. We make plans (mental models) and carry them out, and this helps structure our consciousness for a period of time. Our attention is maintained and determined by the context that we are in and the demands and expectations it has of us. We are periodically reminded of goals we have created for ourselves and need to return to, or drives that need satisfying.

You shift your head and instantly you find yourself looking into the refrigerator, and for a few moments nothing else is on your mind other than scanning those cold racks until you find what you are looking for. What we feel about the situation we are in, our thoughts and emotions, gives us a sense of intentionality in the moment. We react to the present moment on the basis of the very recent past, but also what we have learned from the past, our assumptive world. We are able to hold in mind a number of plans and goals, some short-term and some long-term. Keeping track of one's goals is another matter.

Consciousness may occur in the present moment, but it is constantly being informed and enlightened by new information that may lead us to correct our bearings, and reorient ourselves towards previous goals, or new goals that we set ourselves. That new information takes us to another train of thought, and that may mean temporarily forgetting, or 'losing', one's previous train of thought, which might well have been a plan. This is what we have termed *cognitive drop-off*, when a current train of thought or intention, becomes superseded by a new one and consequently falls off the back of working-memory.

Our minds are deeply enmeshed with our emotions. Emotion immediately comes into play whenever there is a discrepancy between what our assumptions expect (such as pursuing a plan) and what our actual lived experience delivers. This motivates us to reduce the discrepancy by allocating our controlled attention to resolve the anomaly. Meaning is achieved by creating or modifying existing mental models, so that previously unexpected or unexplainable events start to make sense. It is these goals and glitches that direct our attention from one moment to the next, creating a sense of intentionality. There is therefore no single part of us doing the directing.

Finally, the idea that the past has somehow preordained the future is as ludicrous as saying that it is irrelevant to how people behave. People have free will to the extent that they can put together different ideas and create new ones from the vast complexity of their experience. Human behaviour is very much driven by a changing mental understanding of the past, present and the future, not simply by conditioned responses that may have originated in the past.

Every person's mind, brain and body develop over the course of their long childhood and beyond. Children are not born with consciousness, they develop it. They are not born able to control their bodies, but they learn to do so. Young children are poor at regulating their drives and emotions, so they must learn to control them. Children are not born knowing much about other people or themselves but, over the course of their lives, they develop their own assumptions and models about relationships and the world at large.

Children often learn through trial and error, but over time they can also learn to override their drives and emotions, develop a sophisticated understanding of themselves and other people, and ultimately experience consciousness, because they are able to think in symbolic ways and model their own experience and that of other people. Human society is so complex that it takes a long childhood for our minds and brains to develop so that we are able to negotiate and contribute to the world. So we now turn to how our minds develop over the course of our lives.

◆————————◆

Further Reading

Austin J, Vancouver J. (1996) Goal constructs in psychology: structure, process, and content. *Psychological Bulletin*, 120, 338-375

Blackmore, S. (2005) *Conversations on Consciousness.* Oxford: Oxford University Press

Claxton G. (1998) *Hare Brain Tortoise Mind: Why intelligence increases when you think less.* London: Fourth Estate

Craik K. (1967) *The Nature of Explanation.* Cambridge: Cambridge University Press

Damasio A. (1999) *The Feeling of What Happens: Body and Emotions in the Making of Consciousness.* New York, NY: Harcourt Brace.

Dennett D. (1991) *Consciousness Explained.* Boston: Little Brown and Co.

Dixon M. (2015) Cognitive control, emotional value, and the lateral prefrontal cortex. *Frontiers in Psychology*, 6: doi: 10.3389/fpsyg.2015.00758

Donald M. (1995) The neurobiology of human consciousness: An evolutionary approach. *Neuropsychologia*, 33, 1087-102.

Edelman G. (2004). *Wider than the sky: The phenomenal gift of consciousness.* Yale University Press

Elqayam S, Over D. (2016) Editorial: From is to ought: The place of normative models in the study of human thought. *Frontiers in Psychology,* 7: doi: 10.3389/fpsyg.2016.00628

Friston K, Price C. (2001) Generative models, brain function and neuroimaging. *Scandinavian Journal of Psychology*, 42, 167-177

Frith C. (2011) What brain plasticity reveals about the nature of consciousness: commentary. *Frontiers in Psychology*, 2: doi: 10.3389/fpsyg.2011.00087

Geary D. (1999) Evolution and developmental sex differences. *Current Directions in Psychological Science*, 8, 115-20.

Gilhooly K. (2016) Incubation and intuition in creative problem-solving. *Frontiers in Psychology*, 7: doi: 10.3389/fpsyg.2016.01076

Hamilton D, Rose T. (1980) Illusory correlation and the maintenance of stereotypic beliefs. *Journal of Personality and Social Psychology*, 39, 832-845

James W. (1890), *The Principles of Psychology,* New York: Henry Holt and Co.

Kanizsa G. (1976) Subjective contours. *Scientific American*, 234,48-52

Kahnemann D. (2012) *Thinking Fast and Slow.* London: Penguin

Par T, Friston K. (2018) The anatomy of inference: Generative models and brain structure. *Frontiers in Computational Neuroscience, 12:* doi:10.3389/fncom.2018.00090

Power M, Dalgleish T. (1997) *Cognition and Emotion: From Order to Disorder.* Hove, East Sussex: Psychology Press

Rimé B. (2009) Emotion elicits the social sharing of emotion: Theory and empirical review. *Emotion Review*, 1, 60-85.

Schneider W, Shiffrin R. (1977). Controlled and automatic human information processing: I. Detection, search, and attention. *Psychological Review, 84*, 1-66.

Seth A. (2021) *Being You – A New Science of Consciousness.* London: Faber and Faber

Developing Minds

Starting out

My three-year-old asked me if he had batteries inside him. When I told him no, he said "Then how come I can talk?

At the risk of spoiling something as delightful as a three-year-old's thoughts by trying to explain them, its charm surely lies in reminding us that small children possess naive mental models of the world. But three-year-olds are eager to learn more and it is important that that impulse is nurtured because the world is a complex and challenging place.

A child of three rarely has much of a model of the human body, but this child's understanding may well be based on a model that he has already developed that toys which move autonomously run on batteries. And since he finds himself moving autonomously, he has made the assumption that he too must be powered by a battery. A logical deduction perhaps but one based on limited information.

Here are some more preschoolers' ideas about the world:

Dad, I like bald egg.
Do you mean 'boiled' eggs?
Yes, the hard egg, with no hair and skin.

My daughter thinks that the people who came before us are our ansisters.

My daughter thought we were travelling to the island by fairy, so she was disappointed when we boarded the ferry.

Mum, why is it called a higher car when it's the same height as other cars?

Childhood was when we learned about the world around us and formed the psychological templates for later lived-experience. In other words, childhood helped us construct the core mental models that we have been building upon ever since. The world around us only looks familiar because we have learned to expect it to be so, and many of those expectations and assumptions were learned in childhood.

From birth onwards our brains have developed and changed in response to input from the world around us. Minds are not fixed, any more than politics, the weather, or relationships. Consciousness does not simply appear the moment we are born and then remain so for the rest of our lives. Our knowledge of the world, including ourselves, develops over the course of a lifetime.

Jean Piaget, the Swiss child psychologist, recognised this and proposed a theory to explain how cognitive minds develop during childhood, with one model building upon previous models and the mind becoming ever more abstract and sophisticated. This chapter, and the next, reflect many of Piaget's ideas about child development and how we adjust to new information, and also those of Russian psychologist Lev Vygotsky (1896-1934) who wrote about how we learn from the people and culture around us.

As we will see, adults are just grown-up children and childhood is an intimate dance between biology and environment. Throughout our early life, our brains were primed by our genes to learn from certain types of experience at certain times. A one-day-old's eyes are constantly scanning the world, eager to engage with other people and keen to learn about the world around them. They are born biologically programmed to be curious and attuned to other people's eyes and faces, and for the rest of their lives they will go on developing new memories and associations, with a growing understanding of how the world works. The foundation stones of how adults think and make sense of the world were laid in these early years.

The English philosopher John Locke (1632-1704) recognised the importance of childhood on our later lives, writing that "*the little and almost insensible impressions on our tender infancies have very important and lasting consequences.*" Babies and children are keen to observe and learn.

The most remarkable thing about mental development is that the state of the brain at one stage of neurological and cognitive development helps it select the experiences it needs to develop to the next stage. Children's brains develop in response to genetic tendencies as well as the input from the environment around them. That *environment* for almost all very young children is their mother (and the rest of the family), and it is largely the responsibility of parents to provide appropriate *experience*s. Nature and nurture are therefore mutually interdependent – the brain organises itself in response to a social and physical environment that it actively seeks out. Epigenetics at its most elegant.

If the *environment* fails to provide adequate human contact, care, and social stimulation, the brain fails to develop in normal ways. When the communist regime of Nicolae Ceauşescu was overthrown in 1989, there were 170,000 children living in Romania's impoverished institutions. Many had experienced

151

extreme neglect, with almost no stimulation other than being fed and cleaned. It was reported that there was an eery quietness in these institutions because the children's cries had been so long ignored that they had given up seeking connection with other people. The lack of human contact led the children to stimulate themselves through rocking and hand flapping. Most children suffered severe delays in cognitive function, motor development and language, quite apart from enormous difficulties in being able to relate to others, and their brains were smaller than non-institutionalised children.

Thankfully, for most people, childhood was when we learned about the things that we now broadly assume to be true, the things we simply take for granted in the world around us – schools, houses, people, shops, jobs, laws, nations. Whether simple or complex, we develop mental models of where we fit into the vast and intricate world around us. But for young children it can all seem very complicated and uncertain, and sometimes emotionally distressing.

Understanding how the world is structured is just one part of what we learn in childhood of course. We also learn about what we can expect from other people, and what we cannot, and from these experiences we developed a sense of ourselves. These lessons shaped the nature of the relationships we have subsequently formed with other people in our lives.

We are born seeking connection with other people and we inevitably learn useful things from our encounters, so the way that other people behave towards us while we are growing up can forge a lasting impression on our minds, for better or worse. We learn almost everything from other people, and by the time we are adults we have developed assumptions about other people – family, neighbours, friends, acquaintances – expectations that other people will behave in certain ways. We even expect people we don't know to behave in predictable boundaried ways too – shop-keepers, cultural figures, tradespeople, religious leaders, politicians, and so on. Childhood was when we learned many of these implicit social assumptions.

During childhood we also inevitably soak up other cultural assumptions from the world around us, such as a religious faith or what is expected of men and women. After all, children are inheriting a very complicated human-made world, and they must learn about it so they can survive and hopefully thrive within it. Parents and other family members must do their gentle best to provide this information in the early years, but children are quick learners compared with adults and they are soon learning from one another as much as from their parents.

The continuation of human culture can ultimately be attributed to the care and investment that parents make in their children during these early years and the environment they provide for them. In fact, John Locke had some good advice for parents too: he suggested that whoever "*is about children should well study their natures and aptitudes and see, by often trials, what turn they easily take and what becomes them, observe what their native stock is, how it may be improved, and what it is fit for.*" In other words, remember to be responsive to the child's unique temperament, qualities and sensibilities.

But there is an intriguing conundrum, powerfully described by the American academic Melvin Konner.[10] Compared with most other species, human childhood is exceedingly long, and there is relatively little cultural variation in this. Admittedly, elephants do have long childhoods, but it takes human children almost twice as long as chimpanzees and bonobos, our biologically nearest relatives, to reach puberty. From an evolutionary point of view, prolonged immaturity has no obvious survival advantage on its own, so our extended childhood must be a by-product of something else, and its benefits must outweigh its considerable costs or we would not have evolved it (unless, having evolved it, it is no longer useful to us). As we are about to see, the benefits of this long childhood turn out to be critical to human society as a whole.

On one thing we can surely all agree. Babies give irrepressible delight to people all over the world. There is universal wonder in the presence of a new human life. When a baby is born everyone present recognises that something inexpressibly beautiful and spiritually moving has occurred. (Incidentally, chimpanzees are

---

Melvin Konner's 2001 book *The Evolution of Childhood* (London: Belknap Press (Harvard) was an essential source for this chapter.

similarly interested and attentive towards a new baby chimp in the group.)

People delight in the baby's bewilderment. It appears to be stunned by its existence, yet clearly so eager to learn and to survive. Our attention is drawn to the child's vulnerable cries. They howl out to us to care for them. We are moved by the baby's helpless fragility, its big innocent eyes looking up at us, seeking the nurturance of a mother, and later a father.

In this sense, babies are not at all helpless. When they are born they are able to do many clever and useful things. They have built-in reflexes that enable them to root around for something to suck, and when they have found something suitable, like a nipple, they are able to swallow the milk and all the nutrients it provides. If we stroke a baby's cheek it will turn to our hand and try to suck our finger. Sometimes it finds its own thumb and sucking on this may be a comforting substitute for a nipple. Babies certainly know how to cry when they are hungry or tired, so they are very effective at communicating their simple needs. A baby can physically move its head a bit so that it can breathe, and it definitely knows how to urinate, defecate and spit up its milk without having to be asked.

So there was quite a lot that we were able to do as a new-born to aid our own survival. But of course it was not nearly enough. Human babies and small children depend on their mother (and substitutes) for their survival for a very long time, much longer, as we have said, than almost any other animal. Childhoods are long for a reason – there is a lot to learn.

Parents are often happily aware of the powerful caring feelings that well up inside them when faced with their own helpless child, or even someone else's. Their protective nurturing drive, and the emotions it elicits, kick in instinctively. One might even think of this need to care as being a primitive mammalian brain module – 'hard-wired' neural pathways that lie deep in some of the oldest parts of the brain, just above the top of the neck and brain stem. The pituitary gland at the base of our brain responds to parenthood by releasing oxytocin in mothers and fathers, a hormone that not only helps in breastfeeding but seems to underlie most forms of intimate bonding between people.

Human parents usually maintain this posture of unconditional love for their offspring for the rest of their lives, far longer than other animals nurture their young. Of course, parents often base their assumptions about how to parent on their own experience of being parented, sometimes inadvertently copying the behaviour of their parents, and sometimes deliberately avoiding it.

During childhood our brain and mind were developing tremendously fast. Our 86 billion neurons were making new connections (synapses) with one another at an astonishing rate. The synapses we had at birth were those innate skills that ran our life support systems: sucking, swallowing, and so on, situated in the older parts of the brain. But very soon the outer newer parts of our brain were getting to work, developing new synapses in response to what we learned from our environment. From birth to our teenage years the volume of our brain increased by four times, and 90 per cent of that growth occurred in the first three years. Our brain more than doubled in size during the first year of our life and then nearly doubled again in our second year. By the age of two, a typical neuron (and remember, there are 86 billion of them) has made fifteen thousand synaptic connections with other neurons.

We have said that a child's earliest experiences become the templates for all their subsequent learning to build upon. Jean Piaget demonstrated this in his studies of children's cognitive development, showing that knowledge builds on previous knowledge. For example, he noticed that a young child must first learn that things continue to exist even if they can no longer be seen, before they are able to learn that a thing can exist in another shape or form while still being the same thing (e.g. the amount of liquid in a short, wide glass is the same volume as that in a tall narrow glass, or later that ice and water are the same thing).

Mental development starts immediately. As already mentioned, new-born babies orient their gaze towards smiling faces that are directly looking at them. This ensures that from birth they are able to engage other human beings. During those first few months of life, our brain was biologically primed to engage with our mother or, if our biological mother was not available, a substitute caregiver.

In a few cultures, motherhood is shared amongst a group of women, but it is almost always women who perform this role. Your mother's brain, bathed in oxytocin, was also very ready to engage with you, her precious child. Almost all mothers are highly invested in their babies well before they are born. So you looked at her face and stared into eyes that were gazing right back at you. When, after a few weeks, you smiled, you were rewarded by lots of delighted noises and a sudden increase in facial stimulation from your mother and other family members.

So, for a very social mammal like us, learning almost always begins within an extremely intimate bond between a mother and child. This bond, evolutionary biologists believe, has been around since the time of the dinosaurs, when infant mammals would cry at such a high pitch that only their mothers could hear them, and not any reptile predator that happened to be in the vicinity. Intriguingly, it appears that many mammals today even respond to the distress calls of other mammal species.

Although human mothers have long received help from fathers, grandmothers and siblings, the mother-child bond is usually the first relationship that any of us experience, and it is from our mothers that we learn some of the most important lessons of our lives. We were entirely dependent on our mother for our survival, and her breast milk may well have kept us alive.

One of the first things we learned was that not everything we sucked produced milk. Some things don't taste good and most things, including our own thumb, don't deliver milk. And even our mother could let us down. Sometimes she wasn't there when we wanted her. It was a tough lesson. If we were hungry and she wasn't available, we howled with rage and frustration until our need was satisfied or we were distracted. So sometimes the breast was there, and sometimes it wasn't. It was an important but tough life lesson: you can't always get what you want, but if you try sometimes you just might find you get what you need. And sometimes what you want just turns up when you least expect it.

Living in a physical world

During our first year of life, whilst being very dependent, we were nonetheless starting to learn about the physical world around us, and learning to recognise the sensations coming from our body as we swung our limbs around. We began to mentally model where our arms were in relation to the rest of our body, and we gradually learned how to control them. A baby sees where their hand is when they move it, they learn the sensations of touch when they grab something, and they acquire the ability to discriminate sounds when they hear something. So they are not only learning about the physical properties of the world around them, they are also learning about how their body works, and developing sophisticated physical skills along the way – eventually crawling, walking, eating, babbling, singing, toilet training, and so on.

By the end of our first year we were beginning to get around on our own. A crawling baby is not so different from a young puppy, kitten, or other mammal; it explores the world, examining, prodding and tasting what it finds. We were not taught to do this, we are naturally curious about the world. Once a baby can crawl, it begins to discover the physical world around it and in the process the baby's brain learns new lessons in using its senses and controlling its body.

Walking is not something that parents teach their children to do, it is something that the brain is ready to do around the end of the first year of life. As they clumsily take their first steps, a toddler's brain is rapidly forming billions of new neural pathways which strengthen with practice, enabling them to stretch their capabilities further. Of course they will go on to develop many other physical skills throughout their life, for which language is similarly of limited value: riding a bike, playing a musical instrument, playing a sport, driving a car, touch-typing, etc. As we have said, this type of implicit *know-how knowledge,* or procedural memory, is learned by the body and nervous system until it becomes so habitual that we don't even need to consciously think about it.

A toddler is thought to be creating a couple of million new synapses every second, and by the time an infant is three it will have developed a peak of roughly 1,000 trillion synapses, maybe more, certainly far more than they will ever need. Over time these connections are pruned back and discarded, and by adolescence almost half have gone. The child's experiences in their life will have determined which connections were useful to keep.

As adults, we are able to select what we give attention to amidst the overwhelming cacophony of information coming from our senses, but babies and children are having to gradually learn to recognise the patterns that are relevant and useful for negotiating and navigating the world. They are using what they have learned to discriminate things that are meaningful from things that are not. They are learning to apply *selective attention*.

By the time we were three months old our parents found themselves quite naturally pulling faces, jumping about, and making weird sounds, just so they could arouse us, make us chuckle, and entertain us. They did this by surprising our expectations, but they did so in a gentle way that did not scare us. Parents and babies spend a lot of time staring at one another, and during these interactions parents spontaneously mimic emotions for the infant, using puppets, toys and imaginary figures. They are teaching the child the rudiments of audio-visual communication, emotions, and the idea that one thing might stand in place for another. This is how we started to think in *symbols*. "Da-da. Ma-ma" and so on, are sound symbols for the real thing.

Once we were on our feet, a toddler, we could move around more quickly and explore the world more voraciously. However, because we were biologically primed for stimulation, we quickly became bored, something that all parents soon come to know about. Towards the end of our first year, we were able to discriminate a few emotions from one another, but not all. In particular, we still had trouble distinguishing fear from anger. By this time we had already developed a primitive ability to read other people's minds by following their eye movement and the direction of their gaze, and inferring things from it. In fact, those facial communication games that got played out in our 'nursery years', taught us important interpersonal skills, particularly how to recognise emotions.

We may not remember those early games of communication, nor can we remember when we were hungry or tired, the times when we screamed with rage, or when we were just needing the warmth of human contact. But these early experiences taught us fundamental things about other people. When we awoke in the night and our mother was not there we cried, but those peek-a-boo-type games we played with our parents when we were just a few months old gave us a tiny taste of what it would be like for our mother not to be there, while also learning that she would soon come back. When she hid her face behind her hands she was gone and we were concerned, and when she opened her hands again we were delighted by the reassuringly familiar sight of her smiling eyes.

Peek-a-boo (and later hide-and-seek games) involve repeatedly creating and relieving tension in the child by hiding something that is weakly represented in the baby's mind, and then bringing the object back into their view. Once the tension is relieved, and the discrepancy resolved, the baby smiles. These simple repeated games helped us as infants develop neural pathways that represented the rudiments of trust, and the basis for assumptions and models that we developed later in life. We were developing a growing assumption that our mother would always reappear eventually, and that there can still be a bond and connection with other people even when they are not physically with us.

Worldwide surveys indicate that the end of breast-feeding (weaning) generally occurs when the child is about three years old. During those first three years there is rapid growth in the brain, so children need the rich energy and protein that breast milk provides. In the West, weaning often takes place much earlier, but regardless of timing, the child will continue to depend on others for its food. A young child's body is still small and their new, but deciduous, teeth are unable to process the diet or the quantity of adult food needed for adequate brain and body growth. In fact, in some cultures, mothers pre-chew food for their children which has the added benefit of giving the child some of the mother's immunity through her saliva.

Our exceptional middle childhood

Between the ages of five and seven children go through a biological and psychological transition, during which the neurons in their brains mature considerably. By the time they are seven, a pruning of synapses within the child's brain is well under way, though new synapses are continuing to be formed too. This is the beginning of *mid-childhood* when the human brain and mind really begin to sort themselves out. Biologists have noted that humans are unique in having this mid-childhood phase, roughly between 7 and 12 years old. All other animals go directly from infancy to puberty. Other apes, for example, reach puberty between seven and nine years old, around the same time that they are weaned.

The transition from infancy to mid-childhood, is marked by big changes in the way children think. At about this time, our neurons became covered in a sheath called myelin, that electrically insulates neurons from interference with one another, enabling them to conduct impulses more quickly. It also coincides with an improvement in working-memory capacity, perfectly aligning with the peak period when children are actively learning to understand, speak, read, and write language. Language, as we saw in *Chapter 2*, depends upon working-memory. It allows children to think beyond the immediate impression of their senses, and to begin to model the world. Language amplifies the child's use of symbolic thought and allows them to stand back from a situation and see it more abstractly. As we have seen, this improvement in working-memory and language development are essential precursors to consciousness.

There is sometimes a small growth spurt in children just before they enter the relatively quiet phase of *mid-childhood,* when physical growth slows down before the turbulent years of puberty. Around the age of 7 our first adult teeth appear. With adult teeth, children are able to progress to a more grown-up but less nutritious diet. Between 7 and 13 physical growth may be slowed down but the brain is growing fast. There is a vast blossoming of new neural pathways and brain development. In literate societies it is also when children learn to enjoy reading.

Mid-childhood is the time when children in almost all cultures are seen as empty receptacles into which adults can pour their knowledge, skills, morality, ideas... in other words, the time when children learn about how the world works and what is expected of them. Children are socialised into local customs, indoctrinated into one religion or another, enter formal education where it is available, or start to take on some of the tasks and roles of adulthood, if not the responsibilities.

Mid-childhood is the time when we really began to learn and absorb vital assumptions and models about the culture around us. Melvin Konner has suggested that one of the evolutionary (archaeo) 'purposes' of a long middle childhood is to hone the child's ability to detect cheating in others, an essential skill for our very social species and the counterpoint of learning to trust other people. An extended childhood provides the extra time for all this.

So the answer to the conundrum of why human childhoods take so long lies in this unusually protracted *middle childhood*. The evolutionary reason for such a long childhood is that it enables the environment to finish wiring up the brain. If our brain had been fully developed by the time we were born, our head would not have been able to squeeze through our poor mother's birth canal.

By the time they become adults, children will need to have learned the rudiments of how to communicate with other people using language. They will need to be able to regulate their drives and emotions, how to manage relationships with others, and how to survive within the complicated social world they find themselves in. They may not have had time to make much sense of themselves, but they will be trying to find their place within the world. The job of parents, as we have said, is to provide a safe and caring environment in which the young person (their body, brain and mind) can fully mature, preferably developing a degree of self-sufficiency and moral responsibility, and for the child's genetic potential to find expression.

Playing with language

Watching children play may not immediately make you think that something important is going on in their brains, or that they are learning to make sense of the world. But it turns out that **play** is an essential vehicle throughout life for mental, physical, and social development, though it is especially important in childhood. Many other mammals, especially the more intelligent ones, like cats and dogs, engage in rough-and-tumble play when they are young, but only humans continue to play into adulthood, sport being the obvious and abundant example. But there are many ways to play.

One theory is that play enables young animals to learn how to change and improvise their behaviour so that they are better prepared for the unexpected. Play gives children a chance to act out scenarios that mimic the adult world. Role-play games ("You be..., and I'll be ..."), and sporty games, teach small children some of the critical social skills required in adult life: turn-taking, co-operation, leadership, dealing with disappointment, envy, frustration, jealousy, and so on. Siblings and friends of course play a key role in this. However, play in humans is far more than this.

As already mentioned, the state of the brain and mind at one stage of development (with all its developing neural pathways) helps it select and engage in experiences that enable the mind and brain to develop to the next stage. Play is a vital channel for this self-organising process. Children ask to walk along the top of a wall because they are ready and keen to practise the useful physical skill of balancing one's body (with just that exciting frisson of risk). A children's playground is full of contraptions to help them learn how to control their bodies, and they clearly enjoy these challenges. The child's genetically programmed brain selects the optimal experiences necessary for its development. It is believed that language skills are also learned in this same way – children select what they are ready to learn from the language around them.

Small children are particularly receptive to symbolic play, the ability to envisage one thing standing for another, for dad to become a rabbit when he presses his hands against his forehead, for a stuffed toy to represent an animal, and for a teaspoon to be a helicopter. It is this symbolic nature of play, one thing representing another, that provides fertile ground for language development and adult minds. Adults are just grown-up children, but with any luck their models of the world have become far more sophisticated.

Play was our entry ticket to the symbolic world of language and ideas. Learning to use language is a central task of child development because, as we have seen, language really does set humans apart from all other animals. Other species, of course, have communication systems of their own, with some animals using methods of communication not used by humans at all, such as chemical and electrical signalling. But no other creature has anywhere near the human talent for language, or the kind of creative imagination that language has given birth to.

The sound of people speaking provides babies with the necessary input for their brain to form neural pathways and synapses which become strengthened with repetition. They not only learn to recognise the smell of their mother's body and the way she holds them, babies also quickly learn to recognise the sound of her voice, and soon some of the words she is using.

From one to three years old, children all over the world progress from a few words to several hundred. In the process, they learn the grammatical rules that guide their particular language. By the time they are six they will have acquired nearly 3,000 words in their vocabulary, but can understand many thousands more. It has been estimated that children around this age learn the meaning of roughly ten to fifteen new words each day, but that only one of these words is directly taught to them.

When we were a baby and we said "Ma-aa", our parents responded enthusiastically "That's right, Ma-ma!" Our parents were encouraging and shaping our early language skills, and before long we were absorbing the language around us entirely without realising it, doing our best to imitate the words and phrases we heard and, in time, create our own original sentences from these words.

Children mostly learn language by analogy and pattern-recognition, absorbing it from the behaviour of the people around them. One study found that infants are spoken to as many as 7000 times a day, and that, while at first a child is simply learning the names of objects "It's Daddy", "It's a cat...", they are soon learning the *relationship* between objects: "The dog *wants* its food", "See that cat sleeping *on* the wall?" Over time the child begins to spot these relationship patterns in language, without having to be directly taught them. All this is impressive enough, but how does a child learn two languages at once? Or more? Most of the population of Luxembourg can speak four or more languages. How does the mind and brain learn these different languages and keep them separate? Another scientific mystery.

The speed with which small children acquire vocabulary and rudimentary grammar supports the idea that the brain contains an innate module, like a prefabricated network of neural pathways, that is ready and primed for learning certain linguistic skills during these sensitive periods of development. Children grasp language far more quickly than they should if they were entirely starting from scratch. Whether this is down to 'universal grammar' (innate rules that cut across all human languages) is no longer as certain as was once thought. But what is clear is that, without the right input at the right time, the potential of that part of the developing brain will be lost, along with the neural pathways that had been primed for language. If babies do not hear language during this sensitive period the neural pathways will be pruned back and discarded.

Likewise, a child's attempts at *producing* language must begin within a sensitive period. For example, in the second half of their first year, deaf children make normal babbling sounds but, because they are unable to hear themselves, the babbling fades away. But if this babbling is responded to with sign language then their hand gestures can be shaped into signs of their own and in their second and third years they show the customary rapid increase in their vocabulary, albeit in sign language.

Mothers all over the world speak to their children in a kind of baby-talk that has been called 'motherese.' The mother speaks using a simplified language, exaggerating the sounds of the words and the tone of the sentence so that the child is engaged and can understand. As we have said, the playful social games that parents offer their children include a strong element of symbolic or pretend play which acts as a precursor and stimulus for language development. For example, a mother may use a blue clothes peg to represent "daddy" and a red one to represent "mummy" and then pretend the clothes pegs are holding a conversation.

As young children, we began to string words together to form sentences, but we also used to talk to ourselves and try out our new language skills. Over time these external expressions of our developing consciousness became gradually internalised as thoughts and private reflections. So one might think of language as a precursor to thought, and throughout our life it goes on providing a shadowy framework for our internal trains of thought, the inner world of pure thought.

So another reason Homo sapiens have such long middle childhoods compared with other animals is because language and basic social knowledge are essential if the child is to be adequately prepared for the complexity of the adult social world. With language, children no longer need to learn things by seeing or experiencing them, they can be taught. Education passes on the baton of human culture to future generations, so teaching is extraordinarily important to its maintenance. Formal education is the result, and even if it is rarely as interesting as learning by experience, it is far more efficient at transferring complex information into young minds.

Living in a relational world

By the time babies are about five months old they have got used to the faces of other important people. They have learned that there is a world beyond their mother – dad, siblings, grandparents, and so on – but they are already wary of strangers and unfamiliar places. They prefer the familiarity and comfort of their mother's face and the warmth and sustenance that her body gives them, though fathers of course can provide this early physical warmth through holding their babies. Over the next year or two, children will become far more discriminating about who they feel safe to be with, so it is an important time for fathers to engage their children in a relationship that will hopefully last a lifetime.

Towards the end of our second year, a primitive sense of self was developing. We were able to recognise ourselves in a mirror for the first time and we began using personal pronouns, especially 'me' and 'you'. We were beginning to recognise patterns in the information coming from our body and were starting to differentiate our own experience from that of other people. There is good evidence that other apes, elephants, and dolphins are similarly able to make this self-other distinction.

If our parents were able to be responsive and receptive to our needs when we were a small child, there is every chance that by the time we were four or five we were starting to imagine the mental states of other people too. Our parents' attempts to understand and validate our inner world of feelings and impulses, gradually taught us to do this for ourselves. We were starting to recognise that they too have wishes, feelings, goals, reasons etc. We were beginning to realise that other people have minds, much like our own, but with their own different perspectives and intentions. We were learning to **mentalise**, or imagine other people's minds. It is as if we had developed a theory, a mental model, that other people have minds of their own too. This important insight, this theory of mind, is a skill that children develop provided they are exposed to mentalising caregivers. Perhaps, like language and attachment, this is another innate mental ability among everyone, provided that the child has suitable input from the people around them. One of the dangers of our modern hyper-connected and economically-pressured lifestyles is that parents no longer devote the necessary time to read to their children, play with them, or listen carefully to their inner world.

As children gradually become more aware of other people's separateness from them, they begin to develop more sophisticated models and assumptions about themselves. The parents' validation of the child's inner world teaches the child to understand and regulate their own feelings and emotions. If I can have thoughts about other people, presumably *they* can have thoughts and feelings about me. Once we make this assumption, we can begin to form a narrative about ourselves, derived from the way that other people behave towards us and what they say about us, a nascent self-understanding. Perhaps you noticed, for example, that people generally spoke to you in a certain way, or that people were repeatedly telling you something about yourself that even now you assume to be true. Perhaps you feel you have gained a reputation among the people you know for some quality or other, or there is a family story that you are known for. These assumptions may have little evidence to back them up, or they may have become quickly outdated, but we often internalise them as stable assumptions about ourselves just the same.

From these early thoughts and feelings children began to fashion a sense of themselves, what psychologists call an identity or a self-concept. Who we are, as a personality, reflects our genetic disposition, our temperament, our talents and endowments, the particular experiences of our lives, and especially our relationships with other people. All these influences gradually become incorporated into our sense of our self as a separate person in the world, a Self with our own individual perspective, our subjectivity. Subjectivity is having a fairly consistent and coherent viewpoint from which to understand the world, and as we have already discussed, it is critical to consciousness. In reality, our subjectivity varies according to the context we are in, but our autobiographical memory enables us to experience a more-or-less stable sense of ourselves.

Parents help children structure stories to do with what the child has done, or is soon to do, and these stories become integrated into the child's fledgling sense of self. They buttress the child's self-concept and growing consciousness by referring to things the child has done in the past ("Do you remember visiting granny?"), and things they will do in the future ("It will be your birthday soon"). Although young children only possess snatches of personal stories, by the time they reach adolescence they will have developed a more coherent self-concept and life narrative (unless they have been traumatised), and this sense of personal story and identity is likely to deepen as they grow older.

Mentalisation was a hugely important change in our mental development, for it allowed us to move beyond merely seeing the world from our own frame of reference to that of other people. This opened up the possibility of far more sophisticated and complicated relationships. Being able to mentalise another person's mind meant that the child could now try to predict or explain another person's actions, and to infer their intentions and feelings.

This remarkable human capacity to 'mind-read' another person varies from person to person, but it involves being able to use our own feelings to understand another person's emotions and thoughts, and to intuitively imagine other people's motivations. Mentalisation makes it possible for us to feel empathy and connection. Around the age of seven, empathy seems to develop more fully, as the prefrontal cortex finishes myelination (the sheathing of neurons in electrically insulating myelin). This *most* recently evolved part of the brain is particularly active when someone is mentalising and being empathic. If we can infer the feelings and intentions of other people, then we are able to imagine what they might be wanting or needing. This is the core of empathy, a sensibility that therapists crucially rely upon. It may have evolved to enable us to recognise deception when we see it, but it also helps us to know when it is safe to trust another person, and perhaps collaborate with them, leading to mutual benefit. This became another huge evolutionary advantage.

Importantly, mentalisation also enables us to describe and understand our own feelings, rather than our emotions always taking charge of us. Hungarian-born British psychoanalyst and clinical psychologist Peter Fonagy has shown that when mentalisation is lacking, people often fail to form satisfying connections with other people and struggle to regulate their feelings.

People who are labelled as psychopaths are considered sinister and scary because they are often very good at reading other people's feelings, but they fail to experience any compassion for them. They can mentalise but not empathise or care. This is very different from the social clumsiness of people on the so-called autistic spectrum (previously known as Asperger's syndrome), who find it harder to recognise or 'tune in' to the emotional and visual cues that other people are displaying, but once they are told what the other person is feeling, they are able to understand the emotions described. They can usually empathise once told, but in the moment they struggle to mentalise.

Emotional intelligence is the same idea, the ability of people to decode other people's emotions and intentions and intuit how they are likely to be feeling. Incredibly, neuroscientists have shown that roughly the same neural pathways are activated when someone watches another person doing something, as when they are doing it themselves. The neurons in the observer's brain are able to mirror the neurons involved in whatever the observed person is doing. From one person's language and demeanour, another person's mind manages to recognize patterns of embodied sensory information in their own bodies that match those patterns in the other person. As we shall see, this is a sensitivity that therapists work hard to develop, learning to 'read' and intuit what the client is feeling by noticing what they themselves are feeling. This too depends on mentalisation.

Across the world, babies and toddlers invariably cry when their mothers or caregivers leave them. This *separation anxiety* peaks when the child is about 15 months old. It is as if a special bond has been formed between mother and child that allows the child to feel safe. When this bond is even temporarily broken the child is inclined to protest, fearing perhaps that they have been abandoned. When contact is resumed, the child clings to and cuddles the mother until they feel secure again. In the child's mind, she constitutes what is known as a **secure base**, someone they can turn to in times of need. The mother has become an **attachment figure** for the child – the primary one as it happens – someone whom the child can rely upon for their safety. This dependence mirrors the unconditional love that a parent feels for their child.

Attachment is not unique to humans. The Austrian ethologist, Konrad Lorenz (1903-1989), is best known for his observations of *imprinting* whereby some species of animal instinctively bond with and follow the first moving object they see after being born. He made films of newly hatched geese following him around as if he were their mother, and demonstrated that attachment is innate, though once again it depends upon the environment providing an attachment figure at the right time.

Mothers are almost always the *primary attachment figure* for children, though fathers can become a close second if they work at it. Almost everyone has to deal with the fact that their mother was the most powerful and important person in their life for a very long time. We will need to come back to this later, because boys and girls, men and women, often seem to have different ways of reconciling themselves to this fact of life.

As children grow up, they gradually learn to feel safe at increasing distances from their carers. They vary in how confident and skilled they are in being with other people, but if the child is confident in the security of their early attachment relationships, they are more likely to feel confident to separate from them so as to be able to explore the wider world and other relationships. Knowing that we have a *secure base*, that there is someone in the background to return to, someone who really cares about us, gives us the confidence to venture out into the unpredictable world of other people, the big wide world, and perhaps even have an adventure.

People continue to locate their security in their family, their partner, their friends, and by extension, their home, community, and so on. These secure bases enable them to feel comfortable and safe. I once knew a woman struggling with agoraphobia who only felt safe to go outside if she was clutching her deceased husband's umbrella. Similarly, children sometimes become attached to a particular stuffed animal, toy, or even blanket, and these can act as sources of comfort especially when the child is separated from their primary attachment figure or secure base.

Imagine taking a toddler to the park; let us call her Isabel. Isabel knows us well and to her we are a safe attachment figure – someone familiar whom she trusts, like her mother or father. But this is

Isabel's first visit to this particular park playground and when we arrive she stares at the other children playing in the sandpit and looks wary. She frowns and tightens her grip on our hand.

Being a sensitive parent, we don't rush things but walk to a nearby bench and sit down with her. Young Isabel sits on our lap and continues to stare at the other children, now perhaps starting to look just a little bit envious of the fun they seem to be having in the sand. After a few moments she slips from our lap and points to the sandpit. We stand up, take Isabel's hand, and lead her into the sand. We crouch down and start playing in the sand, and Isabel's hands soon join our own. After a bit, we stand up and slowly back away to the bench where we are able to sit down again. Isabel seems happy enough. She occasionally looks up at us, making sure we are still there, but simply knowing that we *are* there means that she can quite happily play on her own. We are her secure base.

But then a calamity. A rather noisy little boy, perhaps a year older than Isabel, seems to have wilfully or probably innocently thrown his bucket in the air and it hits our beloved Isabel on the side of the head. The bucket is only small and plastic and she is not really hurt, but for Isabel it is a shock and she immediately bursts into tears and comes running back to her secure base. We pick her up and hug her until her tears subside. Soon she turns her head back towards the sandpit, and before long she is ready to try again.

Isabel's confidence in us as a secure base has been strengthened by this experience and at the same time she will have grown in confidence in being able to play in a sandpit on her own. Soon she will be able to play very comfortably with other children, and gain many useful new lessons from these encounters.

As Isabel's language skills develop she will be better able to discuss these experiences with us, and we will be able to help her make sense of them, perhaps sharing with her something of our own much broader knowledge of the world. In this way, parental attachment figures help children to discriminate everyday events from unusual ones, and to develop ideas about how better to manage and understand the wider world that they will encounter. At the same time, parents are helping children to talk about their feelings and experiences and make sense of them. By developing a shared understanding of events that is shaped by the adult's more advanced language and understanding, children develop more sophisticated models of the world and themselves within it.

So, to summarise, our early experiences with the people who cared for us when we were young provided us with patterns and templates of how relationships generally work. Not surprisingly we all hold different implicit assumptions about this relational world, based on our culture, and the relationships we have had in the past, and the relationships that we have witnessed (such as our parents'). Young children unwittingly develop their own assumptions about future relationships based upon their experiences and these become the **relational models** they take into adulthood. The father of Attachment Theory, John Bowlby (1907-1990), said that each child develops their own *internal working model* about relationships in general.

So, if a child has been exposed to inconsistent care from her caregivers, she is more likely to be anxious and clingy, and uncertain whether her secure base will be there for her. If the caregiver is indifferent and unresponsive to the needs of the child, the child (such as those Romanian orphans) is likely to show little emotion when separated or in the presence of strangers. It is as if the child has not learned to attach, or wishes to avoid attaching themselves to other people. And when a caregiver is frightening, absent for long periods, or abusive, the child is more likely to show signs of emotional distress such as rocking, and a disorganized, testing, and wary attitude towards future relationships.

But when children have experienced an attachment figure who is not only a secure base but someone who is sensitive and responsive to their needs, who can soothe their distress and make sense of the situation, and help them to articulate their feelings, the child will be more confident and better equipped to form mutually supportive relationships in the future. This is especially important in times of threat or ambiguity when, like Isabel, people naturally turn to the support and secure base of others.

When the world feels uncertain and threatening, even adults seek the reassurance and guidance of a benign, caring figure of authority, like a parent, doctor, priest, or sometimes even a politician. And people often consciously and unconsciously expect their partners to fulfil this role. This need for guidance and support must of course be balanced by a degree of resilience, tolerance, and courage.

The main thing to remember from all this is that our early experiences fundamentally shape our expectations and therefore how we mentally construct what we later experience. These expectations include the assumptions and *relational models* that we draw on when faced with new relationships. Without realising it, we learned (or not) to 'trust our instincts' about other people. But childhood was not just about learning to turn to other people and get their help and support when the going gets tough, it was also learning how to be self-sufficient and resilient, and to be able to regulate our own drives and emotions.

Self-regulation

Infants and toddlers get frustrated by the large gap between the things they want now and whenever, if ever, they can get them. They become infuriated by the chasm between the things they want to do and what they are allowed to do, or are able to do. Because toddlers have not yet learned to regulate their needs and emotions, they have something of a reputation for giving voice to their frustrations in the form of screaming fits and temper tantrums (preferably in public places).

The challenge for children is learning to deal with the mismatch between what they expect and want, and what reality delivers, a state of affairs that adults are also rarely happy about unless it happens to be good news. The challenge for parents is having to explain these mismatches while at the same time soothing the child and encouraging them to develop their own explanations and meanings for how the world is, and how to manage their emotions on their own.

A parent's core job is to provide consistent love, support, and safety because these are optimal conditions for a child to flourish. But parents must also be prepared to absorb, interpret and sooth the child's emotions until the child has learned how to do this for themselves. I didn't get it right all the time, but here is an excerpt from a diary I once kept.

27th August 1999

Tonight I was reminded of the depth of my feelings as I found myself having to go upstairs to quieten Zoë (two years and nearly two months old already) who was crying. I say 'having to' but that's because I was exhausted from work. Actually, this turned out to be a brief but strangely delightful experience. She'd been crying for a couple of minutes, the first bedtime tears in about a week. I waited for a bit and then went into her room and picked her up. She clung to me, and immediately fell asleep in my arms. A deep physical need for the security of being held I suppose. It was lovely.

3rd September 1999

H. was out again this evening so I put the children to bed. Pretty clockwork really, as these things go. But Zoë wouldn't go to sleep. She put up a fuss about "wanting Mummy", always a tricky one to handle. I went in a couple of times and eventually she seemed to go quiet, but it took a while. Then, about half an hour later, I heard her 'crying', perhaps more a sort of angry shouting, interspersed with well-articulated whining. So I went into her room where she was standing up in her cot, and with a firm but calm voice said "Now that's enough Zoë. It's time to go to sleep now." She responded "Okay", one of her new words, and immediately lay down, turned over, and silently went to sleep. I simply pulled the blanket over her. Not a squeak since.

There is something very calming and reassuring for a child to know that there are limits to their behaviour. So-called **boundaries** provide a feeling of safety by reducing the uncertainty and ambiguity of the situation and limiting the range of behaviours within which we can operate. Someone more powerful has taken responsibility and is in charge, and that makes us feel safe. In psychological terms, boundaries provide a form of containment. They help simplify the world. Of course another person's direction may be benign, but it can also be malign. Boundaries can enable people to feel contained and safe, but they can also be imprisoning and unjust. Literally and symbolically, children like to feel held within the secure embrace of a caring parent who is in charge and who knows how things work. This wish for a secure base – to be looked after and led by someone who seems to know what is going on, a responsible grown-up figure, a benign authority – is a powerful force that may continue throughout life, but of course it can also be exploited.

Learning to regulate our emotions and drives is one of the key challenges of childhood, and recent research suggests that it is linked to working-memory. Children who are more successful in delaying their gratification show better working-memory which enables them to keep track of long-term goals. Having to delay our immediate gratification remains a hard lesson well after supermarket tantrums have ceased. Adults, just like children, often struggle with self-restraint and delaying gratification, so these lessons are best learned in childhood.

The famous marshmallow test, devised by US psychologist Walter Mischel (1930-2018), involved putting a marshmallow in front of a four to six-year-old child and telling them that they can eat this marshmallow whenever they like. It is theirs. However, they were also told that if they waited on their own for fifteen minutes and managed not to eat the marshmallow in front of them, they would be given *two* marshmallows when the adult returned.

Mischel found that children varied in their ability to delay their gratification. Some used mental strategies to distract themselves, such as looking away or talking to themselves, but others were unable to resist gobbling up the marshmallow before the fifteen minutes had elapsed. By following up these children over many years, Mischel discovered that children who were able to regulate their drives better (i.e. delay their gratification until they could get the second marshmallow) were generally more successful later in life and had higher educational attainment.

The skills involved in delaying gratification appear to be at least partly taught because children from different cultures vary dramatically in their performance at this test. For example, a 2017 study reported that 4-year-olds in Cameroon showed significantly better 'delay-of-gratification performance' compared with middle class German 4 year olds, using the marshmallow test.

The frontal lobes are important to self-control and working-memory but they are not fully developed until a person is in their early twenties. The frontal pole (the frontal lobe of the frontal lobe) is particularly active when people need to defer immediate gratification, such as resisting a marshmallow, but learning this skill requires practice and input from the environment.

In childhood we learn to control our drives and emotions so that as adults we are able to coexist with other people. Children begin learning about morality as soon as they interact with other people, and parents are there to teach selfish and violent toddlers some important lessons about social conduct. When infants bite or kick, or hit other children with buckets in sandpits, they prompt parents to respond. Happily, by the time they are about three, children are starting to grasp that harming other people is wrong, and thereafter rates of violence towards other children decline.

Adolescence and beyond

Historically, puberty has marked the beginning of adulthood in most cultures. In the late nineteenth century, however, early psychologists, such as American psychologist G. Stanley Hall (1844-1924) in particular, began to recognize that children were continuing to develop throughout their teens, and with this recognition the idea of adolescence was born.

Before puberty, there is a phase of rapid production of neurons and synapses, especially in the prefrontal cortex, which is crucial for higher-order cognitive functions such as decision-making and, as we have just seen, impulse control. Adolescence is often about mastering these more sophisticated mental skills.

In adolescence, the body continues to grow but also develops adult reproductive features. As they enter their fertile years, young people become more socially and sexually aware, and consequently more self-conscious of their bodies and how they are seen by others in the world. These pressures sometimes lead young people to develop eating disorders and other unhappy preoccupations with their changing bodies. The young person may feel awkward, unsure how to dress and behave with others, and this can lead to a morbid fixation on their self-presentation, and excessive worry about what other people think of them. This has become even more pronounced in the age of social media where, unless they remain connected with other people, young adults may be tempted to withdraw into themselves with only their feelings of loneliness and self-doubt to keep them company. Thankfully, at the other end of life, older people tend to care far less about what others think of them, and this sometimes allows them to be more authentic to themselves, something that their younger selves may have struggled with.

'The teenage years' is a time when young people start to look ahead towards the prospect of an adult life, whatever that looks like to them, a time when they are learning to be more independent and autonomous. Nevertheless, adolescents can feel weighed down by the expectations and responsibilities of adulthood, and part of them may wish to return to the safe certainties of childhood.

This oscillation between a wish for adult independence and a wish for childlike dependence makes adolescence a notoriously difficult transition, and not just for the young person in question. It is also a family transition in which parents are encouraging autonomy and independent thinking in their children, whilst themselves sometimes struggling to adjust to the inevitable changes in roles that result from this. Mothers often experience genuine feelings of loss as their children depart the nest, and fathers too can feel bereft when their children leave home, almost as if they have lost a part of themselves. It is not surprising therefore that these oscillating ambivalent feelings can lead to heightened emotion and fraught communication within families.

Yet adolescence can also be an exciting time of existential awakening as the young person, perhaps for the first time, considers what they really believe about the world and their place and aspirations within it. Young adults are developing better self-control, but this is also a time of increased sensation-seeking, as young people begin to flex their new independence and adult power. For young men, it is a time of life associated with a rise in testosterone and loud, showy, competitive behaviour. The adolescent brain is still developing the skills of impulse control, so it is not surprisingly that many young people take far greater risks than adults but with less self-awareness. It is as if there is a tension between impulses from the limbic system's drives and emotions, and a growing self-control exerted by the frontal lobes. As we have already seen, resisting temptation and immediate gratification, whether it be marshmallows or something more intoxicating, takes effort ('will power', 'strength of will'), and this restraint operates a bit like a muscle, becoming tired after prolonged exertion.

In adolescence and early adulthood, young people often begin to explore deeper relationships with people of their own age, and start to experiment with intimate and sexual relationships. This so-called 'pair bonding' (again associated with the release of oxytocin) occurs at this age in almost all cultures. The family of origin may continue to be the primary secure base for many years to come, but young adults are learning to be mutually dependent on other people who are not from their own family. There are many cultural differences in what is permitted, but young people will be trying out the relational models they have learned earlier in their lives, very often from their family of origin.

The ambivalence and conflict between dependence and autonomy that lies at the heart of 'adolescent turmoil' often finds expression in many adult relationships too. Adults are just grown-up children, and their intimate bonds frequently involve mutual dependence in different areas of the relationship, as well as time to oneself and the need for 'a room of one's own'. Faced with a crisis, people turn first to their nearest and dearest, their secure base, but even a relative stranger will sometimes have to do.

It is a common disillusionment on entering adult life to discover that we are each quite ordinary, and in many ways not special at all, and that, for all our increased power in the world, adulthood also comes with the burden of increasing responsibilities. Each of us is unique of course, and possibly clever and skilful in lots of interesting ways, but perhaps not the stand-out extraordinary person that our younger self might have imagined, or was led to believe. Psychological maturity comes with remembering that we are ultimately a perfectly ordinary person. You may be the President of China or a beggar on the streets of Paris, but you are fundamentally just like any other human being, with a body that is ageing and a mind that is changing.

Rather than be disappointed when we realise this, we might instead rejoice and celebrate that we are uniquely ourselves, with a life of our own, however long or short it turns out to be. The sooner we accept that we are the person we happen to be, and adjust our assumptions to the cards that we have been dealt, the sooner we can deploy what assets we have, engage in the world of other people, work on our shortcomings, and live a more interesting life.

————◆————————————◆————

On the whole, children's minds are much more flexible than those of adults. Their minds are used to rapid changes and being exposed to new experiences over which they have little control. But with any luck, they feel confident that someone they trust is in control and will ensure their safety.

As we have seen, over time children gradually learn to be more independent, such as when they first separate from the secure base of their parents to be cared for by others, when they attend school for the first time, or when they eventually leave home. Everyone carries assumptions about their physical and emotional safety in the world and these go on changing over the course of a lifetime. Personal confidence in doing almost anything is derived from our experience of, and exposure to that thing, and likewise our confidence soon becomes vulnerable if we withdraw, avoid, and disengage from it. Confidence is born from experience alone.

In the West, getting older is associated with increasing feelings of invisibility, especially if the person feels they serve no useful function. We all need neo-purposes and it is important for older people to find ways of creating them. Little wonder that so many retired people continue to contribute to society through grandparenting duties, charity work, teaching and sharing their valuable experience, or they pursue hobbies and creative passions. These commitments give them structure and purpose.

But while a child's mind is malleable and adaptable, the assumptions of older people generally become more rigid and resistant to change. Their minds are no longer as willing to hack away at the undergrowth in order to alter or create a new neural pathway. It is far easier and simpler to stick to old assumptions and habitual ways of doing things.

Consequently, older people *tend*, for there are many exceptionally creative and adventurous older people, they tend to be less welcoming of change, because their brains and minds increasingly find change stressful and exhausting to deal with. As people grow older it often takes them more time and effort to alter their mental models of the world, especially if these changes demand fundamental realignments.

There is therefore a *tendency* for older people to become more invested in their existing assumptions about the world. Learning new information becomes slower and harder as neural pathways degrade. Cognitive drop-off (losing one's train of thought) becomes more common, and memory retrieval more laboured. Despite many exceptions, older people tend to become more conservative in outlook and more content with a quiet life in which change is minimised. It is perhaps no coincidence that the amount of noise that people generate and tolerate across the lifespan tends to be inversely correlated with age. Engagement with 'the new' requires ever more effort because, as we will see in the next chapter, change can be exhausting due to the mental adjustments required.

This cognitive conservatism associated with growing older is like a hardening of categories and assumptions: the neural pathways underpinning thought have become so well-worn that new ideas are unable to sidestep or modify existing assumptions. Some areas of the brain, such as the hippocampus and particularly the prefrontal cortex, reduce in size, and there is a greater reliance on top-down processing over bottom-up processing (*see page* 142). This has its own logic of course, particularly when neural pathways take longer to process information, as they do in older brains. The stored representations may still be there, as potentiated neural networks, but they are becoming harder to retrieve and have become more literal and concrete.

So older people tend to stick to what has worked in the past: their long-term memories and their tried-and-tested long-held assumptions. As George Bernard Shaw (1856-1950) famously and wisely remarked, "*We don't stop playing because we grow old, we grow old because we stop playing*".

However, alongside this general cognitive decline, some neurons exhibit yet more branching of dendrites, and there is a strengthening of connections between distant areas of the brain. This corresponds to older brains becoming better at spotting the connections between disparate sources of information, sometimes enabling the person to see the bigger picture. Therein perhaps lies the wisdom of old age.

Further Reading

Abbruzzese L, Magnani N, Robertson I, Mancuso M. (2019) Age and gender differences in emotion recognition. *Frontiers of Psychology* 10, 2371. doi: 10.3389/fpsyg.2019.02371

Bowlby J. (1971) *Attachment and Loss.* London: Hogarth Press

Bowlby J. (1979) *The Making and Breaking of Affectional Bonds.* Tavistock Publications: London

Bowlby J. (1988) *A Secure Base. Clinical Applications of Attachment Theory.* London: Routledge

Case R. (1999). Conceptual development. In Bennett M. (Ed.) *Developmental Psychology: Achievements and Prospects.* London: Psychology Press

Dahl A. (2016) Mothers' insistence when prohibiting infants from harming others in everyday interactions. *Frontiers in Psychology,* 7: doi.org/10.3389/fpsyg.2016.01448

Damon W, Hart D. (1980) *Self-understanding in Childhood and Adolescence.* Cambridge: Cambridge University Press

Fonagy P, Target M. (1997) Attachment and reflective function: Their role in self-organization. *Development and psychopathology,* 9, 679-700.

Gibson E, Walk R. (1960) The visual cliff. *Scientific American,* 202, 64-71

Giedd J. (2015) The amazing teen brain. *Scientific American,* **312**, 32-7

Hedden T, Gabrieli J. (2004) Insights into the ageing mind: a view from cognitive neuroscience. *Nature Reviews Neuroscience,* 5, 87–96

Isen A. (1990) The influence of positive and negative affect on cognitive organisation: Some implications for development. In Stein N, Leventhal B, Trabasco T (Eds.). *Psychological and Biological Approaches to Emotion.* Hillsdale: Erlbaum

Keil F. (1999) Cognition, content and development. In *Developmental Psychology: Achievements and Prospects.* Bennett M. (ed.), London: Psychology Press

Konner M. (2010) *The Evolution of Childhood – Relationships, Emotion, Mind.* London: Belknap Press (Harvard)

Kitwood T. (1997) *Dementia Reconsidered. The Person Comes First.* Buckingham: Open University Press

Lingle S, Riede T. (2014) Deer mothers are sensitive to infant distress vocalizations of diverse mammalian species. *The American Naturalist*, 184(4), 510-522 doi: 10.1086/677677

Locke J. (1693) *Some Thoughts Concerning Education.* London: A. and J. Churchill

Mischel W, Shoda Y, Rodriguez M. (1989) Delay of gratification in children. *Science*, 244, 933–938

Piaget J. (1952) *The Origins of Intelligence in Children.* New York: International Universities Press

Pinker S. (1994) *The Language Instinct: How the Mind Creates Language.* London: Penguin

Vygotsky L. (1986) *Thought and Language (2nd edition).* Cambridge, Mass: MIT Press

Yu J, Kam C, Lee T. (2016) Better working memory and motor inhibition in children who delayed gratification. *Frontiers in Psychology*, 7. doi.org/10.3389/fpsyg.2016.01098

Chapter 7

Living Change

Buddhism emphasises the impermanence of everything. Nothing stays the same for long, even if it is just walking across the room to make a cup of tea, or the experience of subsequently drinking it.

Change can be good or bad but, like it or not, it is the nature of reality, and human minds are constantly responding to it. The covid pandemic of 2020 saw change on a global scale. The Internet has led to unprecedented change over the past forty years, and now with Artificial Intelligence the world embarks on a new social experiment which will lead to inevitable change. The population may not have consented to it, but it remains eager to lap up the new technology, and that technology is heavily capitalised.

Obvious though it may sound, life actually *is* a long series of small and large transitions from one situation to the next, each one requiring people to make psychological and emotional adjustments in response. From being in your mother's arms to spending time with other people, learning to walk, going to school for the first time, leaving home, to falling in love. Or having your heart broken, starting a new job, getting married, adjusting to a disability, becoming a parent, migrating from one place to another, moving to a new home, retirement, bereavement, leaving one room, going for a shower. And so on.

It is the very ordinariness of life's many transitions that makes them seem almost invisible to rational scrutiny, yet these subtle, and sometimes massive, mental adjustments are fundamental to how minds develop and how people live their lives. Change threads its way through the fabric of every person's life story. Some people experience more of it than others, but change is always and inevitably coming down the track towards us in one guise or another. So any plausible description of the mind must account for how we react and mentally adjust to change.

Some changes are the result of decisions we have made, but many more, such as ageing, illness and death, are imposed on us, forcing us, like Nell, to respond as best we can. From birth to death our lives are gently swayed by liminal forces: our bodies change from day to day in mostly tiny imperceptible ways, such as how we look, or how our body feels to us, or how our brain develops and then slowly declines over our lifespan.

Change can also be sudden and violent, and when it strikes it can unleash huge psychological and emotional adjustments. Here is someone traumatised by what she has been told, the moment when she realises that her life has just branched off in a new direction and that it will never be quite the same again.

"It felt like a bad dream. One minute life was chuntering on. The next – well, someone switched the reels... Somewhere, in some parallel universe, life was continuing to chunter on; here, in this one ... where I was unaccountably stuck after some through-the-looking-glass moment... mammograms, ultrasound, core biopsies, sitting in a square at Bart's weeping, apologising, on my partner's shoulder in the soft rain, the world suddenly upside

down, guilty, I or my body had let us down – him, the kids, me..." [11]

———◆———————◆———

We take our assumptions for granted

In the last chapter we looked at how people's brains and minds develop over the course of the lifespan. We saw how people's models of the world, and their brains, grow in response to the world around them. Young adults emerge from their long, protracted childhood with general organising assumptions about how other people behave and how the world is broadly structured, at least within their immediate culture. Over the course of their childhood they were hopefully taught some useful models to do with how the complicated world of adult life is organised. With any luck they developed skills in regulating their immediate impulses and feelings, rather than being ruled by their drives and emotions. And, all being well, they learned that they can't always get what they want, and that in the end it helps if you can trust someone. These, and many other things, most adults simply take for granted.

However, our need to learn about the world and find our place within it is obviously not confined to childhood; we go on learning throughout our lives so that we will be better prepared for negotiating the world in the future. In fact, we are so good at this essential mental process that we fail to notice how much our minds are constantly adjusting in response to new information and experiences. You might try to notice the many times you alter your behaviour, or change an assumption that you had previously held (e.g. "I never realised that...").

It has been emphasised throughout this book that the mind is not a static *thing*. The flexibility of human minds has given our species a survival advantage not only 'in the wild', but even more so in the elaborate and sophisticated social world that we humans have created for ourselves. Søren Kierkegaard (1813-1855) observed that

---

[11] Cancer Diaries Project, cited in Brennan J. (2004) *Cancer in Context*, Oxford: Oxford University Press

life can be understood backwards, but it must be lived forwards. In such a situation, it certainly helps if one can learn from the past and use this information to imagine, predict and plan the future more accurately. Reflectivity and creativity.

The German philosopher Edmund Husserl (1859-1938) came up with the idea of the *Lebenswelt* or **lifeworld** to describe the background world around each of us, the "coherent universe of existing objects", and the basis for all shared human experience. The German-American psychologist Kurt Lewin (1890-1947) preferred to use the term 'life space'. Call it what you like, the lifeworld or life space comprises the objects and ideas that we all broadly agree are there in the world (whether or not we have names for them), the physical and social environment of which we are individually and collectively aware.

Childhood was obviously particularly formative in learning about the lifeworld. Over the course of our lives, as new ideas have nestled in with the things we already know, our once-new ideas soon come to be seen as 'just the way things are'. Knowledge becomes so utterly taken-for-granted that we can afford to tune it out, until it becomes effectively invisible – background unconscious knowledge held in implicit memory (*Chapter 4*). The new reality soon becomes what is expected. The mind is constantly processing information and improving its mental models, even if it is simply registering that nothing much has changed.

In this chapter we examine how our minds adjust and develop in response to change throughout our lives. Change, of course, is not confined to individual people. Couples, families, friends, communities, organisations and nations very often find themselves in a state of transition as they reorganise themselves to meet new demands, opportunities and challenges. However, as we are soon to find out, too much change too quickly can overwhelm the ability of the mind (or any system) to offer up useful responses, and over time the system itself can begin to tire and creak.

Let us once again outline where we have got to so far. The evolutionary advantage of having a mind that uses consciousness to model the world is that it allows us to understand the past and anticipate the future by storing what we have learned in memory. A simple enough idea. Throughout life we develop our own ways of thinking and behaviour, forming routines, intuitive beliefs, heuristics (rules of thumb), and biases. Soon these habitual patterns of thought and behaviour recede into our unconscious procedural memory, and we end up taking all these assumptions and habits for granted. The benefit of having a large bank of procedural know-how memory is that it releases our conscious attention (our controlled mind) to address new concerns, creative ideas, and objectives.

We assume that if we drop an object it will fall, that a chair will support us, and that night follows day. We believe our home will look the same as it did yesterday, that our child is safe at school, and that we will still be alive and well this evening. We expect our body to function consistently, for other people to behave predictably, and we take our own perceptions and beliefs as given. Our automatic mind tries to match our sensory perceptions of what is happening in the moment with the models and assumptions that are being offered up by the assumptive world. This enables us to navigate our experiences effortlessly.

This unconscious or implicit understanding of the world is shaped by emotion-laden memories and associations, but it allows us to interpret and react to events automatically, without the need for slow, conscious reasoning. Such automatic thinking is mentally far less taxing than controlled thinking, and controlled thinking only really kicks in when we encounter questions that our automatic, procedural memory can't easily solve.

A lot of the time what we expect to happen thankfully does indeed happen, and most of the time other people behave in ways that are familiar and predictable. In fact, we rely upon these well-worn habits of thought and normal routines of behaviour to simplify the humdrum requirements of everyday life. This makes fewer demands on controlled thinking and the limited capacity of working-memory, enabling us to think about and attend to other things. The problem is that we are so invested in maintaining the world as we expect it to be, plausible and coherent, that it can be difficult to notice when it has objectively changed. Remember the non-existent white square and 'Paris in the the Spring'?

In summary, our mental models remain unexamined most of the time, and in the absence of change it is hard to alter our assumptions about the world because, as we have said, most of the time they do a reasonable job and are so familiar as to be almost invisible. But change is stressful because it challenges our assumptions and taxes our resources.

Change is stressful but good for us

Social scientists have tried to document some of the most common sources of stress and have labelled these transitions 'life events'. These include bereavement, serious illness, organisational restructuring, retirement, pregnancy, moving home, marriage and the birth of a child. All these transitions were found to be highly stressful, but one might reasonably ask why ostensibly positive events, such as marriage and becoming a parent, are so stressful too.

A world devoid of change becomes stagnant, and for us mentally active humans it is best avoided. Unstructured time and lack of stimulation is intolerable for most people. In fact, some people go to great lengths to avoid quiet reflective time, and feel uncomfortable if they are not busy and externally stimulated. Unless we humans are responding creatively to the world around us in some way, we are left bored, with only our own thoughts for stimulation, and as we will see in the chapter on therapy, our own imaginative thoughts can sometimes lead us into serious trouble.

At the other end of the change continuum, it is clear that too much rapid change can be overwhelming and even traumatic. Most people are therefore more comfortable somewhere between these extremes, but there remains a tension between a wish to be stimulated, preferably by one's own curiosity, and a wish to avoid the stress of the unpredictable, the uncontrollable, and the unknown.

People enjoy new experiences when they retain a measure of control, when they can calculate the risks, and when they anticipate that in the long run they will be safe. Most people are not daredevils, but we have different thresholds for what we find stimulating and exciting. For some people rock-climbing is an thrilling challenge, for others the very thought of it is a nightmare.

Travelling somewhere we have never been before may confront us with new situations that some people find alarming, and others fascinating.

Change seems to have an inherent tendency to expose assumptions that had previously been taken for granted, and this makes it an opportunity to learn something useful. This can happen at many levels. The American philosopher Michael Sandel has observed that the 2020 covid pandemic, for all the misery it caused, also exposed the hollowness of the meritocracy that had been let loose in the West over the previous few decades. It demonstrated how dependent most of us are on people who are poorly paid and rarely valued by the rest of society: the delivery drivers, supermarket staff, the post office workers, the public health workers, the care home staff, the refuse collectors, the technicians that maintain the infrastructure of our society, and many other relatively invisible workers and volunteers.

As we have seen, our mental models of the world do a pretty good job at predicting what happens from moment to moment, enabling us to feel that our existence is coherent and continuous and that everything somehow fits together. Maintaining this consistent and coherent understanding of what is going on around us from moment-to-moment enables us to feel safe and in control. An international survey of nearly 3000 adults, between the ages of 30 and 60, found that psychological 'inner harmony' was almost universal in their definition of happiness, and this was the same for men and women. We absolutely rely on the world to be consistent because we are invested in maintaining the stability of our assumptive world, and therefore highly resistant to its full-scale reorganisation.

But change threatens all this. Change can denote chaos and uncertainty, and we have evolved to know that the uncontrollable and unknown are potentially dangerous. You just never quite know what may be lurking in that cave. On the other hand, there is a lot to be said for having an interesting life. But whenever life doesn't happen in the way that we were expecting it to, our emotions become activated – fear, arousal, vigilance, anger, sadness, guilt, etc. – and immediately summon the conscious mind to find out what is going on.

Change is challenging for individuals, relationships, groups, and organizations because it disrupts routine procedures and habitual trains of thought that people have become used to using. Starting a new job and moving home can be exciting, but are often stressful transitions because of the enormous amount of mental adjustment that is going on. The 2020 pandemic highlighted another feature of significant change: things rarely go back to the way things were, but we are astonishingly capable of mentally adjusting to a new normal. Even when a family goes on holiday, it can take a day or two for everyone to adjust to new routines and settle down emotionally.

So, although change is inherently stressful, it is from new experiences that people learn fresh ideas about the world, and sometimes gain some useful insights along the way. Change can even compel us to re-evaluate the way we have been living, the relationships we have, and what is important to us. It helps to reveal our implicit assumptions so that they can be reconsidered in the cold light of day, making the unconscious conscious.

Some of our assumptions may have been flawed and in need of revision, and that can be helpful. But at the same time it is psychologically and emotionally stressful to adjust the mental models, habits and automatic routines that are affected by serious change, and it is therefore not surprising that life events and transitions can be exhausting and take considerable time.

How the mind adjusts

As we saw in *Chapter 4*, we learn a lot about the world without realising that we are learning it (i.e. *implicit learning*). It is not just that the learning is subliminal, it is that we quickly fit what we experience into models and assumptions that we already have. And if we can't make the new information fit in with what we already know, we are compelled to develop new or modified models of reality. This process is known as **mental adjustment**.

Our mental models are being confirmed or confounded almost all the time, and mental adjustment is arguably at the centre of human thought, the foundry where new ideas are forged. For small things, like losing a pen, the adjustment can be swift; for bigger things, like a divorce, loss, or migration, the personal transition can take considerably longer. So, while we may enjoy the thrill of the new and the excitement of learning or being challenged to the limits of our abilities, we also generally fear and avoid too much that is unknown. Some changes threaten the integrity of our mental models.

Jean Piaget, the Swiss child psychologist, understood more than anyone that knowledge is built upon prior knowledge. By testing and observing children of different ages, he recognised that minds develop and mature over the course of a person's life. Mental models expand and become more elaborate, and they also become nested within broader models of understanding.

Piaget observed that new information always leads to either a strengthening or a modification of existing knowledge. When the changes are small or familiar, they can be easily managed and barely noticed, in the same way that we are unable to detect a child growing taller on a day-to-day basis, or notice how we ourselves are ageing from year to year. But larger, more rapid changes can be stressful, life-changing, or even traumatic. Large changes in one's circumstances (life events such marriage, parenthood, bereavement) tend to involve longer transitions, and the mental adjustments required are often mentally and emotionally exhausting.

It was one of Jean Piaget's great insights to see that minds respond to change in one of these two main ways. Either our mind decides that a change is consistent with our previously-held models of how things work, in other words, more-or-less what we might have expected, in which case there is no need to alter our models of the world. Or our mind decides that the change violates our existing assumptions and that they will need altering or an entirely new model is required.

Whenever possible, new information is interpreted as being consistent with, or confirming existing models, and consequently it is easily assimilated into them. As Winston Churchill (1874-1965) noted, *"Men occasionally stumble over the truth, but most of them pick themselves up and hurry off as if nothing had happened."* This is more-or-less what Francis Bacon had said four hundred years earlier when he talked about people preferring to believe the things they would prefer to be true.

However, if a change has defied our existing assumptions and expectations, our emotions will become engaged and our mind will be forced to recalibrate its existing models, or create new ones, in order to accommodate the new information. This ultimately enables our mental models to anticipate the future more accurately. Change has much to teach, and what is learned can be good or bad, edifying, terrifying, sad, disappointing and so on, but eventually new information must be absorbed by the mind, a process that American psychologist Michael J. Horowitz termed the 'Completion Tendency.'

As we have seen, people are generally resistant to having to alter their core assumptions about the world, and this tendency grows stronger with age, as the grooves of thought become more 'deeply engraved' in neural pathways. This is why people often need time to move beyond their own resistance. Life-altering change, such as the loss of a loved one, serious illness or injury, often involves mental adjustments in multiple areas of the assumptive world, and the implications of the change may be slow to emerge, so this all takes time.

Before we consider a general model of how minds adjust to change, we should once again remember that change rarely affects one person in isolation. A life-changing event may create a punctuation mark in the story of one person's life, but it invariably affects other people too, and this in turn may alter the relationships between any or all of them. Everyone affected by the crisis will need to recalibrate their own mental models, and perhaps restructure their relationships too. For example, following the death of a family member it takes time for those who remain to realign their relationships with one another. Change is therefore almost always a systemic and interpersonal experience, not simply an individual one.

Here is a model of adjustment, published a few years ago, that tries to make sense of what happens in the mind when we are faced with change. The diagram (The SCT *Model of Adjustment*) attempts to summarise the model and is based on Piaget's original ideas. It accounts for both how we adjust to minor changes from moment to moment, and how we adjust to a major life change. It also explains how a personal transition can lead to both high levels of distress and helpful personal growth.

The SCT Model of Adjustment

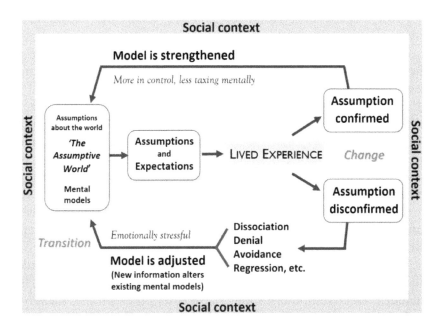

THE SOCIAL COGNITIVE TRANSITION

This model starts from the assumption that everything we experience occurs within a social and cultural world that fundamentally shapes the meaning of everything – the language, ideas, assumptions, models, memes and social constructions that we have internalised from the lifeworld around us.

Starting from the left, our assumptive world provides consciousness with assumptions and expectations with which to understand moment-to-moment lived experience. Now, following the top loop, if what we perceive (our lived experience) appears to confirm our expectations and assumptions, it leads to a strengthening of the models that gave rise to those expectations. This is reassuring for us, in as far as it endorses our existing assumptions about the nature of the world. And, as we have said, we are so invested in maintaining our existing assumptions that we are inclined to perceive the world as confirming our models, even when objectively it doesn't. The world ends up remaining consistent and coherent, and that is reassuring.

Most experiences thankfully *confirm* what we had already assumed about the world (the Sun rises in the morning, our home looks much the same as it did yesterday, our partner gets home at the usual time, the television works, and so on). Life remains generally predictable.

However, taking the lower loop, if our lived experience is different from our expectations, our minds are required to modify our existing models and assumptions so that they will be more predictive in the future (i.e. the Completion Tendency). But, as we have said, it is emotionally stressful to have our assumptions violated, and we would much prefer this not to happen. So if the change is too unwelcome or overwhelming we tend to resist the new information by deploying defence mechanisms, such as denial and avoidance.

New and unexpected events can sometimes profoundly *disconfirm*, or even contradict, our existing mental models. This includes our assumptions about the future, other people, how our body feels or operates, and so on. One doesn't have to look far to find extraordinary stories of people adjusting to profound injuries and disabilities, or conquering other challenges brought on by devastating change. We may not like having our assumptions violated, but we may feel compelled to adjust them, and come up with new ones if they are found to be deficient.

It is helpful to remember that when our minds spot an inconsistency between what is expected and what is happening, our emotions are activated and this draws our attention. The mind responds by applying controlled, conscious thinking to resolve the discrepancy between our existing assumptions and what we in fact experience. We find ourselves thinking and ruminating about what has happened. This discrepancy between our actual experience and what we had previously understood and expected demands an explanation, and this is resolved either by confirming or disconfirming the assumption that gave rise to the expectation. We then adjust our models accordingly.

I invite you to lunch at my favourite restaurant. You get there on time, but I don't show up and you are unable to contact me. The minutes pass and eventually you end up eating alone. Whatever you subsequently discover about my absence, your expectations and assumptions have been gently violated. You feel irritated that I had arranged this lunch but hadn't turned up. You may be worried about what has happened to me, you may be cross that I have forgotten; in fact, you may have many other possible thoughts, assumptions, and feelings as you eat your meal. The experience may also subtly alter your mental models to do with having lunch, having lunch alone, what you feel about me, our relationship, the restaurant, and so on.

Subtle changes are occurring at almost every moment of our day as we move from one place to another, each encounter providing new information, confirming and disconfirming our assumptions. What were you doing two hours ago? It is quite likely that you were not doing what you are doing right now, or what you will be doing in a few minutes time. Our lives are changing every moment.

Whether our models and assumptions of the world are right or wrong, pleasant or unpleasant, change offers our controlled mind new information with which to construct potentially more accurate ideas about the world. It invites us to refine and recalibrate our mental models, hopefully without having to renovate them completely.

However, because controlled thinking takes far more mental effort than automatic thinking, a lot of the time we tend to go along with the story that is on offer from our automatic mind – our initial assumptions, our first impressions, our habits, hunches and 'gut feelings' – rather than going to the trouble of deconstructing the situation and maybe altering our existing models. After all, as we have said, it is much easier and simpler to follow a well-trodden path than be required to hack away at the undergrowth to cut a new path. Happily, this approach gets us by most of the time, though of course our conclusions may end up confirming something that is objectively untrue.

To summarise, when we are faced with significant change our mind tries to maintain the integrity of our assumptive world, our underlying models of the world, either by shutting out the new information and sticking with our current understanding, or being forced to alter our mental models so that they take account of the new information. The first approach, the head-in-the-sand approach, 'explains away' the new information by regarding it is as confirming, or congruent with existing assumptions and models; it says "nothing much has changed, this is broadly consistent with what I already know". This approach minimises disruption and causes little effort or stress because it maintains the integrity and consistency of the mental models that we normally rely upon.

Sometimes this can be done almost instantly, such as when a car ahead pulls out and we are forced to apply our brakes, and sometimes it can be a much lengthier process, such as when someone we love has died or we are adjusting to some other major catastrophe in our lives. The implications of a death for our mental models may be subtle and wide-ranging because the loss can affect many different aspects of our life (involving many different assumptions), so these many implications can take time to reveal themselves.

But when something happens that is both highly threatening and unexpected, it can temporarily overwhelm the capacity of our automatic mind to come up with a plausible narrative of what is going on. In the face of such events, the mind may use psychological defence mechanisms (dissociation, denial, avoidance, etc.) to slow down the rate at which we absorb the new information (*see SCT Model of Adjustment* diagram).

If you were in a train crash or being physically attacked, you would first be immobilised by shock and terror as the trauma begins to unfold. In a state of sudden physical or emotional threat, or entirely unexpected change, the mind is unable to find any mental models that can sensibly account for what is happening or how we should react. People often describe traumatic experiences as a dream-like state of altered consciousness in which time seems to slow down.

In trauma, our controlled mind is soon deployed but it too may be unable to comprehend immediate events or understand their implications, largely because it is swamped with fear, our first line of defence. This rapid emotional response to the catastrophe narrows the mind's focus onto fewer things, but it also becomes less flexible and creative, so we struggle to think logically and analytically. Consequently, in the immediate period following the crash (or any other trauma), our mind may split off these experiences and dissociate them from the world as we know it. We were there, throughout each moment of the event, but our mind has dumped all the information, emotions and memories of it in a place that is sealed off from rational consciousness. This is called dissociation.

However, because the mind has evolved to learn from experience and seeks 'completion', our memories of the traumatic event later re-emerge, intruding on consciousness in the form of nightmares and spontaneous flashbacks. These, and a state of heightened physiological vigilance, are typical post-traumatic stress reactions.

So, in most situations, people quickly get used to small or subtle changes, either by ignoring them or by learning to expect them. But when change is too much, or too fast, we may protect ourselves by keeping the new information at bay until we are ready to absorb it. We may be reluctant to abandon assumptions that have served us well in the past, and risk becoming overwhelmed by our emotions.

For example, confronted with a sudden cancer diagnosis, one woman reflected that *"The first couple of days I suppose I knew I was in denial. I talked about it as if it was someone else; I didn't really feel much."* Such avoidance serves to defend the patient's mind against information that violates their most basic assumptions, such as staying alive, being there for their children, and so on. By disavowing the immediate reality of what is happening, keeping the information at bay, psychological defences have the effect of regulating emotions that would otherwise be overwhelming.

There is usually nothing wrong with psychological defences; they are there for a good reason. Frequently they just slow down the rate at which people have to confront new information, or they are a protection against having to alter the way a person looks at the world. (Incidentally, the idea of defence mechanisms was an important insight of psychoanalysis.) An obvious example is that people sometimes present an image of strength and authority to other people as a defence against being seen as insecure or uncertain. Defensive pessimism on the other hand is a mental strategy that attempts to prepare us for disappointment: anticipate the worst and whatever happens cannot be any worse, but with luck it might just be a bit better. There's clearly a place for it, provided it does not become active pessimism.

In traumatic situations, a person's deep fear of mental fragmentation leads them instinctively to know that, first and foremost, they must keep their mental models intact (consistent, coherent etc.). Such denial was the case for Nell. However, over the next few hours, days, or weeks they will gradually need to absorb the implications of what has happened and begin to alter their mental models accordingly.

Sometimes, however, the person is not able to put the traumatic experience into words, perhaps because the events are too shameful to talk about, or the person has no one to speak to. This incurs the risk that the events go on being denied or suppressed, or they become so dissociated that they remain split off from the individual's autobiographical story of their life. People who have been abused in childhood often dissociate at the time, and gradually learn to suppress and even 'forget' (repress) the abuse that they experienced. Sadly, the psychological and emotional chaos that they are left with occasionally finds expression in so-called 'madness', because, even when someone has repressed memories of events that occurred decades ago, the emotional charge of those events is unconsciously remembered. This can cause havoc for the way people think and make sense of the world. If nothing else, the abused person's mental models are likely to carry an understandable wariness about relationships in general (including that with a therapist if they ever get to meet one).

Almost whatever the change, human minds appear to be capable of adjustment, but these adjustments can be hard and stressful – starting a new job, moving home, having radiotherapy, working through a bereavement. So that is why even apparently pleasant changes, like marriage, having children, or going on holiday, can be stressful, due to the realignment of mental models that is required.

As time passes, however, life gradually starts to feel normal again as mental models incorporate the new routines introduced by the change. Our emotions calm down sooner or later as these new assumptions and expectations become established, and what was once new starts to feel familiar – spouses get used to one another's peculiar habits, parents learn to do their best, new jobs start to feel more manageable, and even going for radiotherapy can soon become a mundane routine. Things you didn't even know about a short while ago gradually begin to seem like common sense and the new normal.

Whatever our initial resistance to the change, such as denial and avoidance, it soon dissipates, and we begin to notice that the world has started to feel coherent again, plausible, continuous, predictable. What was once shockingly new is now taken-for-granted. Our mental models have adjusted to the new reality. Nonetheless, the mental processes involved in these adjustments can become stuck, and when they do it can be helpful to talk to someone with the expertise to help us to find a way forward.

Core concerns

It may seem presumptuous to attempt to codify the assumptive world, but among people with cancer five broad existential concerns are commonly violated by the illness. What is striking from my clinical experience is how often my patients have been oblivious to the core assumptions they had previously held. Like Nell, it took a change the size of a cancer diagnosis to wake them up to the assumptions by which they had thus far been living their lives.

Major life events like serious illness are often described as life-changing for a good reason. The individual at the epicentre of the change, and those close to them, are in transition, as their assumptive worlds adjust to the new reality. Their core assumptions are summarised below under five general headings, and all of them can be fertile ground for the development of emotional distress as well as, sometimes, personal growth. It seems likely that the core assumptions that follow are not unique to people with cancer.

Life trajectory
We each have our own unique life story, a personal history that stretches back into our childhood. It is vital to our sense of who we are. We experience this autobiographical memory as a kind of personal narrative that describes what has happened to us in our lives. However, our current lives are also structured around both

explicit and implicit plans, goals, and assumptions about the future. We look forward and strive towards moments in the future, and we implicitly make assumptions about where we are in our unknown lifespan. We locate ourselves within this unfolding story and project ourselves into the future by having long-term intentions and goals, though perhaps not every culture is as future-oriented as those in the West.

Thus, the idea of life trajectory is simply to do with the fact that people's lives are structured around often tacit and unspoken assumptions about the future. For example, I would venture that you might not be bothering to read this book if you knew you had only a month left to live. Rather, most of us carry an implicit expectation that we will be alive in a month's time.

Goals and aspirations tend to vary with age and the person's stage in life, and they can range from being short-term and clear-cut, such as looking forward to seeing friends later in the day or getting back to reading a book, to being long-term and more abstract, such as ambition, having children one day, grandchildren, a planned holiday, or enjoying a happy retirement. People's drives, aspirations and hopes may have been forged in their past, but they represent an investment in the future. When a person is not invested in their future, they are likely to feel bored, aimless, and low in mood.

It is easy to see how people with serious illnesses like cancer lose their normal levels of hope and motivation when their implicit life goals have been crushed by news of the diagnosis. Longer-term goals no longer seem quite so relevant or important when *survival* becomes the overriding concern. They may well feel an amputation of the future. The threat of death certainly has a compellingly biological tug on our attention. Re-examining one's aspirations, however, can be helpful if it leads to new priorities and more meaningful goals, but equally it can lead to a painful grieving process during which long-held dreams and ambitions must be contracted or gradually relinquished, particularly if the prognosis looks bleak.

Furthermore, after a few encounters with 'bad news', and prolonged uncertainty, people often feel that it would be tempting fate to make any firm plans. Prolonged pain, nausea or fatigue can even diminish the will to make them in the first place. However, without goals to achieve and joyful events to look forward to, we are in danger of losing hope, meaning and self-confidence. Feelings of loss and sadness are therefore common.

On the other hand, as Nell demonstrated, an awareness of one's life trajectory can be a wake-up call, leading to an urgent appreciation of every waking moment.

Relationships

Whatever its objective prognosis, serious illness confronts people with the threat of permanent separation from loved ones, and the very nature of these attachments becomes suddenly clear. The threat posed by the disease can reawaken childhood attachment needs (*see Chapter 6*), as people unconsciously search for a benign parental figure to take charge and make them feel safe. This was why it was symbolically so alarming for the population when the UK Prime Minister was hospitalised during the 2020 covid pandemic.

Patients understandably look to their doctors for this kind of care and benign authority, but they also turn to their loved ones for emotional and practical support. The reality that follows, however, sometimes violates assumptions (relational models) about these relationships. Among couples it can lead to resentment and disappointment at a time when both partners need one another more than ever, yet for other couples it can lead to a confirmation and strengthening of positive qualities within the relationship.

Parents must contemplate the possibility that they will not watch their children grow up, couples must adjust to changes of role as one of them learns to be a patient and the other a caring support. Families must change domestic routines, while still attending to the developmental needs of everyone, especially children. Single people, following their treatment, must face the challenge of making new friends and dating, such as when to talk about their illness and its treatment, how much to tell, and bearing rejection if it occurs. These are significant challenges and demand open honest communication among family members who may or may not be used to being open with one another.

Men and women do not always share the same language of care or the capacity to communicate feelings, and there are often different cultural expectations regarding what should be expressed and to whom. The wish to protect the people we love from our distress can lead to a conspiracy of silence, or a resolute determination to censor anything that is not 'positive'. This has been described as the tyranny of positive thinking.

Control and self-worth

The third area of the assumptive world that is undermined by a life-threatening experience is people's sense of self-worth and personal control. The assumption of personal control is central to a person's self-concept and self-esteem, as well as the maintenance of a buoyant mood, even if it is rarely thought about. Once people become disengaged from the occupational, family and social roles that previously provided them with regular feedback about their value and power in the world, they will soon start to doubt their skills, talents, value to others, and other personal qualities. For example, after months of gruelling medical treatment it often seems that the patient's identity has been starved by the illness.

Cancer and other serious illnesses are frequently seen as uncontrollable threats over which the patient has little influence, and this can induce a sense of helplessness and a dependence on others, particularly medical staff, to make the situation safe again. This loss of control is compounded by feeling ill and housebound, or having to adopt the role of a powerless patient within the complex, intimidating world of hospital medicine.

The main point is that we all hold implicit assumptions about our identity (who we imagine ourselves to be), as well as a sense of the value, personal control, dignity and power that we have in the world. These assumptions are frequently violated in the face of illness.

The Body

Our bodies are so central to our sense of self that we rarely stop to consider the assumptions we have developed about them. Yet it is through the sensory apparatus, limbs and functions of the body that we interact with the world and one another. The effects of noxious disfiguring treatments, distressing symptoms, and chronic disability caused by the disease and its treatment, can soon undermine life-long assumptions about the reliability, appearance, capabilities, and sensation of our body. Chemotherapy, radiotherapy, and hormone treatment can have corrosive effects on mood, while symptoms like pain and fatigue can wear down the patient's resilience, leaving them emotionally and physically exhausted. The particular site of the cancer or the side-effects of the treatment may also hold particular meaning for the patient. For example, a breast may be integral to a woman's body image, but it may also be important to her sexuality, or to her capacity to breastfeed.

Following treatment, many patients retain a residual suspicion, if not a morbid fear, that one day the body will once again provide shelter for the enemy, and this can further alienate them from their habitual relationship with their body. For a smaller number of people, this takes the form of intrusive ruminations or compulsive urges to check for signs that the disease has not returned. Living in a state of uncertainty often means that the person maintains a heightened state of physiological arousal, a form of vigilance based on the threat response.

Existential-Spiritual

The fifth and final group of core assumptions concern a person's existential or spiritual beliefs. Being able to contemplate one's mortality is often considered a defining feature of what it is to be human. The existential-spiritual side of a person is that which expresses their deepest convictions about the nature of existence. Questions of existential meaning usually involve notions of fundamental causation and purpose, and the preciousness of being alive. These questions are naturally important to people but especially so when they are in mortal danger, because, as we have seen, it is our human nature to strive to understand the world we inhabit, and to anticipate our future.

The search for meaning and purpose is certainly not limited to the belief systems embodied in formal religions. Everyone has core beliefs about the nature of their existence, and these are not always framed with reference to a god, but of course for many people they are. In response to a life-threatening illness, people often become interested in constructing a moral summary or overview of their existence in the world, asking such questions as 'Why me?', or 'What is the point of going on if I will die from this disease?', or 'What has my life been about?'. The wish to attribute blame or causation to something or someone is also common and understandable. God may be an obvious target for blame, or not, but this need for accountability is sometimes directed towards others, such as doctors or employers, and sometimes the self ('I should have stopped smoking').

Finally, like Nell, people sometimes become intensely aware of their existential isolation, realising, perhaps for the first time, that they will never transcend the boundaries of their own consciousness. Such existential-spiritual questions may leave people highly distressed, feeling lost and lonely in a sea without meaning, or buoyed up by a belief in an after-life.

Positive Transitions

> *"An illness in stages, a very long flight of steps that led assuredly to death, but whose every step represented a unique apprenticeship. It was a disease that gave death time to live and its victims time to die, time to discover time, and in the end to discover life."*
> Hervé Guibert (1955-1991)

One of the strange paradoxes of war is that while it invariably leads to unspeakable suffering and distress, it also often leaves a legacy of innovation, social bonding and personal growth. This paradox is also evident in life-threatening illnesses and other personal traumas: the person affected often reports that, despite the emotional roller-coaster of their treatment and its aftermath, valuable lessons have been learned. Catastrophic changes like cancer, or in French writer Hervé Guibert's case, AIDS, can reveal important assumptions that the patient, partner or family member had previously taken for granted. And although such revelations may be stressful they can also sometimes be helpful and paradoxically life-enhancing, as they were for Nell.

When a person manages to embrace change they often grow and develop as a person, and this can obviously lead to positive emotions such as a sense of achievement, pride, insight, the feeling they have fulfilled something of their potential, or simply the sense of a job well done.

As we have seen, change can lead people to confront assumptions that they may have held for many years but almost entirely taken for granted. It can bring our implicit assumptions into clearer focus and lead us to abandon false or outdated assumptions. For example, if you find that your partner has failed to support you during your illness, after having spent many years supporting them, you might consider whether it is wise to continue with this relationship. If you learn that the long hours you used to spend at the office are now a far lower priority in your life than spending time with the people you love, you may decide to change your lifestyle. If you learn that you have sailed through life largely unaware of the beauty of the world around you, you may choose to live with more awareness of the simple pleasures to be had from engaging with it.

> *"Just something about the word makes you think of the end. I'm thinking of all the things I have done. I really do appreciate what I've got from life, but I also want a lot more, not material things, just ordinary things like enjoying my garden, the birds, playing hide and seek with Harry in the garden... I really appreciate the simple things in life now, things we normally take for granted.*
>
> *It's a pity we have to go through something as awful as this to bring you back down to earth and start life – looking through different glasses – almost like a child, learning all over again."* [12]

Art, music, puzzles, and jokes

People enjoy jokes, illusions and magic because they playfully violate the assumptions and mental models that we hold. We feel

---

[12]   Cancer Diaries Project. See Brennan (2004)

delight at being surprised in this way. If four out of five people suffer from diarrhoea, does that mean that one person enjoys it? The joke, such as it is, centres around the switch we are forced to make from our initial automatic assumption to a completely different one that we had not anticipated, one that may be absurd to contemplate but could logically be implied by the first statement.

Doctor: You're overweight. Patient: I think I want a second opinion. Doctor: You're also ugly. Again, the humour comes from forcing us to switch our assumptions. Humour has a way of defying our expectations and mental models, pleasantly surprising us with a new, often absurd perspective that had not occurred to us. Something is only 'absurd' because it flies in the face of commonly held assumptions.

Puzzles have a similar allure. Eeing xble po eake rense if ehe norld day qave jmplications hor a werson's cower. The built-in redundancy of language makes a sentence that on first glance looks unintelligible, fairly easy to decipher. People enjoy solving puzzles because, again, it is in our nature to apply our assumptions to make sense of the world. We also enjoy having our assumptions played with... to a point. We do not like to feel we are being manipulated.

Magic works along the same lines, and one could reasonably argue that the Arts similarly help us see the world in a way that we hadn't before, exploiting our extraordinary potential to reimagine the world. The pleasure of music, for example, is derived from having our melodic, harmonic, and temporal expectations violated or confirmed from one moment to the next. Listening to music is an experience that occurs over time, just like consciousness. As the music progresses it evokes emotional reactions and associations that make our hearts flutter, our foot tap, and send shivers down our spine. The memory associations we have with a particular piece of music can ineffably bring to mind some previous experience, along with all its past emotional connotations.

EH Gombrich (1909-2001) made essentially the same point about fine art. How you experience a painting, a depiction of something, an object, or thought, is based on the emotional dance between the expected and the unexpected, *"the interplay between explanation and observation, the waves of fulfilment, disappointment, right guesses and wrong moves that make up our daily life."*

Reading a novel enables us to escape into another mindscape, engaging us in a story that requires us to imagine scenes and mentalise the minds of other people. Our mental models of what is happening are constantly being shifted and surprised by the author, such that we feel delight when things go well and concern when they don't. As the story unfolds, we identify with and feel emotionally invested in the characters, just as you might have done with Nell when her story was being described.

What helps us adjust to change?

Just imagine that you had seen a gruesome road accident earlier today. There is a good chance that by now you will have told someone about it. That is usually what people do. They spontaneously try to put their experiences into words, not just the facts of what happened, but how they felt emotionally, what they thought at the time, and what they now feel about what happened. As we said earlier, people turn their experiences into stories and this enables them to remodel their mental understanding of the world, although admittedly some people find this easier to do than others.

A change of any consequence causes emotion, and this leads people to seek out the support of other people with whom they can talk. Finding words to describe our experiences helps us shape them into a story that structures and makes sense of what has happened. In forming those sentences, we are (re)constructing a more coherent mental model of the world, integrating what has happened into our ongoing life story and the many assumptions it contains. The value of telling our story and forging a narrative is that it enables us to represent and arrange experiences into meaningful wholes. Speaking (or writing) words helps us to coagulate nebulous experiences into identifiable ideas, and in the process we update our mental models, leaving us feeling more in control.

So it really helps if you can talk, or at least put things into words. Talking to a friend, praying, writing about it, and all psychological therapies rely upon the power of this process. All these language-based methods help us comprehend stressful changes, and integrate their implications into our assumptive world. The evidence strongly suggests that confiding support, emotional disclosure, and 'finding the words' are vital to emotional and psychological health, even if cultural practices vary across the world in terms of how this is done. Art, music, dance, crafts, and other forms of creative expression also have a role in helping people to represent their experiences symbolically.

Talking to someone about our experience is a powerful way of integrating what has happened into a more coherent story, particularly if we feel that the person we are speaking to is genuinely listening and validating those experiences. But this is not the only way we adjust our models. Self-reflection, mulling things over, pondering the past, and talking to oneself, are all methods of making sense of one's experiences in order to learn from them. Writing things down works in much the same way; it helps us formulate and understand what we think and feel.

Some people adjust to change more easily than others, either because they are used to change and accustomed to flexibly altering their mental models, or because they have learned to embrace change as a sure-fire method of personal growth and development. On the other hand, some people shun change as much as they can, preferring the sense of control and predictability that familiarity brings. Change can feel like stepping into the unknown and this may entail many unwelcome emotions. However, while some caution and a fear of the unknown may be both rational and adaptive (dark caves sometimes do have a sabre-toothed tiger lurking inside), if taken too far it can also lead to inertia, indolence and boredom. Minds have evolved to be active. They require stimulation, but not too much. Without the stimulation of other people minds, our own can become dull. As the writer Gore Vidal (1925-2012) once said, "The unfed mind devours itself".

Yet, while human minds need stimulation and change if they are to grow and develop, people have long recognised that their minds can be too noisy, too full of stressful thoughts about the past and the future. The complexity of the social world means that we are bombarded with change and the stimulation of other people, so it helps if we can regulate our emotions and calm our minds. Achieving that balance is important if we are to survive in the complex, information-rich social world that we have created for ourselves and in which most of us now live.

◆————————◆

Further Reading

Austin J, Vancouver J. (1996) Goal constructs in psychology: structure, process, and content. *Psychological Bulletin*, 120, 338-375

Brennan J. (2001) Adjustment to cancer – coping or psychosocial transition? *Psycho-Oncology*, 10, 1-18

Brennan J. (2004) *Cancer in Context – A practical guide to supportive care*. Oxford: Oxford University Press

Delle Fave A, Brdar I, Wissing M *et al* (2016) Lay definitions of happiness across nations: the primacy of inner harmony and relational connectedness. *Frontiers of Psychology*, doi.10.3389/fpsyg.2016.00030

Gombrich E. (1959; 1977) *Art and Illusion – A Study in the Psychology of Pictorial Representation*. London: Folio Society

Guibert H. (1991) *A l'Ami qui ne m'a pas Sauve la Vie* (To the Friend who did not Save my Life). Paris: Editions Flammarion

Horowitz M. (1976) *Stress Response Syndromes*. New York: Jason Aronson

Janoff-Bulman R. (1992) *Shattered Assumptions: Towards a New Psychology of Trauma*. New York: The Free Press

Parkes CM. (1971) Psycho-social transitions: a field for study. *Social Science and Medicine*, 5, 101-115

Pennebaker J. (1993) Putting stress into words: Health, linguistic, and therapeutic implications. *Behaviour Research and Therapy*, 31, 539-548

Pennebaker J. (Ed.) (1995) *Emotion, Disclosure and Health.* Washington: American Psychological Association

Piaget, J. (1936) *La Naissance de l'Intelligence chez l'Enfant.* Paris: Delachaux et Niestlé

Rimé B. (2009) Emotion elicits the social sharing of emotion: Theory and empirical review. *Emotion Review*, 1, 60-85

Sandel, M. (2020) *The Tyranny of Merit: What's Become of the Common Good?* London: Penguin Books

Sue D, Sue D. (1990) Counseling the culturally different: Theory and practice. (2nd Ed.) New York: Wiley. Cited in Enelow A, Forde D, Brummel-Smith K. (1996) *Interviewing and Patient Care* (4th Ed.) Oxford: Oxford University Press

Taylor S. (1983) Adjustment to threatening events: A theory of cognitive adaptation. *American Psychologist,* 38, 1161-1173

Taylor S, Brown J. (1988) Illusion and well-being: a social psychological perspective on mental health. *Psychological Bulletin*, 103, 193-210

Tedeschi R, Park C, Calhoun L. (Eds.) *Posttraumatic Growth: Positive Changes in the Aftermath of Crisis.* Mahwah, NJ: Lawrence Erlbaum Associates:

Zatorre R, Salimpoor V. (2013) From perception to pleasure: Music and its neural substrates. *Proceedings of the National Academy of Sciences*, 110 (S2), 10430-10437

Chapter 8

Therapy

Psych fights
Psych therapies
Distress
Relational distress
Telling stories
Doing therapy

I once worked with a woman in her late twenties called Jane. She was a pleasant young mother of two young children, and she had recently been treated for cervical cancer. In our first session she told me that, as far as she was concerned, her cancer was a punishment for having been sexually promiscuous earlier in her life. Jane had made the link between cervical cancer and the human papilloma virus, which is sexually transmitted, and from this she had concluded that she was responsible for her predicament, and she was feeling guilty about it.

What she described felt broadly familiar to me. I had met other people who believed that their cancer was a form of punishment or retribution, and these assumptions usually meant that we would have to dig deep to understand a bigger story. This was confirmed when she said that she was anxious she might have accidently given her children the HIV virus. As the meeting progressed, Jane explained that she was afraid she might have inadvertently used one of her children's toothbrushes, even though she admitted that she had no memory of ever having done so. She conceded that she could see no reason why she would have used one of their toothbrushes, but she said she doubted that her memory could be trusted. Perhaps she had had a moment's amnesia and had simply forgotten.

And although the three HIV tests she had obtained over the past two months all said that she was HIV negative, Jane was convinced they were all wrong. She was certain that three times she had been given somebody else's test results, and therefore she was a potential threat to her children. After all, she had slept with several men in the past, albeit over eight years ago and before she was married, but any one of them could have carried the virus.

It soon emerged that Jane was boiling her children's toothbrushes, sometimes more than once a day. She would check all the rubbish bins, inside and out, to ensure that a drug addict had not left a dirty needle in them. If she even imagined herself touching some rubbish in her kitchen, just having the thought, she would have to wash her hands for the umpteenth time that day, doubting her memory of the last time she had washed them.

It was all just a bit magical and slightly mad, but I could also see that these convoluted, rabbit warrens of thought were the problem. They were making Jane miserable, never achieved anything useful, and they were wasting an enormous amount of her time, precious time that could be put to something more interesting. But of course it all felt very real to this warm and likeable woman before me, and as she spoke I could see that she was emotionally exhausted.

And it wasn't just her obsessive cleanliness. Jane was equally afraid of knives, fearing that she might sleepwalk during the night, grab a kitchen knife and stab her children to death. So, every night before going to bed she would check that the kitchen drawer that held the knives was locked (she had had a lock fitted) and that the key was safely stored in her husband's bedside table.

Obsessive-compulsive problems almost always involve a fear of having to take personal responsibility for something awful happening – gas will fill the house until it explodes, burglars will walk into the unlocked house, other people will become poisoned or infected, and all because you didn't check or clean well enough. The more terrible the fear of one day being held responsible, the more powerful the threat, and therefore the more it intrudes on consciousness. Performing a compulsive behaviour manages to quash the thoughts for a while, and that feels good, but the thoughts are always returning.

Then I took Jane's history, and this is what she told me.

She grew up on a farm on the edge of a country village. When Jane was 12 years old she was sitting in the living room near the front door when a loud BANG! made her drop her magazine. Moments later she watched in horror as her 15-year-old sister, and only sibling, staggered into the room with shot-gun wounds to her chest and through her back. She died in front of her sister, my patient, drowning from the build-up of blood in her lungs.

It was a freak accident. Her sister had often borrowed her father's shotgun to shoot a rabbit or two, and the coroner concluded that, coming through the back gate, she had accidentally shot herself. Terrible grief followed of course. Jane recalled that one of her first thoughts was that now she would be getting her sister's much larger bedroom. I felt deeply moved by this dreadful story, but I remember finding it interesting that she chose to tell me this guilty detail.

Throughout the rest of her childhood Jane watched her parents writhe in the agony of having lost their beloved eldest child. As she told me about the rest of her childhood, it seemed that she had always done her best to compensate her bereft parents for the loss of her dead sister, but they continued to feel guilty for having allowed their child to carry a gun.

Jane did well at school, was never any trouble, and became a tax accountant. She enjoyed a couple of years as a single young woman up in London where she had a few boyfriends, and then moved to the West Country where she married the manager of a local bank, and became the mother of two children, a girl and a boy, now aged eight and five. She had wanted to make her parents proud, yet now there was this.

Her obsessional fears clearly had nothing to do with her psycho-sexual development, as classical Freudian psychoanalysis might have assumed, but it certainly did have a lot to do with what she had experienced in childhood. She was no longer traumatised by her sister's death because she spoke freely about what had happened, and explained that although she had been intensely upset at the time, she had talked about it a great deal over the years.

However, what Jane had learned was that terrible catastrophes can occur out of the blue when you least expect them. She also concluded, quite sensibly, that some dangers are avoidable, and that easy access to a loaded gun may be one of them. Getting cervical cancer re-triggered a sense that she was somehow to blame, having been the daughter that had survived, and that she had brought her illness upon herself.

The worst possible thing that could befall Jane now would be finding herself responsible for the death of one of her beloved children. At the same time, Jane didn't want her children to lose their mother in the way she had lost her sister. So she was physically tense and vigilant for threat. Her life had become so governed by her superstitious and magical thoughts that it was almost as if this part of her was disconnected from the rational tax accountant persona she adopted when she was at work. Things that were merely possible, no matter how unlikely, were now thought probable. She was doubting the veracity of her own perceptions and memory because she was taking far too much account of her own thoughts and beliefs, and they were ruling and ruining her life. It took considerable time before Jane could begin to see that these were just thoughts, and that she was living her life according to assumptions she had perhaps not fully considered.

Astonishing as it is that our minds can model the world, this unfortunately comes with its own problems. Anxious worrying ruminations are certainly one of the drawbacks of having a clever creative mind, because it is all too easy to draw unhelpful conclusions. Jane's memories engendered such emotional distress for her that they had distorted her life, and until she was able to disinter her memories with me, and reflect upon her assumptions, she was a helpless victim to their power over her.

Human civilisation, the world that we humans have built for ourselves since the dawn of Behavioural Modernity, can be harsh in so many ways, and nowhere is its impact felt more than the mind. Psychological therapy is the Western world's relatively recent response to people's emotional distress.

Therapy addresses the need for people to make sense of the things that have happened to them over the course of their lives, and the assumptions, residual emotions, and behaviour they have developed as a result. The therapist responds to the client's distress by providing them with a benign, trustworthy, and interested listener, albeit with iron-clad boundaries that ensure a safe professional relationship. Historically, this role has been fulfilled by relatives, friends, priests, elders, sages, healers, doctors, fortune-tellers, hairdressers and taxi drivers, albeit not always safely or professionally.

Every one of us is trying to make sense of our lives in the short time that we have in this world, but it is easy to become lost, stuck, or confused at times, or simply overwhelmed by our thoughts and emotions. In the course of our lives we experience change, we form relationships and feel pain when these relationships end, which in the end they must inevitably do. We find happiness, or not, depending on our luck, our experiences, our expectations, and the social conditions of our lives. We face hardship, self-doubt, dashed hopes, loneliness, frustration, confusion, loss, and uncertainty. But of course, with any luck, along the way we also experience love, friendship, joy, appreciation, achievements, music, victories, good food, poetry, dancing, sensual pleasure, and general delight. Such is life.

We are generally happy when our experiences exceed our expectations, and distressed when they fall below those expectations. Our cognitive minds are enveloped in our emotions and nervous system, so when our needs are not being met our emotions let us know about it: we feel afraid, angry, frustrated, dejection, shame, indignation, and so on. We seek connection with other people because it can provide security, friendship, love, comfort, stimulation, and many other good things, and yet on the flip side, as everyone knows, relationships can also engender conflict, rejection, hurt, loss, and unfair expectations.

Jane grew up with a feeling that she was required to be the perfect daughter for her parents; disappointing them would be catastrophic and she imagined that everyone she loved would suffer. This was how her mind had modelled the world, how she had made sense of her life. As we saw in previous chapters, habits, routines and taken-for-granted assumptions make life simpler, more efficient and more predictable, providing us with a feeling of control and safety. It is stressful and tiring to have to consciously think all the time, so our minds quickly develop short-hand assumptions about the world, and we use these rules-of-thumb to guide our interpretation of the world and what is happening. In a similar vein, our autobiographical memory of what has happened to us leads us, like Jane, to assume, largely unconsciously, that history may well repeat itself.

In the last chapter we saw that people rarely question their taken-for-granted assumptions unless the events of their lives force them to do so. Most people are heavily invested in maintaining the integrity of their mental models of the world so as to keep themselves safe and life predictable, but for Jane this meant living in a heightened state of vigilance for many years.

Any one of us can draw conclusions from our past experiences that are misguided, unwise, or unhelpful. The models we develop about the world are not always in our own or other people's best interests. The person with agoraphobia believes to their core that going outside will be dangerous for them. The person who feels depressed believes that they are worthless, and feels so hopeless about their life improving that they no longer initiate things to achieve, or things to look forward to, thus sustaining their beliefs. The fanatic becomes fixated on the certainty of their ideas. The person with obsessive thoughts believes that if they don't compulsively do something, or think something in a particular way, they will ultimately be held responsible for some future calamity. All these people remain committed and obedient to the particular conclusions or assumptions they have reached about the world.

Talking therapies aim to slow everything down so as to uncover the implicit, often nebulous, assumptions underlying what the client is feeling and believing about their world. Articulating our assumptions in words helps us to make them conscious, so that they can be thought about and possibly amended if they are deemed to be unhelpful. And in finding the words we sometimes gain a new perspective with which to view our lives, our behaviour, and our future.

But talking therapies have not been the only game in town when it comes to responding to psychological and emotional distress.

Psych fights

A friend of mine once told me that her medical colleagues could be differentiated by their attachment to one of two fairly distinct philosophies: the list-makers and the model-makers. She described how, for some doctors, the simple labelling of phenomena, such as making a diagnosis, was enough, as if the label somehow explained the illness. These doctors, she said, are comfortable trusting and rigidly following lists and protocols. Other doctors, the model-makers, are more concerned with how processes and systems within the unique body of the particular patient interact and develop over time. She admitted that this differentiation might seem a bit crude, but I could see what she meant.

In his book, *The Birth of the Clinic*, French philosopher Michel Foucault (1926-1984) coined the term 'the medical gaze' to refer to the way that medicine has too often dehumanised people by reducing the complexity of the whole person to body or brain parts that need fixing. This stance assumes that there has to be something wrong with the patient, and that symptoms define the problem which can then be reduced to a label. In physical medicine this 'medical model' has been extraordinarily successful because list-making and model-making have worked together.

However, the list-making philosophy finds its limits in the way that medicine, in the form of psychiatry, has developed cataloguing systems such as the Diagnostic and Statistical Manual of Mental Disorders (DSM) or the International Classification of Diseases (ICD). These ever-growing compendiums list all the possible 'mental disorders' that are thought to exist, and are used as a reference for psychiatrists (and other people who use this framework) so they can pattern-match the patient's symptoms with a particular diagnosis.

A psychiatric diagnosis is derived from seeing to what extent an individual's symptoms conform to a list that describes a so-called 'disorder'. So, for example, the symptoms of 'clinical depression' include: continuous low mood or sadness, feeling hopeless and helpless, having low self-esteem, feeling tearful, feeling guilt, feeling irritable and intolerant of others, having no motivation or interest in things, finding it difficult to make decisions, not getting any enjoyment out of life, feeling suicidal, and so on. You immediately see the problem. These are all subjective 'feelings' that may be strongly or weakly held, and all of which may be caused by any number of factors.

There is no x-ray or blood test that can determine whether or not someone 'has' depression, or that can distinguish between depression and sadness, because clinical depression is not a 'thing' that exists in nature like a book, a wound, or abnormal cell growth. 'Clinical depression' is a human construction or judgement – a fuzzy demarcation beyond which people qualify as having a 'mental disorder'. This makes it an entirely social judgement as to where 'experts' choose to draw that line.

Human minds exist within biological *things* called brains and bodies, but as we have shown, minds are not things as such, so much as complicated informational (and relational) processes that go on developing over time. Feelings of loss, hopelessness and despair are expressions of sadness born from experience, not malfunction.

Many psychiatric treatments are based on abstract theories about chemical interactions and their effects on neurotransmitters, hormones and emotions, but it is hard to see why neurotransmitters have anything much to do with *meaning*. Their general function is one of signal transmission between neurons, not lived experience. Some psychiatrists have come to believe that psychotropic medications induce their own abnormal brain states, and professor of psychiatry David Healy has said: *"No one for whom Prozac has been prescribed has ever had their serotonin levels checked to see if they really are suffering from what the drug supposedly corrects."*[13]

---

[13] Healy D. (1998) Gloomy days and sunshine pills. *Openmind*, 90, 8-9.

It is important to note that many psychiatrists these days do not hold to this purely medical model of human behaviour. Happily, many progressive psychiatrists subscribe to a more nuanced psychological and social view of human distress, rather than the crude biomedical model that still prevails in most parts of the world. Many of the most important insights in psychological therapy have been made by psychiatrists. However, despite this progress, doctors continue to prescribe antidepressants in ever greater numbers. According to NHS England, more than one in four women and one in ten men were taking an antidepressant in 2021. In the US, over 13 per cent of adults were prescribed an antidepressant between 2015 and 2018, including almost one in four women over the age of 60.

Although quick and easy to dispense, anti-depressants however are unable to accurately target specific emotions. Instead, they effectively act as an emotional analgesia or sedative, blunting all emotions, not just the negative ones. It is therefore little wonder that when people withdraw from taking them, sometimes after many months or years, they often report not just unpleasant withdrawal or rebound effects such as insomnia, nausea and hyperarousal, but also a sense of reawakening into a world in which they are able to feel once again.

This drug-dependent, symptom-suppressing approach simply fails to address the far more important question of cause and effect, such as what has happened to the person in question to cause them to feel so low in mood. What are the effects of the social circumstances of their lives, what has the individual concluded from their life experiences and complicated relationships, what assumptions do they hold that are borne from their experiences? This complexity cannot be sensibly reduced to a simple list or diagnosis, and it certainly cannot be alleviated by a pill that merely blunts one's emotions.

Parenthetically, there may occasionally be a role for drug-based emotional analgesia within medicine (e.g. sometimes in end-stage palliative care), but most of the time a person's emotions are an important and functional part of their mind and personhood. It is perhaps telling that Amitriptyline, an older tricyclic anti-depressant, is commonly used these days as an actual analgesic, to treat nerve or neuropathic pain.

Hardware can go wrong of course; according to the World Health Organisation, 55 million people across the world were living with dementia in 2023, and by 2040 it is estimated there will be 12 million patients with Parkinson's disease, not to mention the many other neurological disorders. And some people do become so 'mentally disturbed' as to need temporary containment, or so withdrawn that they become inaccessible. But it surely possible to recognise human *distress* without having to define it as a form of mental illness or disorder? Having a highly emotional life plainly does not mean that a person is mentally sick and needs medicating. Minds are as powerful as bodies at healing themselves, given the right support and conditions, and people patently have enormous power to help themselves.

Far from being 'ill', it is more likely that people are merely doing their best to manage chronic stress, such as social deprivation, an abusive relationship, fears, losses, and changes that they have yet to adjust to. The person may have been damaged by their experiences, or are feeling overwhelmed by their emotions and drives, but it is far more likely their distress is a reflection of how they are perceiving the world than a nervous disease of the brain.

Minds are not computers, but they are computational, yet in the face of that complexity there has been an unfortunate historical tendency to apply the medical model as if the mind were simply another physical organ, rather than a sophisticated emotional information processing system that is housed within the physical brain, the nervous system and the body more generally.

The medical model of diagnosis is in stark contrast to the psychological approach which starts from the ground up with each and every client or patient. It starts by recognising that everyone has had a rich and complicated life thus far, one that has taught them lessons and models about how the world works, where the dangers lie, and what to expect from other people, etc. Instead of a diagnosis, a psychological assessment results in a unique formulation, one that is co-created with the client and which changes and develops as the therapy proceeds.

Psychology is the study of human behaviour, where humans have come from, how we function (e.g. perception, memory, learning, etc.), how we behave, how we think, and how we feel. Many psychologists work as university academics, researching and teaching these many scientific topics. *Clinical* psychologists attempt to apply this knowledge in the form of psychological therapies.

The psychology of the mind is far more complex than anything that one could sensibly list because it involves the uniqueness of each person's life experience, the social conditions of their lives, and the relationships they have had and perhaps are currently having. Human behaviour is enormously complex and does not have the sharp edges that lists require. We are continuous, not categorical creatures. Even night and day blur into one another twice a day.

Of course, people often find it reassuring to be given a diagnosis, believing that their distress is perhaps understood by other people, but a diagnosis is little more than a very short-hand description. There are radically divergent ways of understanding human distress, but psychiatry and psychology have had very different starting points, both historically and philosophically, even if 'in the field' their roles often overlap.

A clinical psychologist starts from the premise that people are able to mentally represent and model the world, and that many clients have endured harsh, confusing, and impoverished lives in which the lessons they have learned have not always served them well. These meaning-making processes are far more plausible, albeit more complex, than clusters of neural pathways or chemical transmitter malfunctions.

So psychologists are simply not interested in listing what is wrong with you, they are interested in what has happened to you, the threats and losses you have faced, the relationships you have had, the social conditions of your life, the emotions you are feeling and have felt, the things you have learned, and the meaning that you have derived from these experiences. Any decent therapist is interested in understanding how people live their lives, but do not assume that their clients' distress is pathological or some form of system failure. Having a human mind also gives us agency so, while our lives are shaped by the social world around us, we also get to make choices.

Psych therapies

The philosophical tussle between psychology and psychiatry is nothing compared with the raging arguments within psychological therapies as a whole. As a field of study, psychology has had more than its fair share of bigotry, purges, and dogmatic orthodoxies. These battles have been particularly acrimonious in the area of applied psychology, or psychological therapy.

Just a few years ago, modern scientific psychology, the field I first trained in, had entirely dismissed psychodynamic therapy and its theoretical basis, to the extent that any talk of 'the unconscious mind' was considered profane. In fact, when I began my training in the late 1970s at the Institute of Psychiatry, Britain's bastion of behaviourism, we were even forbidden from ever using the admittedly tricky term 'the mind'.

The psychodynamic movement, which is broadly based on the insights and views of Sigmund Freud and his many disciples, was condemned by the scientific community for being...well, unscientific. This was mainly due to its central claim that there is a 'subconscious' world of experience and knowledge, a hidden and largely invisible part of the mind that influences what people think and do, their verbal slips, their dreams, and also the cause of their neuroses. There was no research being done to back this up however. Behaviourism, by contrast, confined itself to measuring what could be observed, and that meant behaviour and physiology (i.e. emotion: heart rate, sweat response, etc.).

Psychoanalysis is largely about how people symbolically represent the world, their emotions, and the nature of their relationships. Whether or not Freud's overall conception of the mind was accurate, his belief in a subconscious remains an important insight, if not entirely original. Such therapists accept Freud's contention that a lot of people's memory is hidden from view. The unconscious, as it is generally known these days, is seen as a mental repository of hidden memories, conflicts and impulses from the past that guide a person's behaviour in the present. Psychoanalysts believe that our memories can become repressed (effectively forgotten by the conscious mind), leaving the person unaware of these dynamic driving forces. Thus, another term for this therapeutic approach is psychodynamic therapy (which, confusingly, is often shortened in the UK to the term 'psychotherapy'. Other countries tend to use the term psychotherapy to refer to any form of psychological therapy).

For many years, the unconscious continued to be a source of great dispute and acrimony within the discipline of psychology. For the behaviourist, the idea of an unconscious mind implied too much that could not be measured and was therefore condemned as untestable and of no scientific interest. By today's standards this seems narrow-minded when one considers how much mental experience this excludes, such as, for example, the feelings that are evoked when you simply think of your mother's voice.

These two warring branches of psychology had been approaching the same problem using different assumptions, different frames of reference, and different units of analysis. The behaviourists were rigidly bound by a Rutherford-like straight-jacket of only being able to consider things they could directly observe and measure. Drawing on learning theory, which had been derived from animal experiments, behaviour therapists showed that, with practice, emotions and behaviour can be learned, unlearned, and effectively regulated. And behaviourism obtained verifiable results. Meanwhile psychoanalysts got on with seeing patients and learning more about how relationships are symbolically represented in the unconscious world, such as what happens in the relationship between the therapist and the client. But the psychoanalysts undertook almost no research that could be validated or replicated by behavioural scientists, and they regarded the advances being made in behaviour therapy as trivial and superficial. Thus, the antipathy and stalemate continued, though progress continued to be made in both camps.

In the mid-20th Century, ethology and evolutionary psychology had begun to emerge as a paradigm through which to understand modern behaviour. This approach attempts to understand the many ways in which human behaviour is a product of adaptation and natural selection, a way of thinking that gradually seeped into the consciousness of both the warring camps within psychology. It became increasingly recognised that people react to the world with evolved appetites, archaeo-purposes, and behavioural propensities – such things as language, emotions, social instincts like cheat detection and incest avoidance, but perhaps also conformity and obedience and other more specific behaviours.

Evolutionary psychologists recognised that the big survival advantage of modern minds is that humans can think; we can model the world and anticipate it. This cognitive species perspective has influenced both psychoanalysis and behaviourism, arguably drawing them closer together.

In the psychoanalytic camp there was a growing realisation that humans *need* connection with other people and that this is fundamental to how people relate to the world. This was perhaps where Sigmund Freud went a bit adrift, despite his many extraordinary insights.

Being a typical young man in repressed Vienna, Freud was perhaps all too aware of how sexually aroused he was feeling, yet he was also aware of how shameful and taboo it was within Viennese society to acknowledge these primitive biological impulses. So he was naturally inclined to believe that sexual energy is the core, albeit unmentionable, drive at the centre of the psychological universe, the main driving force within mental life. And from this idea he understood that people sometimes suppress (mentally push away and avoid) and even repress (block out, dissociate and forget) feelings and memories. He thought that taboos plus sexual fantasies led to conflict within people, even if they were not aware of it.

In some respects, Freud was right about sex; it is a powerful expression of the drive to procreate, and it is indeed a subject that is considered taboo in many cultures across the world. But 'sexual conflict' became the intellectual *cause célèbre* of Freud's thesis: repressed sexual feelings or fantasies supposedly become expressed later in the relationships and internal conflicts of everyday life. Well, perhaps this was the case for Professor Freud, but the essential need for all children (and ultimately adults) is having trusted bonds with other people: human connection. In the interests of our selfish genes, sex is not the most valuable drive, it is connection with other people. Before we reach sexual maturity, we need to have survived, and until that time children are very obviously dependent and vulnerable, so they seek connection with other people to obtain their protection and care. Once again it seems that adults are very much grown-up children: connection with other people continues to remain a primary need. Psychological wellbeing, as we will see in the next chapter, is very much the result of social support and being connected with other people.

The Scottish psychoanalyst Ronald Fairbairn (1889-1964) was one of the first to break with the orthodox Freudian idea that people's primary drive is sexual gratification. Instead, Fairbairn suggested that Freud had got the wrong end of the stick, and that people have a primary biological need to *connect* with other people. This, he argued, is the fundamental drive or 'libido' within the *psyche*.

It was Fairbairn, incidentally, who coined the term *splitting* to describe the tendency of people, particularly infants, to think in simple binary ways; black or white, good or bad, idealising other people or feeling contempt for them and devaluing them. He regarded it as an infantile way of thinking, but one retained by many adults. Decades later cognitive therapists would call it all-or-nothing thinking.

Around the same time, the 1940s, psychoanalyst Melanie Klein (1882-1960) recognised something that she called the 'object-seeking' drive, a need for connection. She derived her insights from an almost obsessive interest in the mother-child relationship, though Klein was certainly onto something in her fascination with this bond. She argued that you began learning about the relational world during those early days when you and your mother used to stare lovingly into each other's eyes while she fed you. At those moments, and hopefully many others since, you symbiotically needed one another.

Psychoanalysts such as Fairbairn and Klein came to realise that people need connections with other people if they are to flourish. And not just when they are babies but throughout life. However, more than anyone else, it was John Bowlby who understood the influence of a child's early bonds on the assumptions that they develop and which they later bring to relationships in general.

Bowlby's Attachment Theory is predicated on the fact that we humans are an evolved species. Chimpanzees and bonobos, our closest evolutionary cousins, are similarly highly social species. If a rhesus monkey is given a wire figure to feed from (to act as its mother) it will not thrive and soon become sickly and despondent. However, if it is given a cloth-covered wire figure, even one that provides no food, it will readily attach itself to it, and end up physically healthy. Rat pups that are licked and groomed a lot are more likely later to lick and groom their own young. It is a mammalian thing, and it is essentially the same for us humans – early relationship experiences shape later ones.

From his studies in ethology, such as Harlow's sad experiments on baby monkeys deprived of a mother figure, mentioned above, and working closely with ethologist Robert Hinde (1923-2016), Bowlby realised, like Fairbairn and Klein before him, that the human need for relational connection is the central organizing principle of human development.

Bowlby came to see that early relationship experiences, or their absence, deeply influence how people subsequently look at and think about future relationships with other people. He aptly called these relational assumptions 'internal working models'. Like any other part of the assumptive world, a person continues to learn about relationships throughout their lives, so relational models are important templates, and like models in general they are not cast-iron or inevitable.

Bowlby's Attachment Theory provides a scientifically more plausible and coherent account of people's development of emotional and relational intelligence than the traditional Freudian model, but what they both share is an understanding that early experiences profoundly, often unconsciously, shape subsequent expectations and relationships. This is an important insight when it comes to understanding and ameliorating relational distress.

Around the same time, in the late 1960s, a few psychologists, notably American psychiatrist Aaron Beck (1921-2021) and psychologist Albert Ellis (1913-2007), began to make the now rather obvious point that we humans think and have ideas. Our thoughts and beliefs can lead to very different behaviours and outcomes. In other words, our behaviour is governed by our thoughts as much as our bodies. Hardly surprising, you may say, when it is the very thing that defines us as a species. This may seem self-evident now, but Beck and others were clever enough to show that one can study and model thinking itself in fairly scientific ways.

Beck noted that people with low mood were experiencing trains of negative thoughts that seemed to emerge spontaneously. These he termed 'automatic thoughts'. He also noted that people did not reflect on their automatic thoughts, but just assumed they were valid. He realised that people simply *'feel'* their beliefs to be true, and therefore live by them, but by helping his patients identify and evaluate their thoughts, and regard them more objectively, Beck enabled them to think more realistically and coherently, with positive effects on their behaviour and mood. He concluded that people's automatic thoughts are often based on distortions or biases, and that these are a function of core beliefs (i.e. models) that have been acquired earlier in the person's life and are now taken for granted.

The advent of this cognitive psychology and the resurgence of evolutionary psychology was a turning point. With such fierce conflicts in its past, applied psychology was perhaps ready for a more ecumenical approach, one that recognised that, despite their rivalry, psychoanalysis and behaviourism both had truths to tell.

Historically, our psychological understanding of the mind has tended to reflect the prevailing cultural assumptions of the day. We are currently passing through a neuroscience boom, made possible by massive advances in digital imaging technology, electrophysiology, molecular biology and computer science. The neurosciences are getting ever clearer maps of how information passes through the brain, and one suspects that minds are increasingly being thought of as mere brain circuitry.

But the neurosciences are perhaps not the most helpful explanatory framework when it comes to understanding the nature of relationships, or questions of meaning. Brain science is fascinating, but it can tell us little, for example, about how someone mentally adjusts to the prospect of dying.

Mara

I once met a 49-year-old woman called Mara. She was from Cyprus and had thick curly black hair. Her hair is my main visual memory of her. I remember that she had a high voice but not shrill, and wore lots of chunky colourful jewellery and bright lipstick. She was dying of lung cancer, and was very distressed. She told me that her teenage children still very much needed her.

As if this were not bad enough, she was suffering with horrible images of her children weeping with distress, standing by her grave as her coffin is lowered into it. And of course in this recurring fantasy Mara is unable to do anything about it. She is hovering above, watching it.

Mara's thoughts frequently became stuck with this looping image until she became so distressed that, in floods of tears, she would tear herself away from her thoughts and distract herself by getting involved with something else. Mara was very tearful during our first session, but it felt that she was releasing feelings she had been holding back for a long time. She said it was a relief to be telling someone, and by the end of the session the wastepaper bin was full of tissues.

Mara said she was happily married to Georgios, a reliable and steady man who worked as a bus driver. He was not a big talker, she said. She was immensely proud of her daughter and son who, she said, were managing the news of her illness well. She told me that her own mother had died when she was 14 and that her father was now married to someone who Mara didn't think was good enough for him. Her one brother lived in Australia and she rarely spoke to him, though since her illness he had phoned a couple of times.

At one point Mara mentioned that she and Georgios had always fallen asleep together every night as spoons, with Georgios gently holding her breast, and she cried telling me how he would miss this after she was gone. It was all terribly sad, her anguish was total, and I remember feeling depleted at the end of the session, but I felt we had established a good relationship.

At the next session Mara seemed more composed. We returned to the intrusive images she had told me about in our first session and she confirmed that they were still troubling her every day. I asked if we could talk about them a bit more, and she agreed for me to ask her some potentially upsetting questions about her thoughts. We began by acknowledging that, being their mother, she was naturally finding it unbearably painful to imagine her children in such distress. Mara became distressed again. Then I asked her

"When you have these thoughts, what do you imagine will happen after the funeral?"

"What?" she asked.

"What do you imagine Georgios and the children will be doing after the funeral?"

There was a pause.

"I don't know. I suppose my dad and his… wife may still be there…" Over the next few minutes she began to imagine with me that there would actually be a reception after the funeral, and that everyone would be talking about her. She noted that her father might stay the night with the family.

"Okay, and what about the next day? I'm sure it will be another difficult day for all of them, but perhaps not so bad as the day of the funeral?"

"No" she said sadly, "perhaps not". I noticed that her eyes were brimming at this point, but she was still not actively crying.

"And I wonder what it will be like a week later; no, a month later. They will all still be missing you terribly of course, and very sad, but do you think the children might be thinking of returning to school by then?" Mara paused again before she spoke.

"I suppose so… well, I hope so." She looked up at me and burst into tears again, but it was different. She had begun to see the future through a different lens, framing it as less of a catastrophe and more as part of an adjustment that her children would go through. In time their lives would move on, they would adjust and adapt, albeit without her. It was a reassuring thought, and a different model or story of the future.

Mara had never allowed herself to look beyond her most horrific nightmare. She assumed it could only get worse so she never imagined the next frame in the film, or the next, culminating in her children's grief dissipating, as it naturally would in time. By allowing herself to watch a bit more of her fantasy of the imagined future, she could begin to see that her own death would be a devastating loss for her family, but that their tears would eventually stop. They would adjust to a world without her, but this did not mean they would ever forget her.

At our third session Mara initially seemed more business-like with me. I remember being surprised by this in view of how helpful and reassuring she said she had found our previous session. There was something slightly abrupt about her manner. I am tempted to use the word brittle, but this would be overstating it. She said that she was feeling much better in herself and was trying to get on with living life in whatever time she had left. The intrusive images had all but stopped. We talked about this for a while, and then she turned to me and said

"Georgios and I are not getting on."

"I'm sorry to hear that. Can you say more?"

"He won't talk to me about my illness. He says I am being unreasonable."

"Sometimes men find it hard knowing quite what to say. I remember you saying when we first met that Georgios is not much of a talker."

"No, he just thinks I'm being unreasonable."

"Why would he think you are being unreasonable? Is it because you are expecting him to talk?"

"No, it's not that. You know he's Greek?"

"Yes, I know."

"Well after... when I'm not here... he plans to go back to Greece and buy a place there." She trailed off into silence. I thought I had understood.

"So are you perhaps worried that the children will feel they have lost their mum and then they would be losing their dad and their home?"

"Well, yes, that is one thing, but he says the children will be able to visit him and for them it will be nice to have somewhere warm to visit."

"Okay, so what do...?" I began to say, feeling a bit confused.

"I've told him that if he goes back to Greece, he mustn't marry anyone else."

At this, I paused. "So... Mara, you're saying that you have forbidden Georgios from marrying again if he goes to live in Greece?"

"From marrying."

"You mean anyone, anywhere?"

"Yes"

It all seemed a bit odd. Certainly unusual. She always spoke of Georgios so fondly, and in my mind I imagined him as a big friendly teddy bear of a man. Mara said that she could not bear the thought of him being with another woman, and later admitted that she had demanded that Georgios swear that he would never marry anyone else. When he refused, apparently in some distress himself, she screamed at him and they have barely spoken since.

"What do you think Georgios is feeling about this request of yours?" I asked.

"He can't wait to get rid of me." That just didn't sound very likely, but it strangely also didn't feel right to challenge Mara too much, no matter how unreasonable her demand seemed to be. I tried to explore it further with her but she was resolute, so I asked if I could speak to Georgios at our next scheduled meeting.

Georgios turned out to be short, with thick curly black hair of his own and a bushy moustache, surprisingly similar to the image I had imagined. This rarely happens. He had a broad smiley face that, as we talked, would occasionally and momentarily crumple into a grimace of despair. He seemed like a lovely man.

No, he said, he had absolutely no plans to remarry and certainly hadn't raised the subject. He loved Mara and didn't want any of this to be happening. He had only mentioned Greece because he thought it might cheer everyone up to think that he and the children would be all right after Mara had died. He now thought that it was the stupidest thing for him to have said because since then Mara had become obsessed about him remarrying. But at the same time he didn't like the fact that Mara was asking him to promise that he would never marry anyone else. He said he just didn't feel that that was right.

At my next session with Mara, on her own, we went over her history again in a bit more detail. We returned to discussing the death of her mother. She told me that after her mother died, aged 14, she had taken over the running of the household. Mara had cooked and washed for her father and brother, neither of whom, she said, had a clue what to do. This went on for the next three and a half years, and then, just before her eighteenth birthday, her father announced that he had been seeing a woman Mara had never met and that they were planning to get married the following summer. This came as a massive shock for Mara and her brother.

When Mara met her step-mother-to-be, she was appalled by her vulgarity compared with her beloved mother. The word 'vile' was used several times as she described her to me. She was furious about her father's betrayal of her mother's memory, and within a week of her father's new bride moving in Mara had moved out of the house.

At this point I found myself suggesting that we stop there for a moment so that we could both think about what she had told me. I briefly summarised what she had told me. A minute passed. She began gently crying again, but the silence between us felt so rich with meaning that I said nothing.

"I know what you are thinking" she eventually said, "and yes, you are right. It is happening again. I hadn't realised..." She could see that the situation was different, but she was damned if she was going to be supplanted and replaced again by another vile intruder.

In the last session we had, a couple of weeks before she died, Mara said that she had told Georgios that he must feel free to live the rest of his life in whatever way he wished, but that she hoped that he would never forget her. I reassured her that this would be impossible. She was much calmer generally and I was glad that she and Georgios were at peace with one another.

Several years later I ran into Georgios in a pub. He looked well. He had not moved back to Greece and he was still single. He told me that he was happy enough, and was enjoying his time at his garden allotment where he had several friends.

Distress

We experience distress as a mental, emotional and/or physical state of discomfort, but although distress is invariably a mental experience, something that one subjectively feels, the source of the distress is obviously not always psychological. Poverty, hunger, and physical pain may be experienced in the mind, but the mind is not necessarily the cause of the distress so much as its casualty. Consequently, most psychological therapists are trained to think about a person's distress in terms of its bio-psycho-social causes. They try to think about the power and threat the client is up against, the social and interpersonal conditions and context of their lives, and the meaning they are making about their situation.

This approach to understanding distress is known as the Power, Threat and Meaning Framework, a recent alternative model to traditional psychiatric diagnoses. It starts by acknowledging that a huge amount of human distress is caused by the social conditions of people's lives: deprivation, migration, unemployment, imprisonment, loneliness and isolation, noisy neighbours, racial prejudice, domestic abuse, and so on. These very real social factors. Inequalities.

Therapists, like everyone else, are only able to see the world through the prism of their own assumptions and are therefore always in danger of adopting an overly psycho-centric (intrapsychic) line of enquiry rather than thinking about the bigger social picture in which the unfortunate client is embedded. So therapists must periodically renew their vow to think holistically about people's distress, and from multiple perspectives. This is one of many reasons why it is good practice for therapists to review and reflect on their work with other therapists in what is known as clinical supervision.

Psychological distress occurs when a person's needs are not being met, such as when their need for safety, relational connection, or sense of purpose is being obstructed, or when their expectations are violated. In *Chapter 3,* we saw that emotions are entirely normal and an important source of information about what is happening in our lives, so it helps to be able to read them accurately.

If you get to work and discover you have been fired, you are likely to be unhappy. However, if you were expecting to be in as much pain as you were yesterday, but today the pain has lessened, you might feel you are having a relatively good day. Our emotional experience of what happens moment to moment, as well as the larger events of our lives, is always in relation to our expectations, which are of course themselves based on assumptions and mental models. Put simply, a mismatch between expectations and lived experience is likely to generate stress, but when the mismatch is particularly negative it is likely to generate *di*stress *(See SCT diagram on page* 193).

For therapists therefore, understanding the client's assumptions and expectations is as important as understanding their needs and emotions. The client's personal context, social conditions and autobiographical history are critical to understanding how they are making sense of their lives and the assumptions they hold, so understanding these factors is invariably a key to understanding their distress. This unique aggregate of information must be learned afresh with each and every client.

Therapy creates the space and time for clients to (re)construct a plausible narrative of their troubles, as well as perhaps learn how to tame their wilder thoughts and calm their emotional responses. This may involve learning how their bodies work and how their emotions can be better understood and better regulated. For example, many people can be helped by simply learning to relax their tensed up, vigilant bodies. Emotional distress can have myriad psychological causes, but for many it has become so familiar that it is taken for granted and considered normal. Unmet needs, mental distortions of reality, and high levels of emotional arousal, can all seem 'just the ways things are', and soon they are rarely questioned or challenged.

Fear

First appointments are interesting for therapists. I always notice my clients' natural nervousness, or not, on meeting me for the first time. Some people sit on the edge of their seat looking physically tense for nearly the whole hour, despite our genial conversation, or at least until I point it out to them and encourage them to allow the chair to do its job. But even then, some people find it manifestly difficult to sit back in the chair, because relaxing their body feels unnatural to them. It is not a part of their assumptive world. Their habitual bodily state is one of vigilant physiological arousal, which as you may recall, is part of the threat response, a preparation to escape or defend oneself.

So, sometimes a good place to start is helping the client learn how to regulate their emotions better, perhaps through muscle relaxation exercises and learning to breathe more calmly, the two areas of the threat response that are amenable to voluntary control (by contrast, we cannot directly cause our hearts to beat more slowly).

The job of the therapist is to formulate with the client a plausible model for what may have caused this fear, whether it is still justified, how it has been learned in the body, what may be maintaining it, and what steps can be taken to overcome it. You may recall that the man who had panic attacks in the Blackwall Tunnel initially assumed that his fear was to do with the tunnel. It took time to formulate an understanding of the true source of his distress, his frustration and anger towards his boss.

Anxiety, the clinical term for the fear response, is often maintained by the way the client is thinking about their fears: Will I be safe? Will I survive? Will I be overcome by another panic attack? And so on. These powerful thoughts and ideas may be driving the anxiety, so they need to be identified, challenged, and undermined.

Finally, in addition to physiological arousal (heart palpitations, muscle tension, etc.), and persuasive thinking, fear usually involves the avoidance of whatever is provoking it. So at some point the feared and avoided place, person, or thing must be confronted. The client must learn to approach the feared 'object', whilst trying to maintain a state of physiological calm, and simultaneously deploying more realistic, less catastrophic thoughts about the situation. This obviously takes practice, but it can also work.

Distorted thinking

There is a big difference between *thinking* someone doesn't like you, and *knowing* that they don't like you. We can think anything we like, but knowing something means basing our assertion or assumption on evidence of some kind. The problem with thinking is that it is beset with illusions and distortions.

The fact that we human beings are able to model the world in our minds results in a promiscuous tendency to get lost in our own thinking. Our propensity towards establishing coherent models of the world can also lead us to draw the wrong conclusions, perhaps unfairly blaming ourselves or others for our misfortune or unhappiness, or making unhelpful generalisations on the basis of specific experiences (if one person said this about me, perhaps everyone thinks the same thing). These are broadly known as cognitive distortions.

Cognitive distortions come in many different guises. As said earlier, Daniel Kahneman has described these numerous distortions of reason in fine detail. We tend to dread calamity more than we appreciate the good things that we do have, and we dwell on slights and criticisms more than feeling uplifted by praise. We feel shame when we compare ourselves to those we see as more successful, talented, or worthy, while overlooking those who struggle more than we do. We overvalue our own thoughts, treating them as if they must be real, simply because we thought them. We fear things that in all probability are not very likely to happen, and we can feel deep hopelessness whilst having so much to feel grateful for, and so on. In a similar way, cognitive therapists like Aaron Beck began to notice typical ways in which people's minds misrepresent reality, with the unfortunate effect of reinforcing unhelpful models and leading the person to feel distressed.

Here are a few cognitive distortions:

Emotional Reasoning

"I feel lonely because no one cares about me." This is when we allow our emotions to lead us to a distorted conclusion. Because of how we feel about ourselves in one situation, we believe that this accurately reflects how we are in life more generally. For example, if you feel inadequate when starting a new job, you assume that you are generally a bit of a failure. Contrary evidence is disregarded or dismissed.

All-or-Nothing

Any form of negative outcome affects our view of the entire event. If we are not perfect at something, we see ourselves as a failure. If someone is not good, they must be bad. This black-and-white way of thinking fails to allow for shades of grey, or for people to be simply good enough. Infants tend to think in these simplistic ways, hence 'infantile thinking'.

Personalisation

We automatically assume that if things are not going well it must be our fault, entirely discounting other factors which may be playing a part. We take things too personally. We are critical of ourselves, rather than seeing that other people or other factors may bear some responsibility.

Shoulds and Musts
If we internalise rigid high standards for ourselves, we may be setting ourselves up to fail or be disappointed. Rather than allowing ourselves and our behaviour to be 'good enough', we only see our shortcomings.

Labelling
We label ourselves with some term that may have once been said to us, and assume that this is generally true – shy, humourless, clumsy etc. Or we generalise from one event: we make a mistake and say to ourselves "I'm such an idiot".

Filtering
Any slightly negative outcome affects our view of everything. So, while the rest of that talk you gave at work went quite well, you allow the small slip-up that you made at the start to frame how you feel about the entire presentation. We also fail to internalise when something goes well. Instead, we dismiss and filter out good experiences as being a fluke or little to do with our own contributions.

Mind-reading
By assuming we know what other people are thinking, we imagine them having all sorts of thoughts, feelings and intentions that they simply may not be having.

Catastrophising
We leap to imagine the worst possible outcome, and begin to feel the emotions we would feel if that outcome had already happened. We confuse what is possible with what is probable. It is possible that if I go to that party no one will want to talk to me, but in real life it is not very probable.

Obsessing
If you place a hungry pigeon inside a box and give it food at regular intervals, as BF Skinner (1904-1990) famously did in 1947, after a while it will develop ritualised tics of behaviour, such as bobbing its

head or spinning in circles. The pigeon has developed a superstition about the source of its food, linking its own behaviour with the expectation of the continued arrival of food. This is an example, incidentally, of conditioned memory (*see Chapter 4*), the source of many personal superstitions.

I once worked with a man in his late twenties called Trevor, who believed that everything he touched had germs. Consequently, he wore gloves a lot of the time. When I first met Trevor, I noticed that his gloves were not particularly new or even 'hygienic'; they seemed rather grimy. However, he seemed willing to shake my hand because he took off his gloves and they remained off for the whole session and did not go back on even when he left the room.

Fortunately, Trevor had quite a clear memory of how his difficulties had started. He told me that his beliefs about germs had started when he was at school. He was in a biology class when his teacher began talking about bacteria and viruses. He could remember imagining what his teacher was describing, the world covered by a thin layer of invisible bacteria of different sorts. He said that soon after this class he became fixated on using the phrase 'colonies of germs' because he could imagine quite vividly what they would look like.

Then the teacher went on to describe some of the horrendous epidemics and plagues that had ravaged humanity. And that is what got to Trevor. He imagined that by touching things he might inadvertently pick up a combination of bacteria and that these would evolve into 'mutant bacteria', as he saw it, and that he would end up infecting everyone. He became terrified that he might cause another plague, so he avoided touching things as much as possible and would wash his hands exactly three times whenever he had taken off his gloves. When I later came out of my consulting room, after our session, I saw him leaving the washroom with his gloves back on. He had presumably felt compelled to wash his hands three times after touching mine, the superstitious ritual he had told me about.

Obsessions and compulsions are often lumped together, as in the term obsessive-compulsive disorder, but while they often do occur together, they can also occur apart. People, like Jane and Trevor, spent agonising hours worrying and ruminating about threats that were very unlikely to be real. Such obsessional thinking is closely related to rumination and worry.

Worrying about the future (i.e. mentally modelling it) is a highly useful cognitive skill, for it allows us to anticipate threats in the future and take evasive or mitigating action. For example, worrying about an impending exam may prompt us to study for it, and that is most likely to be in our best interests. So worry can be highly functional.

However, obsessional thinking, or obsessional ruminations, as they are sometimes known, involves people believing that unless they *think* in a particular way, or in the case of compulsions, *behave* in a particular way, they are putting themselves or other people in danger. The threat has become overstated and overinvested in. A cognitive distortion indeed. At the core of the unfortunate person's beliefs is invariably a fear that they will be held responsible for some catastrophe in the future, and that the finger of blame will be pointing directly at them. Remember that Jane ended up boiling her children's toothbrushes.

Consequently, people often perform mental rituals such as counting things, doing things a certain way, or saying particular phrases a certain number of times, as a way of cleansing or neutralising their minds of the original triggering thought. BF Skinner's pigeons merely had simpler superstitions, and most people sustain a few. For Jane, no amount of risk was acceptable if there was even a possibility that she might infect and kill her children, and for Trevor, no amount of risk was acceptable if he might cause a pandemic.

It is interesting to consider with the client where these overcharged assumptions and cognitive distortions may have come from. Our sensitivities and assumptions are of course born from our experience of life. For example, if someone is humiliated as a child, they are likely to develop sensitivity towards shame, and therefore worry about it, perhaps developing all sorts of defences and cognitive distortions along the way. It may lead them to be vulnerable to self-doubt, fear of rejection or criticism, or perhaps reticent about self-expression.

But wherever our particular sensitivities and sensibilities originated, mental rituals and ruminations can take up an enormous amount of time. Many people detest unstructured time because they would prefer not to be left alone with their own anxious punishing thoughts and, as we have said, solitary confinement is a punishment for this very reason. But obsessive thoughts effectively fill in this time with the rituals.

Therefore, one of the sometimes overlooked but key challenges in overcoming both obsessions and compulsions is finding alternative ways of filling in the time vacated by the rituals. Obsessive cleaning at least gives people the feeling that they are accomplishing something useful; consequently, alternative, more meaningful goals need to be found (e.g. art, craft, charity, hobby, sport, etc.). No mean feat.

As seen earlier, we can easily distort reality by how we frame our experiences. As imaginative creatures, humans can think of things that don't exist, and while this is a remarkable skill, simply having a thought doesn't make it *real*. For example, it is easy to imagine a man without a spacesuit sitting on a chair on the moon, but that doesn't make him real – only a representation in my mind, and now yours. Thoughts are just that: models, symbols, and fleeting neural patterns. But problems arise when we take these thoughts too literally or interpret them in unrealistic ways, giving them more power than they deserve. The long-standing and sure-fire antidote to the uncertainty of not knowing whether our thoughts are valid, accurate or reasonable, is to use other people's reactions as social reference points. This is one of the reasons why social support is so important for us, and why social isolation can be so damaging.

Sadness and low mood

To feel sad occasionally is part of the human condition, but it can lead to profound psychological pain. Consider the much maligned midlife crisis. It may be easy to denigrate the turmoil caused by a midlife crisis as being self-indulgent, and it does appear to be more commonly reported in economically developed countries. However, there is often a deep and genuine sadness within this life transition.

A midlife crisis may be triggered by reaching a certain age, children leaving home, or sometimes by the death of a loved one, or a crisis at work. Typically, the person becomes aware of assumptions they had neglected, such as aspirations of their younger selves that may now seem unattainable. They often feel trapped within a lifestyle they have created for themselves, and are now questioning whether this was the one they had imagined, and whether there may still be other options available? Ruminating on the loss of one's youth, a time when the future seemed limitless, may be temporarily alleviated by escapist fantasies of reclaiming that youth, starting again, buying that sportscar, and abandoning one's (seemingly imprisoning) commitments to other people. But often-as-not the midlife review leads to the resigned conclusion that, for better or worse, 'this is the bed I have made for myself', and perhaps it is simply time for new purposes to be found.

Sadness, such as a midlife crisis, often occurs when progression towards a goal has been blocked (or sometimes completed), a drive has been thwarted, or when there is a divergence between what we expected would happen and what is actually happening. It invariably involves a loss of some kind. Sadness is the emotional reaction to this discrepancy, stimulating the mind to close the gap and regain equilibrium through a search for meaning and explanation. As we saw in *Chapter 3,* despite its many negative connotations, sadness is a normal emotion that evolved to help us survive. Indeed, it can be helpful to withdraw temporarily so that we can re-evaluate our position in the changed world following a loss (including that of one's youth).

The problem is that a person can get stuck in their sadness by withdrawing for too long, becoming psychologically and emotionally fearful of re-engagement. Withdrawal can lead to a loss of investment in the future, a loss of purpose, a loss of confidence in being in the world, and a diminishing sense of self-worth. In other words, hopelessness. Depressive withdrawal reduces the opportunities for feedback from other people who would normally remind us that we are loved, valued and respected, and it limits the likelihood of any joyful sense of achievement. As prospects decline, the loss of motivational structure enables hopelessness to seep in, leading to a further loss of confidence and further withdrawal. In other words, it becomes an unhelpful feedback loop. The orientation towards any loss must therefore also bend towards 'restoration' and re-engagement with the world of other people and finding a meaningful purpose to one's life.

Being stuck in sadness is exhausting and is often listed medically as 'depression', which, as already discussed, has for too long been seen as a mainly biological or medical disease. The reality is that there is no biological difference between sadness and 'depression', and nor is there much evidence that anti-depressant medication does anymore than act as an emotional analgesic, just as aspirin is to pain. Anti-depressants may numb our emotions but they are not addressing their cause.

Therapy, instead, aims to help clients take stock of what they have understood about their lives and the things that have happened to them. In the face of sadness, the client may well need to grieve the original loss and recalibrate their mental models of the world, but they may also need to examine their habitual (automatic) thoughts and develop new meaningful goals for the future: things to look forward to and things to achieve. The patient thereby develops a deeper understanding and a different narrative, with new assumptions and new goals that they can take forward into the future.

The opposite of sadness is happiness and hope, and that necessitates an investment in a wished-for future which provides us with a sense of purpose and direction. Creating a structure to follow, setting ourselves a challenge to achieve, and planning things to look forward to, all increase the likelihood that we will feel engaged and delighted by the world, and begin to feel effective and valued within it.

Trauma

Change and surprise are ultimately what delights and enriches the mind, but people don't like too much change too quickly. This is as true for organisations as it is for individual people. Catastrophic sudden change can lead to psychological trauma, and trauma early in life can lead to a shutdown of various parts of the person's developing mind, resulting in many of the other psychological difficulties discussed above.

As we have said, people are naturally resistant to sudden change because we are motivated to maintain a consistent and coherent rendering of moment-to-moment reality. We also need to develop a plausible account of our experiences so that we are able to ascribe meaning to the events and relationships of our lives. This mental 'completion tendency' is all about constructing a credible model of what has happened and is happening, one that is consistent with our other mental models. Traumatic experiences thwart this tendency.

It is difficult to make sense of something when it is bewilderingly new and unexpected, or when we simply do not have the words to describe it. Faced with anything new, it can be unclear at first what is happening, what we are dealing with, what things mean, or what is expected of us. We don't yet have a *model* available that makes sense of what we are experiencing. Yet that is invariably the situation when faced with traumatic change. Trauma invokes powerful emotions, such as paralysing fear, that can overwhelm our sense of cognitive control, leaving us feeling utterly helpless.

Instead of being able to make sense of what has happened following a trauma and integrating it with what we already understand about the world, events and emotions can be pushed into a place where they are not even acknowledged. They are broken off from awareness, so they are no longer consciously remembered. This is known as **dissociation** and it is another psychological defence mechanism that serves to protect the mind from fragmentation. As we saw in the previous chapter on adjustment, people need time to integrate the many implications of massive change, and dissociation, denial and avoidance do an effective job in slowing down the rate at which new information is absorbed into the assumptive world. The problem with dissociation is that it can lead to the more permanent state of **repression** in which memories are rendered invisible to the conscious mind, effectively forgotten.

I once met a woman who felt relatively calm until she was required to lie down under a radiotherapy machine, whereupon she had a massive panic attack followed by the sudden onset of debilitating sadness that she was unable to account for. It took weeks of slow painstaking work for us to piece together the fragments of memory that were intruding on her consciousness as she lay on the radiotherapy table, entirely vulnerable, her chest exposed and her arms above her head.

We gradually reassembled her memories from when she was eight years old and had been left with her grandfather to be looked after. Instead of caring for her, he had sexually abused her. But in the years that followed, these unacceptably shameful memories became avoided to such an extent that they became repressed, locked away and hidden deep in her unconscious. Lying under the huge linear accelerator, once again feeling helpless and vulnerable, had reawakened these dreadful memories.

Trauma is the source of many psychological troubles, but the processes involved are not always the result of truly catastrophic events such as violence, a life-threatening accident, or being raped. Psychological responses to trauma are an extreme version of the normal psychological need to adjust to new information. Many other experiences can also be poorly integrated into a coherent rendering in long-term memory, perhaps because we failed to reflect on our experiences at the time.

Telling and creating a story about emotionally painful experiences is essential, because in the process of telling of the story we hear ourselves joining up into sentences the elements of what we have experienced, which helps provide a sense of coherence and control. Talking, reflecting and writing help to create a continuous plausible story that begins to make sense of what we went through. Later, when we come to remember the experience in question, we will be able to recall a more coherent story that is better integrated and more consistent with our understanding of the world.

Traumatic memories generally lack these properties. Parts of the experience have become dissociated or split off from the main body of our personal narrative. These traumatic fragments are 'remembered' as intrusive flashbacks and nightmares, and the body remains in a highly charged state of vigilance.

The purpose of therapy for trauma or other terrifying experiences is to help the client reintegrate the traumatic memories into a plausible narrative that no longer evokes the overwhelming emotions associated with the traumatic events. The trauma must be rethreaded into the person's life narrative as something awful that happened but an experience that can be later recalled for what it was.

Sarah and Peter

Sarah had been diagnosed and treated for breast cancer and was referred to me because she had been having panic attacks. At our first meeting she said she no longer knew who she was: "I don't recognise the person I have become." She was wearing a scarf on her head but took it off as soon as we sat down, so we briefly talked about her hair regrowing. She pointed out that her hair was now grey and wavy where it had been straight and black before her chemo. She went on to say that she was unable to find a bra to fit her 'grotesque' body, as she described it. She was suffering with post-treatment fatigue and had no confidence in her body staying well.

As far as I could see, her hair was still short but it was not long since her chemotherapy. A fear of recurrence is common and natural, and her alienation from her body was again not uncommon. But I was particularly interested in how she expressed these feelings. She was breathless and sat nervously on the front edge of her chair.

"Do you feel you have changed in any other ways?" I asked. She talked about having felt emotionally knocked about and that she was feeling utterly depleted. She thought she had let herself down by not being as emotionally strong as she had imagined herself to be, but equally, she reluctantly admitted that she sometimes felt annoyed that other people in her life were already expecting her to be fighting fit and to have put the illness behind her, now that active treatment was over. She said "They just see what they want to see. They only look at the surface, not what's going on inside me."

Despite her annoyance there was something particularly moving in the way that Sarah talked about the other people in her life, her parents, her children, and her husband Peter. There was a kindness in the way she spoke about everyone, a caring concern that rang through. From what she said, it sounded as if she had done her best to protect everyone in the family from the more distressing aspects of her illness. She was even generous-spirited and understanding about two of her friends who had become disappointingly distant since her diagnosis.

She had grown up as the eldest of three children. Her parents were kind and caring but her father was much older than her mother and had suffered with chronic emphysema throughout Sarah's childhood.

As for Sarah's panic attacks, they seemed to be associated with a sudden overwhelming realisation of what she had been through over the past 18 months and just how much her life had changed. This led her to have catastrophic images of her oncologist telling her that she had a recurrence, followed by a further string of appalling images: more chemotherapy, more radiotherapy, dying in a bed in the hospice surrounded by her distressed family. Despite her kind and gentle presentation, I felt more than a slight whiff of irritation in the room, and found myself wondering whether perhaps there was suppressed anger behind what she was saying.

In our second session, Sarah was more open with me and began to hint at concerns about her marriage. She said that she used to regard herself as the stronger partner in the relationship, but since she had been ill their roles had changed and now she felt that she was the more vulnerable one. She soon admitted that Peter had shown little sensitivity or apparent interest in what she had been going through, and she worried that they were becoming estranged from one another. Unlike any other time in their marriage, they were sniping and being irritable and mean to one another. We agreed that it might be helpful to consider inviting Peter to our sessions, but she was sceptical that he would attend.

I did eventually meet Peter on his own and, in the event, he came along quite willingly. In fact, he seemed quite grateful to be seeing me, but there was something hesitant and nervous in the way that he spoke. I asked him what it had been like since Sarah's diagnosis, and how he thought Sarah and he had been managing as a couple. He said that at first he had been terrified he would lose her, but admitted that he found her neediness and vulnerability irritating. He confessed that he had sometimes been nasty towards her, making snide comments that he knew would hurt her, but he didn't understand why, and had immediately regretted it.

As the session unfolded, it became clearer what a vulnerable man he was. He said he had had a difficult childhood in which his mother had suffered with 'manic depression'. His description made it clear that she was inconsistent in her care of him, as well as his younger sister. Sometimes his mother was emotionally engaged and responsive, and at other times she seemed strange and withdrawn. His father, incidentally, had left the family when Peter was four years old and had moved abroad, never to be seen or heard of again.

I asked him more about those early years of his life and he said that the first image that came to mind was seeing his mother lying in bed looking helpless and vulnerable, and that this used to make him feel something very similar. He went on to describe his troubled adolescence when he had become mixed up with a gang of teenagers that used to steal bicycles and get into trouble with the police. He met Sarah when he was 19, and his mother died the following year, but from then on his life had become more stable.

I gently put it to him that the relationship he had had with his mother seemed rather similar to what had recently happened with Sarah. From being something of a rock in his life, she was suddenly vulnerable. He was now expected to look after her but he didn't know what to do, and seemed to be frozen by his helplessness. He agreed that he could not bear the uncertainty that her cancer represented, and her lack of hair was a constant reminder that she was ill and how scared he felt at the idea of losing her. He said he felt angry towards Sarah's cancer, not Sarah of course, but he again admitted that he had been very short and distant with her.

From then on, I saw them as a couple and over the next few months they managed to develop a new understanding of their past, both individually and as a couple, culminating in this illness and what it meant to them both. As the sessions progressed, they became more engaged with each other, but also with me. Sarah no longer worried about the state of her body and the panic attacks ceased. They gradually developed a story that felt plausible to both of them and one that they could share: the story of where they had individually come from, their coming together as a couple, how they had made their own family, what they had been through together, how they could support one another better, and the things they needed to continue to work on, including "this bloody illness" as Peter described it. We agreed that they were still entitled to feel angry, but perhaps they could be angry about the cancer together and not with one another.

Relational distress

The psychology of relationships is exponentially more complex than that of the individual. But, as it is, a huge part of our lives is spent in relation to other people, and making sense of our relationships can therefore often be difficult. Our relationships can bring us intense pleasure but also painful anguish, and sometimes within the same relationship.

The couple remains the most popular form of adult relationship the world over. In the West it is often reified as the answer to all our problems if we can only meet that one person with whom we were destined to spend our life. That puts a lot of pressure on a relationship.

In reality, long-term relationships can be complicated and challenging. There are often underlying power imbalances, and partners may feel disillusioned by 'having to work at it' so much. People may feel trapped in relationships that they know are not good for them, or they hold relational expectations that are a poor fit with those of their partner. Some relationships are more emotionally intense than others, some are good, some are bad, and some are downright toxic.

From the very first patients with cancer I met, it was obvious that their relationships with their loved ones were often under immense strain. Parents were anxiously worried about their children's future welfare, domestic roles had been quickly reconfigured as family members adjusted their lives to support the patient and accommodate their treatment routines, dying patients sometimes emotionally withdrew from their loved ones in the misguided hope of sparing them later pain, and the relationship between patients and their partners sometimes became a source of tension when normal ways of operating with one another no longer seemed to work.

Time and again I found myself listening to middle-aged women telling me how disappointed they were with their male partners. They complained that while their husband was able to demonstrate their support in practical ways (perhaps taking on a greater share of domestic work, attending appointments, and so on), he rarely provided the emotional support that she was looking for. When she wanted to speak about what she was feeling, such as her fears for the future and her family, he appeared lost and unresponsive. At best he would either insist that she should be positive, thereby shutting her up, or he would simply keep himself at a silent distance. Not surprisingly, women often turned to other women for support: friends, mothers, and sisters. Men, by contrast, almost never turned to other men for support but seemed generally content with the support from their wives, mothers, daughters or sisters. When I looked into it, clinical research tended to back up my impressions.

Even more disturbing, it seemed that some men were actively needling and undermining their sick wives at the very time when their partners needed their support most. Peter was just one example. Women would often, usually guiltily, tell me how angry they felt that no one in the family seemed to be interested in what they were going through. And it was not hard to understand her outrage and disappointment after she had spent the past umpteen years thinking about and caring for the needs of everyone else in the family, whilst sacrificing many of her own aspirations. At the one time when she might have assumed that her husband and family would be there to support her, they were floundering. And whenever a member of the family *did* do something helpful for her, she felt guilty that she was no longer able to fulfil her normal role of caring for others. It seemed that many men were emotionally lost, and most women, having been locked into their role as universal family carer, were discovering how little they knew about their own needs.

Initially I was mystified by how my patients' husbands could be so callous and uncaring when their wives were clearly tortured with fear and despair, and so obviously in need of their support. I began to invite men to my consulting room, and increasingly saw partners together as couples. Two things seemed to be going on.

The first was that men very often seemed to lack the vocabulary to describe their emotions and relationships (*see Gender in Chapter 9*). He seemed unable to engage in a meaningful conversation with his partner about the issues at stake, let alone what was happening in their relationship. He appeared to be quickly lost for words and, if pressed for them, would become defensive, even hostile towards her. He experienced her as demanding and intrusive, and he felt criticised, backed into a corner in what seemed like an interrogation.

The second was that the traditional roles that the couple had previously adopted had been upended. No longer was the woman the source of everyone's support in the family and, just like Peter, it seemed that most men did not like to be reminded of their unconscious dependency on their partner. Her pleas to be listened to irritated him, so he needled her back. It was not that he did not care, but he felt impotent in his attempts to support her and was cross and guilty at feeling deprived of her attention and support.

Hannah and Joy

It began with a rather vague phone referral from the hospice. Could I help out with a family conflict? A 24-year-old woman was dying of an unknown primary tumour, always a particularly distressing situation. It was in the days before the hospice had a psychologist of their own, and before I had a colleague of my own. So I made a detour on my way home that evening and met with the medical staff as they were about to go home.

The patient was Hannah, a geography student. She was a local girl attending the local university. I was told that it was too late for further oncology tests or treatments; she was dying, so the hospice staff were expecting to look after her during her final days. However, the relationship between her partner and her parents had broken down. Both saw themselves as Hannah's primary caregivers, and relations between them had become tense and brittle. I noted with interest that even the medical staff seemed conflicted about the situation and what should be done.

I walked round to Hannah's room. Despite the morphine, she was still fairly lucid and told me she was comfortable, but she went on to say quite bluntly that her 'organs were packing up'. She told me that a year ago, entering her third year at university, she had moved into her first flat with her first girlfriend Joy. Her parents were fine about the arrangement and seemed to accept Joy into their lives. That is until Hannah was diagnosed two months ago. Immediately they wanted her back home so they could look after her, but Hannah had made it clear that she wanted to stay with Joy. Once at the hospice, however, the parents had put their foot down and asked the staff that Joy not be allowed to visit. The medical team had explained that the patient's wishes must take precedence, but her parents were making it difficult for everyone. Hannah knew that she only had weeks or less and was distraught that her parents were behaving so unreasonably.

So I asked if she thought if it would be a good idea if I met her parents first, and then maybe Joy and her together. She said this would be fine.

During my lunchbreak the next day I met her parents. They were warm, lovely people but they were heartbroken. They told me that their only other child, Hannah's much older brother, lived in Canada but had not spoken to them for years. They had contacted him but he had made it clear that he would not be coming back for Hannah's funeral. Their distress was palpable. I asked about Joy and they were quick to protest that they didn't mind Joy being involved. Of course Joy should be involved in Hannah's support, but 'we are her parents' was how they saw it.

As they talked, it seemed that they had been feeling left out by Hannah and Joy, almost as if Hannah now wanted them out of the picture. This was mostly articulated by Hannah's father who spoke in a rather stiff formal way. Her mother looked at him, nodding. I said that I imagined that all of them were struggling with appalling distress and how sorry I was. I can't remember quite how I said it, but I do remember how terribly sad it was in that room. At this they both cried, and then Hannah's mother started talking about her beloved daughter and, amidst her tears, the father occasionally chipped in.

At the end of the meeting they were still weeping, but with arms round one another, and when I saw them again at the hospice the next morning, Hannah's mother said that they had both found our meeting helpful because it had somehow brought her and her husband closer together. They were now able to talk more openly with one another about their terrible anguish. It was as if they both felt that their unspeakable pain had been heard, first by me and then one another. They agreed for me to speak openly with Hannah and Joy about what we had discussed.

A few minutes later I phoned Joy and asked when she was likely to be at the hospice. I met with both young women an hour or two later, around lunchtime. Hannah and Joy were clearly very much in love and, despite everything, they were still making little jokes with one another. I told them about my meeting with Hannah's parents and what they had said. They responded as one, saying that they had always wanted Hannah's mum and dad to be there. They just felt that her parents didn't seem to want Joy to be around, and they seemed to snub her whenever they came into contact. There seemed to me to be a fair degree of mind-reading going on.

We carried on talking for another few minutes but Hannah was getting tired, so before I left we agreed a time when we could all meet with Hannah's parents. That evening I stopped by the hospice again on my way home. I walked into Hannah's room with her parents. Hannah's parents sat to her left and Joy was already seated to her right. There were no other chairs to be had, so I stood at the end of the bed facing Hannah. It was tense at first. They all looked at me to start the meeting which I did by summarising all that I had heard. When I had finished, I invited Hannah to speak first, and then Joy. And then they all spoke, and I was soon able to withdraw.

•————•

Relational therapy

When I was working as a couple therapist I always tried to remember that I was seeing only a snapshot of the relationship at a particular moment. While my time with the couple might be revealing, it is the complexity of change that has occurred between these two people in the time they have known one another and what they now think about that, that is really interesting. How has their history, both individually and as a couple, informed the present relationship and its challenges, and what do they now wish for their relationship?

Relationships are often in conflict because people's different assumptive worlds do not easily mesh. Different expectations, different beliefs, different values. Once that is understood, the issue of blame becomes irrelevant. In couple counselling I am more interested in the assumptions both partners are bringing to the relationship, assumptions that may well be born from their attachment history.

We saw in *Chapter 6* that when a child has been exposed to inconsistent care they are more likely to be anxious and clingy, unsure whether their secure base will be there for them or not. If these relational models persist into adulthood, as they had for Peter, the individual is likely to continue to be unsure of themselves, and dependent and insecure about their relationships. Even so, these 'dynamics' can be altered in time with insight, practice, and perseverance.

If the caregiver is indifferent and unresponsive to the child's needs, the child may well show little emotion when separated, and is more likely to prefer a detached distance from an adult partner. On the other hand, when a caregiver is frightening, abusive, or absent for long periods, the child is more likely to grow up with more disorganized assumptions about relationships, becoming more wary about them in general, and perhaps needing to test the fidelity of the relationships they find themselves in. Too much testing of course can result in the very thing that one fears: the new partner eventually has had enough and withdraws.

The combinations are infinite, but the evidence does seem to indicate that if children are securely attached to consistent, caring, parental figures who are able to mentalise their experiences, they are more likely to grow up to expect that other people will be responsive and caring too, and they are more likely to behave this way themselves.

When I am with a couple, of course I am thinking about each of the two partners, how they are feeling, and how they each understand what is going on between them as a couple. But I am also trying to notice how they work together (often as parents), and what sort of joint relationship they have managed to forge and sustain. What is the system they have worked out for themselves, the reciprocal roles they each inhabit? How do the partners' attachment histories knit with one another and what is the bigger whole? What is working, and what is not? Whose needs are being met and whose are not, and what are these needs? What is shared, and what is not? Who has power and control, and in what areas? What is happening in that space between the two people I am meeting? Whatever comes up.

I tend to imagine the relationship almost as if it is a living organism that exists in the space between the two partners. This imaginary thing, this relationship, is fed and kept alive by the verbal and physical communication between the partners. It takes effort, communication, and shared reflection to build a creative relationship that is receptive and responsive to one other's needs. Therein lies my job as a therapist.

Of course, relationships exist within a social world of beliefs, ideologies and customs, and these inevitably shape the way that men and women approach couple relationships. In most of the world men still have far more privilege, power and opportunity than women, and this power difference naturally leads to tension between the sexes.

Couple relationships can have long, complicated and rich emotional histories, but equally, what was once appreciated about the other person becomes 'normal' and part of the background. Earlier, in the chapter on memory, we saw that our minds are particularly good at storing procedural memory, remembering a sequence of ideas or behaviours until they have become automatic. People quickly take for granted what has become familiar, and unfortunately in a relationship that can easily apply to one another. There are fewer expressions of joy about being in the relationship than there were at its start, and soon we become preoccupied with what irritates us about our partner, rather than what we still value about them. Partners become reluctant to show affection, or concern, and rarely celebrate the relationship by reminding one another of what still works well between them as a couple.

When I am working with couples, I sometimes find myself introducing terms and ideas about couple relationships and associated emotions, words that I occasionally notice the couple deploying later as they understand and describe what has, and is, happening within their relationship. It is as if I am unwittingly teaching them, more often the man, a set of conceptual tools, an emotional vocabulary, with which to make sense of the relationship, or, if you prefer, to model it.

For some couples the biggest challenge is something that sounds deceptively easy. It is simply allowing the other person to be the person they happen to be, rather than wishing that they were someone else, or some idealised fantasy of who we might prefer them to be. This can be far harder than it sounds. It does not mean tolerating an abusive or controlling partner of course, but it may mean finding the compassion to see the other person as someone with their own feelings, their own relational history, and their own assumptive world. In other words, the perfect must not become the enemy of the good enough.

Couple relationships sometimes become isolated systems, joined at the hip, cut off from the stimulation of the world around them. Both partners may have withdrawn into the safety of the couple relationship itself but, like the person with an agoraphobic fear of the outside world, the relationship becomes not merely a haven but a bastion and sometimes a prison, with both partners becoming ever more fearful of the outside world and possible change. Closed systems soon become stale and uncreative, with little to communicate and little to keep them alive. It is sad to see a couple share a meal together with barely a word to say to one another.

Reflexivity enables systems to learn, so it obviously helps if couples make the time for it. Many of the couples I have met have simply not talked about their relationship, or the reciprocal roles they have unwittingly adopted in relation to one another. There has been little sense of a shared narrative, a joined-up understanding of what has happened thus far in their lives together, nor any discussion of common aspirations.

As we have seen, expectations and assumptions play a huge part in how we feel. If we have unrealistic idealised expectations of our partners, we are likely to feel disappointed. If we can allow them to be the people they happen to be, rather the person we would ideally wish them to be, this in itself can sometimes be enough to remove a dynamic in the relationship that may have inadvertently been creating our misgivings in the first place. Rather than wanting our partners to be someone other than the person they are, we might instead think about what we can do to support them better to be the person *they* wish to be, while working on our own shortcomings within the relationship. Reflexivity is a strength provided it is given exercise.

Telling Stories

If you had seen a road traffic accident earlier today, there is a good chance that by now you will have told someone else about what you saw, and perhaps what you felt. When something very unusual happens, people are confronted with information that violates their expectations, and their instinctive reaction is to tell someone. But it is the *telling* of the story that is most helpful.

People tell one another stories all the time: what they did, what they heard, what they saw, what they plan to do, what they feel, what they think, what they imagine. Describing what has happened is helpful because it coheres our experiences into meaningful wholes, such as words and ideas, that are integrated with what the person already understands about the world.

Turning experiences into words, whether spoken or written, enables people to make stories about their lives and helps them congeal otherwise nebulous experiences into more coherent trains of thought and identifiable ideas. When we talk out loud, whether to ourselves or someone else, we often get to hear what we actually think and feel. And sometimes we don't even need to talk, we just need the time to think, to formulate our own understanding, on our own. Words help to anchor experience by disentangling rational thought from fantasy. Talking therapies are a chance for people to reflect on their experiences and to examine their assumptions.

However we do it (speaking, thinking, writing, creating), turning things into words and ideas helps to give shape to our experiences. It enables us to find other ways to frame the events of our lives. Merely talking or writing about our experiences, and hearing our own story reflected back to us by the therapist or by the words on the page, may help us to question and perhaps even change some of the assumptions that we had taken for granted.

The originator of Attachment Theory, John Bowlby, was alluding to similar ideas when he advocated these two tasks of therapy:

- Encourage patients to consider how their current expectations, perceptions, feelings and actions may be a product of events and situations encountered earlier in life.

- Enable patients to see that the models they hold about themselves and others may not be appropriate or justified in the current circumstances. Enable them to consider alternatives more in line with their aspirations and values.

Bowlby pointed out that people often become stuck with assumptions that were once useful, and perhaps even accurate in their time, but are no longer fit for purpose. In the telling and the hearing of stories, the client and the therapist are able to construct a new narrative of the client's life, a version of the past and present that perhaps contains more understanding and compassion. Such reflection allows us to learn from experience, draw conclusions, reconsider priorities, and adjust our mental models accordingly.

Doing therapy

As I hope is clear by now, psychological therapists do not start out with the question of what is *wrong* with the client. This, as we have seen, would be the traditional medical approach. Instead, we are curious about *what has happened* in the client's life that has resulted in their emotional distress. We are interested in the client's emotions and feelings, the problems they face, their relationships with other people, their stories, their understanding of what has happened to them in their life, the habits they have formed, the conclusions they have reached, the stresses they face, the power of others to which they may be subjected, the assumptions they are making, and the values and aspirations they hold. The wider context.

We aim to achieve this complex understanding collaboratively, so that when the client feels stuck and unable to see connections, I am sometimes able to suggest a way forward, or help the client reflect on how they are looking at something. In the very telling of their story they are constructing a new version of it.

If my client's thinking seems to be saturated by their problems, I try to help them remember and recognise their strengths, and what may be working well for them. Often their compassion for other people simply does not extend to themselves. Most people are also remarkably resilient, resourceful, and long-suffering, but sometimes they need to be reminded of this. Together we might consider what small steps they could take towards resolving or mitigating whatever they are dealing with. I therefore usually invite the client to tell me not only about what has been hard in their lives, but also what has perhaps gone well. What has sustained them and what sustains them now?

Clinical psychologist Jack Chalkley, describing the role of therapists, says that *"listening to someone else's account of what troubles them, depends in part on how one views the sheer complexity of it, its highly charged, personal, idiosyncratic, particularised, even disorganised nature, and especially on whether despite all this one feels one can in some way bring constructive order to it."* [14]

One way to bring constructive order to the complexity of patients' difficulties is to try to understand with them what they have concluded and understood based on their past experiences. What models and assumptions are they drawing on as they tell me about their troubles? Clients themselves often do not realise the conclusions they have reached, even when their lives may have been profoundly shaped by them. But by reflecting, contextualising and sometimes reframing their experiences, we can begin to formulate a new understanding, often accompanied by new goals and aspirations.

Of course, it is impossible to hear someone else's story without imposing one's own models and judgments, so therapists must work

---

[14] **Chalkley J.** (2015) *The Content of Psychological Distress: Addressing complex personal experience.* London: Palgrave (p.10)

hard to be as compassionate, dispassionate, and non-judgmental as they can. They inevitably make sense of their patients' distress through the prism of their own mental models of the world, though ideally their training has provided them with a somewhat broader understanding of human behaviour. Critically, we must allow our client to be the person they happen to be, respect their agency, and never imagine that we know what is right for them in the context of their lives, even when we think we know. Therapists therefore need to reflect on whether they might subtly and unconsciously be influencing the client, or perhaps teaching them lessons that they themselves most need to learn.

Therapists try to understand the client's frame of reference, intuiting the emotions that they are feeling and the assumptions they are using. This is commonly referred to as empathy. The aim is to use this understanding to help the client think about their situation in different ways, name their feelings, and consider their cause, and perhaps even reflect on their current needs and aspirations. After each appointment, I myself try to find the words to reflect on what happened in the session, and in doing so reformulate my own understanding of it. In these clinical notes I also try to capture the spirit or tone of the session so that both can be drawn upon it as an aide memoire for future sessions.

As a therapist allied to medicine, it can often be helpful to consider what we represent for our clients, and the relationship we are having with them, in the context of everything else that is happening in their lives. In psychodynamic terms, this is known as **transference**: what the patient feels towards their therapist. Consequently, competent therapists reflect on the quality and tone of their interactions. Where do these infrequent sessions sit in the client's life? How does the client relate to us and how might this inform our understanding of their needs and their attachment history?

Attachment Theory predicts that in situations of threat and uncertainty, such as serious illness in the family, people unconsciously seek out figures of benign authority and safety, people who will help contain our fears, our rage and our loss. Remember what young Isabel did in *Chapter 6* when she was hit on the head by a bucket in the sandpit? Therapists attempt to assuage this need for containment. Accordingly, patients arrive in my consulting room hoping to meet someone who will be able to hear their distress without judgment or fear. So, rather like a parent comforting a distressed child in their arms, my role is to provide a calm strength, and a benign and trustworthy container into which they can pour their anguish.

As a therapist, I try to listen very actively to my clients' words and observe their face, tone and posture. I provide them with my full attention. But in order for me to understand their feelings, I need to mentally model their experience. Consequently, some part of me recognises something in my own internal body state that is mirroring a feeling that the client is experiencing in their body state (via my so-called mirror neurons). This intuitive sensibility draws on unconscious, often inchoate associations, but with practice it can be refined.

The therapist's feelings in relation to their patient/client is known as **counter-transference**. The therapist's own emotions and feelings are a useful and important source of information for the therapist in 'reading' and understanding the patient. Consequently, while I monitor the patient's emotional responses as they tell me their concerns, I am also trying to track my own, so that I can more easily intuit what the client is feeling.

Finally, I am almost always intensely engaged with what my patient is talking about, so when I feel my attention starting to drift, or feel that I am becoming bored in a therapy session, and it is very rare that I do, I have learned to be curious about why this is happening. When this does occur, I may well find myself saying "I wonder if there is perhaps something that we are not talking about that you feel we should be talking about." Clients are usually surprised by this question, but they often quickly acknowledge that they have been actively avoiding something that has indeed been playing on their mind or has been difficult to talk about.

On rare occasions I have found myself becoming irritated in the session. So I quickly have to think about where this is coming from.

Is there something passive-aggressive going on in the room? Am I reacting to something that I myself might feel sensitive about?

Now and again, I meet someone who makes me feel put to the test. I become aware of my own raised anxiety, as I initially did with Nell, and I have to consider whether it is coming from the client. And I try to think about whether there is anything within me or my own life that may be making me feel this. I have to consider, for example, whether my client is worried that I might judge them to be not good enough in some way, or perhaps they may be unconsciously testing out whether I will abandon them, as others have done so often in the past. So when a client elicits this sense of self-doubt in me, I wonder whether perhaps it is they who are carrying this very burden, and perhaps the need to explore that..

But while therapists have to be open to the feelings and beliefs of their clients, they also have to be careful not to draw conclusions entirely on the basis of what they themselves feel, or come to a viewpoint without good evidence. We must remain reflective, responsive and willing to change our assumptions about the people we meet. Our supportive neutrality is there to provide a safe and containing relationship in which our clients can reflect on their experiences and assumptions. Our role is to remain curious, supportive, and authentic.

The vast majority of my patients over the past 30 years have been people with cancer, so you may well imagine that my patients and I spend a lot of our time together talking about death. Well, we do a bit of course, but most of the time we talk about living, and a lot of that has to do with the relationships they have had, or are currently having with other people. We talk about what it really means to them to be alive, and what in the end is valuable and important to them. People naturally fear their death, and many of the patients I have worked with have died, but in their struggle with their mortality most people seem to learn a great deal about themselves and the nature of their lives. So we focus on living life, yet also making sense of the life that has been lived.

Of course, if a therapist is to contain the powerful emotions of their clients day after day they must also remember to look after themselves, something that I have not always done well. Here is another diary entry:

24ᵗʰ September 2000

I can't quite believe what just happened. Harriet is out, the children are asleep, and I am otherwise alone at home. Sitting here at the computer screen, writing down my thoughts from the day, I found myself thinking about my patient Joni, and the fact that she told me this afternoon that she has brain mets [metastases]. I feel so sorry for her. Such a lovely person.

Anyway, I began to think about how we therapists may recognise our patients' experiences and try to understand them, but there is this level at which, no matter how brilliant we may think we are at empathy and so forth, we simply can't reach in and fully understand. There is a reaching-inside-someone quality about empathy, a sort of excavation of their experience, but it's just never the same as what they themselves are actually experiencing. It can't be.

Well, as I was thinking about all this and poor Joni, I found myself starting to cry… I mean sobbing, a real outpouring of emotion. I'd had a glass of wine and that had probably loosened me up. And after a while I realised it wasn't just Joni that I was crying about, but for all the distress I have been listening to over the years. Maybe it was tears of self-pity, I don't know. But I suppose it felt cathartic. It is so unfamiliar for me to cry like this. It went on for about five or six minutes, quite a long time while it's happening. It was a mixture of emotional release, wonder at what was happening, and later a sense of relief, I suppose, that I am still able to cry like this, along with a mild sense of lightness and gratitude for the life that I have, and that we are all currently well.

●————————————●

Further Reading

Albee E. (1962) *Who's Afraid of Virginia Woolf?* New York: Atheneum Books

Beck A. (1967) *Depression: Clinical, Experimental, and Theoretical Aspects.* New York: Harper and Row

Bowlby J. (1971) *Attachment and Loss.* London: Hogarth Press

Bowlby J. (1978) *A Secure Base. Clinical Applications of Attachment Theory.* London: Routledge

Brennan J. (2000) Changing tack: the importance of the therapeutic relationship. *Primary Care and Cancer*, 20, 31-34

Brennan J. (2001) Adjustment to cancer – coping or psychosocial transition? *Psycho-Oncology*, 10, 1-18

Brennan J. (2004) *Cancer in Context – A practical guide to supportive care.* Oxford: Oxford University Press

Brody D, Gu Q. (2020) Antidepressant Use Among Adults: United States, 2015-2018 *NCHS Data Brief*, No. 377. Hyattsville, MD: National Center for Health Statistics

Chalkley J. (2015) *The Content of Psychological Distress – Addressing complex personal experience.* London: Palgrave

Cuijpers P, van Straten A, Andersson G, van Oppen P. (2008). Psychotherapy for depression in adults: A meta-analysis of comparative outcome studies. *Journal of Consulting and Clinical Psychology*, 76, 909-922. doi.org/10.1037/a0013075

De Timary P, Heenen-Wolff S, Philippot P. (2011) The question of "representation" in the psychoanalytical and cognitive-behavioral approaches. Some theoretical aspects and therapy

considerations. *Frontiers in Psychology*, 2:
doi.org/10.3389/fpsyg.2011.00071

Fairbairn W. (1952) *Psychological Studies of the Personality.*
London: Routledge & Kegan Paul

Fonagy P, Target M. (1997) Attachment and reflective function:
Their role in self-organization. *Development and
psychopathology*, 9, 679-700

Fonagy P, Bateman A, Bateman A. (2011) The widening scope
of mentalizing: A discussion. *Psychology and
Psychotherapy: Theory, Research and Practice*, 84, 98-110

Freud S. (1971) *New Introductory Lectures on Psychoanalysis.*
(Pelican Freud Library, Vol. 2) Harmondsworth: Penguin.
Originally published in 1933

Galanti G. (1991) *Caring for Patients from Different Cultures:
Case Studies from American Hospitals.* Philadelphia:
University of Pennsylvania Press

Gottman J. (1994). *Why Marriages Succeed or Fail.* New York:
Simon & Schuster

Healy D. (1998) Gloomy days and sunshine pills. *Openmind*,
90, 8-9.

Holmes J. (1998) Narrative in psychotherapy. In Greenhalgh T,
Hurwitz B. (Eds.) *Narrative Based Medicine: Dialogue and
Discourse in Clinical Practice.* London: BMJ Books.

Horwitz A, Wakefield J. (2007) *The Loss of Sadness: How
psychiatry transformed normal sadness into depressive
disorder.* New York: Oxford University Press

Johnstone L, Boyle M. (2018). *The Power Threat Meaning
Framework: Towards the identification of patterns in
emotional distress, unusual experiences and troubled or
troubling behaviour, as an alternative to functional
psychiatric diagnosis.* Leicester: British Psychological
Society.

Klein M. (1975) *Love, Guilt and Reparation and Other Works
1921-1945.* New York: The Free Press

Lecours S, Sanlian N, Bouchard M. (2017) Assessing verbal elaboration of affect in clinical interviews: Exploring sex differences. *Bulletin of the Menninger Clinic*, 71(3), 227–247

Lilienfeld S, Schwartz S, Meca A, Sauvigné K, Satel S. (2015). Neuro-centrism: Implications for psychotherapy practice and research. *The Behavioural Therapist*, 38, 173-181

Mirowsky J, Ross C. (1989) *Social Causes of Psychological Distress.* New York: Aldine de Gruyter

Moncrieff, J. (2007) Diagnosis and drug treatment. *The Psychologist*, 20 (5), 296-297

Parkes CM. (1971) Psycho-social transitions: a field for study. *Social Science and Medicine*, 5, 101-115

Pennebaker J. (Ed.) (1995) *Emotion, Disclosure and Health.* Washington: American Psychological Association

Pilgrim D. (2019) Philosophy of science and clinical psychology. *Clinical Psychology Forum*, 318, 2

Pistrang N, Barker C. (1995). The partner relationship in psychological response to breast cancer. *Social Science and Medicine*, 40, 789-797

Public Health England (2019) *Prescribed Medicines Review: Report.* tinyurl.com/y5hqfld4

Russell R, van den Broek P. (1992) Changing narrative schemas in psychotherapy. *Psychotherapy*, 29, 344-354

Shafir T. (2016) Using movement to regulate emotion: neurophysiological findings and their application in psychotherapy. *Frontiers in Psychology*, 7: doi.org/10.3389/fpsyg.2016.01451

Stein H. (1985) Whatever happened to countertransference? The subjective in medicine. In Stein H, Apprey M. (Eds.) *Context and Dynamics in Clinical Knowledge.* Charlottesville: University of Virginia Press.

Stiles W, Shapiro D, Elliott R. (1986). Are all psychotherapies equivalent? *American Psychologist*, 41, 165–180

Stroebe M, Schut H. (1999) The dual process model of coping with bereavement: Rationale and description. *Death Studies*, 23, 197-224

Wallston B, Alagna S, DeVellis B, DeVellis R. (1983) Social support and physical health. *Health Psychology*, 2, 367-391

Chapter 9

Cultural Storage

Social connection
Conformity and obedience
Simplifying the world
Superstition
Religious beliefs
Gender
Men-women relationships
Progress

"The Ede of Krong Buk in Dak Lak believe a baby has a weak soul that could be taken by evil spirits. The ritual master invokes spirits to protect the baby and give her good health. A young rooster is sacrificed for a boy. Offerings for boys include working tools such as a crossbow, a jungle knife and a fishnet. A young chicken is sacrificed for girls and the offerings include women's tools such as a weaving loom, a basket and a mortar and pestle. The ritual master asks that the girl excel in weaving and household tasks and for the boys to excel in hunting and farm work."
Sign in the Vietnam Museum of Ethnology, Hanoi (January 2012)

This enquiry into the mind began with the archaeological and evolutionary evidence that modern human minds are extraordinarily recent within the natural history of our planet. We have since travelled far, from planetary physics through the evolution of life, to human beings with clever modern brains that are capable of sustaining a mind, a species that can learn, teach, and build things with other people. The world that we know today has been built over historical and prehistorical time all the way back to the dawn of modern thinking.

With Behavioural Modernity came the start of a slow accumulation of artefacts, buildings, customs, beliefs, institutions, infrastructure... all of which one might think of as **cultural storage**. Archaeologists refer to this as symbolic storage, whereby objects carry meaning beyond their functional use. For example, beads, figurines, cave paintings, burial mounds, and so on, indicate the development of complex societies with structured ways of transmitting and preserving knowledge across generations. These objects also provide evidence of the cognitive abilities of these early humans and their capacity for abstract thought, communication, and cultural expression.

Imagine a person 2000 years in the future finding a simple ballpoint pen and working out what it once was once used for. The material world of cars, buildings, schools, and so on, carries within each object, symbolic meanings of different kinds, just as the pen would convey information about the people who had once had use for such an object and the world they must have inhabited. But cultural storage is not limited to objects, buildings and institutions. It is embodied in the way we commonly think and behave as a species.

It doesn't matter whether you are an old farmer eking out a living in southern Spain, or a mother of four in rural Zimbabwe, or an urban Chinese factory worker, or an executive running a huge corporation in California, your life is fashioned and framed by the social and cultural world around you. It cannot be otherwise.

Every person inhabits a different social world, a different combination of family, friends, community, society, nation, ethnic and religious culture, and so on. In other words, each person is exposed to a unique aggregate of cultural information and ideas. Everyone's autobiographical history occurs in a certain period of historical time, in certain places, within a particular culture. I am sure you get the idea. Each person's software is unique. This of course is just another way of saying that every person's mental representation of the world is a unique combination of assumptions drawn from their culture, their experiences, and their innate propensities. It results in their own world view, their own assumptive world.

So little wonder that human beings sometimes find it hard to agree with one another. The formidable complexity of the human-made world has given rise to a similar diversity of perspective. Every person is entitled to their own perspective, their own understanding, their own beliefs, this being the most basic of human rights.

This book's journey from physics, through biology, psychology to the social world is one of increasing complexity and increasing conjecture. Rutherford may have been a fundamentalist, but he did have a point. Any commentary on human culture inevitably runs the risk that other people will despise the author's views as profane and misguided. And that danger is there for you and me too, as we now venture into that world. However, I hope that by this point there are some things we can agree upon.

If you have travelled with me this far I hope that we can agree that minds emerge from brains that have unusually big frontal lobes, sitting at the front of an impressively large neocortex (the outer folds of the brain). We humans possess a powerful working-memory that enables us to mentally represent and model the world and to communicate our thoughts and ideas to other people in sophisticated ways using language. Yet this modern way of thinking only began about 50,000 years ago, the last seven and a half minutes of 31st December, according to the LUCA scale (*see page 31*)

Archaeologists continue to reconstruct a plausible narrative of these past fifty millennia, but *recorded* history only represents the last ten per cent of it, or thereabouts. For example, the Great Pyramid at Giza in Egypt was built about 2560 BCE, or 4,580 years ago, over a twenty-year period. It was built as a tomb for the Egyptian pharaoh Khufu (often Hellenized as "Cheops"). The Great

Pyramid, incidentally, remained the tallest human-made structure in the world for the next 3,800 years, until Lincoln Cathedral in England was completed in 1311.

The earliest writing (i.e. external symbolic storage) is thought to have originated in Mesopotamia (modern-day Iraq and Syria) at roughly the same time as the pyramids were built, just over 5000 years ago, probably as a method for keeping accounts for trading. Writing enabled people to *record* complex ideas and communicate them over time, allowing cultural knowledge to accumulate far more rapidly than oral history. And it was soon recognised to be far more durable and reliable than human memory.

The complexity of the social world that we have since created for ourselves, and must now negotiate, has grown exponentially since this dawn of modern minds. The accumulation of human knowledge began very slowly and it took until the Bronze Age, less than five thousand years ago, for people to work out how to smelt copper and tin to produce bronze. It took another thousand years or more for us to work out how to do the same with iron. It is 600 years since Gutenberg made the first printing press, only 200 hundred years since a steam train began operating commercially, and less than 150 years since people began driving cars. And not even twenty years since we all had smart phones.

This exponential speed of change has culminated in our digitally communicating world, now with Artificial Intelligence to clarify and muddy the waters. Our technological brilliance is taking humanity on a massive journey into the unknown, a social experiment that involves the entire population of the world, even though no one signed a consent form.

Cultural diversity amongst the people of the world only adds to that complexity, albeit it is often of a fairly superficial nature. Every face and body is unique, we have different languages, different ways of speaking; we dress and present ourselves differently, we have different levels of education, skin colours, religions, customs, ethnicities, communities, families and relationships. But underneath this surface diversity there is actually far more that we have in common than divides us. We are genetically homogenous as a species, our brains and bodies work broadly the same way among everyone, and we all have the same primary emotions.

So, like the mind, human culture is not just immensely complex, it is never fixed for long and is always changing. As a species we may have superior intelligence, but we mostly manage the complexity of everyday life by simplifying it into habits, routines, beliefs, rituals, customs, and taken-for-granted assumptions.

These past 50,000 years have left many legacies within the social world that we all share today: cheat-detection, compassion, competition, conformity, obedience, superstition, gender relations, religious beliefs, and much more. So we will start with a brief look at some of the more common aspects of what is known as social psychology. Tadpoles come into the world expecting water, we humans come into the world expecting human culture and other people.

So yes, it is now time to emerge from the shady woods of biology and individual minds, and walk out into the dazzling and convoluted ecosphere of other people.

Humans are quintessentially a social species, something that Aristotle (385-323 BCE) observed nearly two and a half thousand years ago. Without other humans around us, our intelligence and reasoning ability would be little more than your average chimp. Other animals may be able to learn, but we can teach. Not just that, but we are the only species that has ever developed moral reasoning and the rule of law, and the only species that can override its primitive impulses and exercise moral responsibility for the benefit of other people, even if that just means being kind, decent, and sticking to the local laws.

Throughout our lives therefore we are attuned and reactive to the expectations and beliefs of other people, and this sensibility has helped forge each of us into the person we are today, with all the assumptions that we have managed to pick up and develop along the way. The family and social milieu in which we have lived during our life may have led us to be arrogant, lazy, apathetic, and selfish. Or perhaps we are attentive, kind, respectful and generous. Or any combination of all of these and many more adjectives. The point is that our qualities are not merely the result of our genes but also what we have learned from our lives thus far.

Our temperament and many of our sensibilities will have been shaped by genetic predispositions but, as we have said, the *content* of our minds, the assumptions and models we hold, are derived from the customs we have individually grown up with, and the extent to which we have tried to conform to, or subvert them. This 'content' also includes the idiosyncratic personal experiences we have had, the people we happen to have known, and what we have learned from these relationships with other people.

Thanks to our long childhoods, human minds are not at all like tadpole 'minds'. Instead, they are cognitive and computational, and built to make sense and meaning out of lived experience. Being able to model our experiences using mental symbols enables each of us to construct our own reality. The essential *function* of the mind therefore is to model the world. But the main *content* of these mental models involves the social world of other people and the vast complicated landscape of human culture. It is easier to unravel this complexity a little if we stand back and take a natural history perspective.

Social connection

Like other social mammals, human genes enable our brains to make the most of social and physical environments so as to improve our chances of passing on our genes to the next generation. In humans, this especially involves building and maintaining relationships with other people.

Most evolutionary psychologists believe that the clever brains of modern humans enabled people to outwit and out-scheme one another, and that the slightly cleverer brains of our ancestors enabled them to survive and woo members of the other sex. In order to survive as an early human on the African savannah, you didn't need to defeat the lion if you were attacked by one, you only had to outrun other humans. And this was also true in the cognitive arms race. Dominance and survival in the wild or in the city is not as much about outwitting other species, so much as outwitting and taking advantage of one's own. In either case the results can be brutal.

Hearing, seeing, and to a much lesser extent touching, are the perceptual systems most commonly involved in human communication, and much of it is non-verbal, such as smiling, frowning and laughter. The white area of human eyes, known as the sclera, is three times larger than our primate ancestors and enables us to follow the path of another person's gaze (and for them to follow ours). It has also long been noticed that a person's level of emotional arousal slightly alters the aperture of their eyes. If we look at someone we love, our pupils dilate. So, in Victorian times, tincture of belladonna, or deadly nightshade, was used by women to enlarge their pupils to make them appear more loving and lovable.

As a social primate there is a clear advantage in being finely attuned to the social world around us. Minds not only emerged from clever human brains because they enabled humans to trade, collaborate and solve practical problems, but because successive generations were better able to 'read' (mentalise) and outsmart one another, thereby gaining sexual partners and social power. Happily, empathy and compassion are benign off-shoots. It is little wonder that new-born babies can almost immediately recognise human faces, and it is no accident that the human perceptual system is unusually weighted towards processing audio-visual information, in contrast to most other animals, which rely more upon smell and taste. People go on developing that acuity in detecting subtle changes in other people's faces and voices throughout their lives.

But it is not only our visual sense that is attuned to the social world. Studies have shown that people laugh differently when they are with friends than when they are with strangers, and other people can tell the difference, regardless of where in the world they come from. So, just listening to other people's laughter can tell us something about them.

Humans not only have a sophisticated capacity for outwitting and deceiving one another, they also have the capacity to detect this in others. Advanced communication and co-operation could not have evolved in our species, or be sustained in a social group, unless the participants had the brain capacity to detect individuals who cheat. As soon as humans were able to develop trading relationships with one another, they soon learned to spot cheaters, so that thereafter they could be excluded from further trade. In fact we humans are particularly aroused by feelings of injustice and unfairness, and the anger underlying these social emotions tends to remain dogged and persistent. Social insects, like ants and bees, by contrast, live in extremely organised societies in which survival depends upon the entire society functioning in prescribed ways.

Like the peacock and his tail, humans are out to impress, but like the fox they can also be crafty about it, so people are often excellent at detecting a fake smile from a genuine one. Euripides (480-406 BCE) astutely observed that *'Man's most valuable attribute is a shrewd sense of what not to believe'*. Otherwise known as our 'bullshit detector', we have virtual antennae for spotting fraudulence in another person's appearance or behaviour. We can quickly sense from the other person's demeanour and words that they are not to be trusted or are hiding something. It obviously helps if we can learn to trust these unconscious 'gut feelings' about other people.

Experiments have shown that this capacity to detect a cheat is not even something that has to be learned; it can be demonstrated in contexts that people have never come across before. By the age of three, children have developed a sense of trust and fairness and will not only remember who they previously shared their toys with, but are more likely to ask the other child to reciprocate and share their toys with them. Trust and cooperation are the essential alter-ego of cheat-detection; by being able to recognise one, we learn to recognise the other.

Some degree of mentalising is essential for social cohesion and trust, but it is not limited to humans. Ethological research has shown that chimps, elephants and dolphins all appear to be capable of adopting the perspective of another member of their species, albeit usually a family member. Only human social exchanges are full of glib tokens of false empathy and concern – 'Have a nice day' – but of course these simple customs lubricate what might otherwise lead to ambiguous and awkward encounters between strangers.

When we employ someone to come into our house, take our bike to be mended, or we buy something, we trust the other person to keep their end of the bargain. These non-intimate interactions are important in our daily lives, but it is our intimate interactions that really count because we obviously have a far greater investment in the people we are closest to. Our survival may even depend on these relationships. In intimate human interactions, mutual trust and dependency take on a whole new meaning, which is why the words we use in these contexts are so much more important. But even without words it takes only a facial expression, eye contact, or a hand gesture for us to know we have made an authentic connection with someone else.

Compassion towards someone we do not know personally is a mark of our humanity; it is what anthropologists call altruism. It probably developed among modern humans alongside the development of language and barter. As favours were given and received, early humans learned that when they could trust one another it benefitted both parties. Reciprocity did not always have to be simultaneous. As more complex relationships developed, common practices became customs, rules and eventually laws. These social expectations came to include folk ideas to do with the common good. But our ancestors also developed taboos, superstitions, the supernatural, and eventually religions and moral reasoning. The ethic of self-sacrifice and care for the less fortunate is a common theme of religions the world over. In short, it seems likely that reciprocal altruism evolved as a social process, a win-win strategy, that potentially allowed everyone to survive and feel safe, even when it was not a zero-sum scenario.

We are constantly reading each other's faces for indications of intention and emotion, although there are cultural differences in how well we are able to read these cues. One experiment in 1978 involved Japanese, British and Italian people being filmed, without sound, expressing different emotions. Later, a different group of Japanese, British and Italian subjects were asked to watch the films and identify the emotions shown. Which nationality was the most accurate in detecting the emotions across all three nationalities? It turned out to be the Japanese who, whilst being the most understated and subtle in expressing their own emotions, showed the most acuity in detecting it in others. The Italians were the opposite, the British somewhere in the middle.

My sentimental grandmother used to say "Smile a while and while you smile another smiles, and soon there will be miles and miles of smiles." Smiling is a universally recognised facial expression that communicates trust between human beings. In other primates, the smile-like exposure of teeth can indicate a threat warning. But among our cousins the chimpanzees it is a sign of submission, and this may well be the same for the human smile: we paradoxically bear our teeth to show one another that we are not a threat and not planning to use them.

Human smiles of course can convey many things: joy, amusement, compassion, empathy, hospitality, patience, indeed even threat, but probably its most common use is that of conveying love, trust and respect to family, friends and strangers alike. Notice how many times you smile at people during the day. If you generally don't smile a lot, then try spending a whole day when you do, and notice the difference in how others respond to you and how your day feels.

Smiling conveys different emotions depending on the social context, culture, and fashion of the times. Too much smiling may be seen as a sign of dishonesty, anger, shyness, embarrassment, or even lack of dignity. Photographs taken in Britain before the 1930s rarely depict anyone smiling because people preferred to maintain a serious demeanour for fear of looking like a 'smiling idiot'.

Go out into the street and, from a discrete vantage point, have a good look at someone you do not know. It could be anyone: a cleaner, a shopkeeper, a young man, an old person. Who are they? What is their personal story? Why are they holding that tall jar? What are they wearing, and how did they come to buy those red plastic boots? Why are they here in this same place as you? Notice their demeanour and how they present themselves, their facial expression, how they move, how their eyes look around at the world, the emotional tone of their behaviour. Try to capture your own feelings in reaction to what you see. What can you infer about them, and what do you imagine they might be thinking and feeling?

You do not actually need to do this of course because you immediately recognise that what I am describing is merely what people do a lot of the time all over the world. Here is my term for it: **Pollocking.** Pollocking is essentially people-watching but it is a far less clumsy term for it.

When I was about seven years old, in the early 1960s, our family lived near Notting Hill Gate in London. Whenever we would leave or return to our house, our next-door neighbour, Mrs Pollock, would be staring out at us from behind her net curtains. She was trying not to be seen but we noticed that she took great interest in our comings and goings. Our family thus coined the verb 'to pollock'. Go to any public place, a restaurant, shopping mall, rambla, or beach and you will find yourself and other people pollocking one another. You only have to walk down any street to notice the fleeting eye-contact between people. Notice other people averting their eyes, and you averting yours. Just look at how much pollocking is going on.

Like other apes, humans are fascinated by one another and spend a lot of time staring at, listening to, and learning about one another. The entertainment industry, internet, and much of the arts serve this deep fascination we have with one another and ourselves. Other people provide us with a useful yardstick with which to compare ourselves, so we should not be surprised that we go to elaborate lengths to consider what image we are presenting to others. The world of fashion and cosmetics caters to this preoccupation. Likewise, we cannot help but notice other people's self-presentation and the information it conveys, so we understandably worry about our own.

The way we present ourselves to others often serves as a shield, guarding us from exposing the vulnerabilities or insecurities we fear others might perceive in us. For example, most people would prefer not to think of themselves as vulnerable or ignorant, so we have a defensive vocabulary of nervous habits that emerge in certain social situations, particularly when we feel shy, uncertain, or out of our depth. Self-presentations can be all too transparent, such as when a young woman feels she has to be the most socially active, self-confident, and even outrageous person that she can be, in order to camouflage her inner feelings of shyness and insecurity. Or the man who treats waiters with contempt because of his wish to be seen as commanding and powerful, rather than the insecure person he fears other people might assume him to be. Perhaps another meaning of psychological maturity therefore is to be consistently our authentic selves, presenting more-or-less the same person in all social situations.

Eavesdropping and pollocking are social and interpersonal taboos of course because, like Mrs Pollock, we don't want to be caught being too interested in other people's business (though again there is some cultural variation in this). Gaining information about someone else might mean that you are planning to take advantage of them. Children are therefore often taught not to pollock other people ('Don't stare'), and told not to listen in to their conversations too obviously, because these behaviours are considered rude, even if children are merely showing the same impulses as their equally nosy elders. Women are pollocked more than men, and not just by men on the lookout for a potential mate, but also by women who are interested in other women's self-presentation.

While pollocking is very common among all primates and seemingly universal among humans, only humans gossip, chat and discuss one another, and they do it an awful lot. The main reason we are so fascinated with one another is that this is how people have long learned about the social world around them, and how they can best survive within it. A farmer in Alberta, an attorney in Delhi, a boat-hand in Vietnam, and a migrant mother in Germany may all be quite different, but they all pollock other people, and often tell others what they have seen in order to make sense of it, and make use of it. We exchange our views and experiences of other people so that we can gauge the reaction of the people we are speaking to. In this way we validate our feelings and opinions by bouncing them off other people, and in the process we learn what others think and feel (sometimes about us). This ensures that people do not stray too far from the norms of the society in which they live.

In this very real sense, we are a socially enmeshed species. Most people unconsciously mimic other people, and also tend to like people who mimic them. We mirror each other's body language and facial expressions, we match the speed and tone of the person we are talking to, and we are affected by the emotional tone of those we are with.

'Social support' has been one of the most widely cited terms in the social sciences, largely because it has been shown to play such an important role in people's wellbeing. Perhaps not surprisingly, it has been found that people with many relationships live longer and have better physical and mental health than those with few such 'social ties'. The research suggests that people's social network enmeshes them in a web of relationships, not necessarily intimate ones, that helps sustain them through good times as well as bad.

Another way of studying social support has been to work out what type of social support is helpful in what sort of situation. There are several forms of social support but the three most important types are *practical* help, *informational* help, and *emotional* help. To take a simple example, moving house is a stressful experience for most people. The support given by a friend might involve their *practical* assistance shifting furniture, providing *information* about where to find a good removals company, or simply being around to talk to about how exhausting it all is.

The support we feel we have from other people keeps us going from day to day. In 1978, George Brown and Tirril Harris published an interview study of 458 mothers living in south London. Eight per cent of these women were found to be depressed and almost all of them had experienced a serious loss or adversity, such as an abusive partner. Brown and Harris showed that mothers were at higher risk of depression if they had three or more children under the age of 14, were unemployed, had lost their mother before they were 11, and lacked a confiding intimate relationship. However, if they did have a confiding intimate relationship it was much less likely that the mothers were depressed.

In other words, relationships can be good or bad for people, and often they are a mixture of both. But when our relationships work well they can help protect us from the slings and arrows of daily life, as well as help us cope with the stress of a major life event.

Now let's look at one or two of our significant limitations.

Conformity and obedience

In the 1930s a Turkish-American psychologist called Muzafer Sherif (1906-1988) put several people into a completely dark room and showed them a small stationary dot of light. If you do this yourself, you will find that the slight movements of your eye muscles causes you to perceive the light to be moving. It is called the autokinetic effect.

While they were in the dark room Sherif repeatedly asked his participants to say out loud one after another how far they thought the light had moved. He found that over time their estimates gradually converged. They were unwittingly conforming to a norm that they had created for themselves as a group.

As any immigrant or rookie will tell you, it helps if you can learn about the cultural norms around you so that you can fit into the local social milieu and negotiate its challenges. Conforming to social expectations and norms is socially (and ultimately biologically) adaptive, because it reduces the risk of being thrown out of the group because you are different. Those who are unwilling to play by the rules, for whatever reason, are in danger of being marginalised, imprisoned, killed, or cast out of the tribe or society. Conformity may seem more common in totalitarian and repressive societies but it is also evident in more egalitarian ones too. In the individualistic West it can be a badge of honour to demonstrate that one is capable of *not* conforming to norms, even though the expression of one's nonconformity may be superficial (clothes and appearance). Most people still conform to the behaviour of the majority (including the prevailing fashions). Relatively few people are consciously prepared to go against social and cultural norms.

Cultural norms of course are changing all the time. For example, in medieval Europe it was quite normal for people to weep openly in public and this was still common in the 18th century, but by the 19th century it came to be seen as a sign of 'womanly weakness'.

The main benefit of conformity is that we are accepted, included, and feel safe within the group, tribe or society. However, the ease of conformity can leave us vulnerable to exploitation by others, and stifle personal growth, leading to a dull, unfulfilling existence. In the interests of conformity, people tend to go along with accepted wisdom, the views of the local majority, and the dictates of authority or leadership figures, even if in the process they risk surrendering their own capacity for reason, the one thing, as Aristotle also noted, that differentiates humans from other animals.

The problem with loyalty to one's own group is that it can lead to suspicion and hostility towards those outside the group, particularly if those outside are perceived as thwarting or in competition with one's own group. This fear and suspicion of the unfamiliar 'other' typifies xenophobia and social discrimination, like racism, nationalism, homophobia, and so on.

Conformity can even lead people to behave in ways that are cruel, disrespectful and unkind, attributes that people generally do not value in themselves. Citizens can only make moral choices if they think about what they are doing, but a lot of the time they fail to do even that, preferring instead to follow an 'authority' figure or the simple dictates of the people around them. The (in)famous 1963 experiment by American social psychologist Stanley Milgram (1933-1984), exploring the limits of human obedience, took place shortly after the trial of the Nazi, Adolf Eichmann, who was responsible for the logistics of the Holocaust. Facing the charge of crimes against humanity, Eichmann's defence was that he had 'merely been following orders'.

In Milgram's disturbing (and frankly unethical) experiment, volunteer research participants were told that they were helping in a study to investigate 'learning'. They were instructed by a white-coated scientist to administer electric shocks to a fellow volunteer participant in another room, whom they could hear but not see, whenever the second participant answered a question incorrectly. In reality, the second participant was one of Milgram's research assistants and no one was getting electric shocks. But two-thirds of the volunteers were prepared to increase the level of shock to potentially lethal doses (it said so on the dial) and continued in this way despite hearing screams of agony from the next room. They did so in order to obey the 'scientist' who merely encouraged them when they resisted with prompts like "The experiment requires you to continue."

As children, we were dependent on powerful figures of benign authority, such as our parents, and we were inclined to do what we were told, trusting our parents to know best. Similarly, in situations of threat or ambiguity, adults often revert or regress to this early attachment behaviour by seeking out figures of comforting authority – doctors, priests, police, and so on. Politicians similarly leverage this symbolic authority because the electorate looks to leaders and authority figures to assume responsibility, providing them with a sense of security and reassurance. Like Milgram's participants, it can feel reassuring to follow someone who appears to have strong convictions about the correct direction of travel.

When times are especially uncertain or threatening people are even more receptive to figures of authority, particularly if they appear to understand the situation and promise to restore order and safety. However, as Naomi Klein has pointed out, rulers can deliberately generate insecurity, such as warning of an 'invasion of migrants', and thereby exploit the resulting public uncertainty by taking advantage of it for their own ends.

As if this were not worrying enough, it seems that people quickly habituate to lying, something that has clear resonance with recent American politics. Cognitive neuroscientist Tali Sharot asked volunteers to lie for their own benefit, at the expense of someone else. At first, there was a strong reaction in their amygdala, a sign of heightened emotion, but over time the reaction faded as the volunteers got used to lying. Lying quickly became an easy habit, and other people equally quickly habituated to it.

Simplifying the world

Our controlled mind, the conscious mind, works with information in a sequential manner, and our capacity for reason is therefore ultimately constrained by how much our working-memory can 'hold in mind'.

In terms of information, the social world is an immensely complicated place and no one can ever understand it all, so we use shortcuts, habits, rules of thumb, generalizations and, as we have seen, distortions, to reduce the amount of information we have to process. In other words, we simplify the world. We categorise information into fewer, bigger and simpler chunks, and create routines for repetitive procedures. While this quickly causes information to become more automatic and assumed, saving us time and effort, simplifying the world runs the risk of glib solutions to complex problems, and leaves us vulnerable to neglecting the intricacies of real-life situations.

Simplifying the world takes many forms. It is simpler to conform to the behaviour and beliefs of the people around us, it is simpler to see the world in binary or dichotomous ways (black and white, all-or-nothing, good or bad etc.), it is simpler to unquestioningly obey figures of authority, it is simpler to maintain (often ignorant and prejudiced) stereotypes, it is simpler to use hunches and rules of thumb (biases and heuristics), it is simpler to deploy habits and routines, and it is simpler to designate some information as simply 'given' or taken on faith. We saw in the last chapter how people often mind-read their partner's thought, feelings and intentions. There is a constant tendency for the mind to package up ideas and experiences and turn them into simpler units. Generalising and drawing conclusions ("comparing past impressions" as Darwin put it), is the first step in making them routine and habitual until (particularly if they recur) they become background, taken-for-granted, *automatic* assumptions. This is enormously useful in terms of efficiency, but again potentially dangerous because of the many biased, redundant, unhelpful, and wrong assumptions that can creep in.

It may have been an urban myth, but there circulated a story of two men wearing hard hats and high visibility jackets who stopped their van in a busy street in central London. They placed red traffic cones in a circle and proceeded to dig a hole in the road. Then they left, leaving the traffic cones and the hole behind them. The story goes that traffic continued to pass around the cones for several weeks before anyone questioned why the cones or the hole were there. Everyone assumed that someone else had authorised the digging of the hole, so everyone went along with it. Many ideas are like this, we just assume they must be true because they are there.

The more familiar an idea, whether or not it is true, the more we are inclined to believe it. A lot of the time we base our decisions on what we intuitively feel is the right or obvious thing to do but, as we have said, this automatic thinking is based on our unconscious taken-for-granted assumptions. We rarely question the memes and cultural assumptions we have imbibed from the social world around us, so our assumptions remain largely invisible to us. We prefer to believe what we would prefer to be true.

Aphorisms, proverbs, rules of thumb, traditions, superstitions, and binary thinking, all help to simplify the world, but often they are insipid, lazy shorthand solutions for living an easy life. We stick with our beliefs mainly because doing so keeps the world consistent and coherent, and this saves us the time and effort of having to alter our mental models. It is far simpler to pass around traffic cones than take the trouble to question why they might be there. In this way, beliefs, assumptions, and memes concerning the nature of the world become established and get passed around between people with enormous ease, embraced as accepted wisdom or articles of faith, rather than critically examined. Accurate knowledge is expensive to produce.

Yet another view of psychological maturity regards it as the ability to see the world in complex ways, rather than in these more simplistic ways of thinking. It is about seeing things as existing within their context, comprising shades of grey, not merely black or white. Complexity arises from asking the questions 'why' and 'how'.

That proverbial apple falling on Newton's head led him to formulate a question. The idea of cause-and-effect, that one thing causes another thing, is present in all languages. It reflects a central organising principle within the human mind, the power generator behind human reason. People feel a sense of discomfort when they are unable to find the cause for something that has happened, and they feel compelled to seek a plausible explanation until one is found, sometimes with enormous persistence (like those air crash investigators). Education is all about providing the language, ideas and skills to enable people to ask critical questions and develop more sophisticated ways of thinking about the world.

Of course, words can be bent to convince others to do and believe all sorts of things, and political leaders know that citizens are more likely to believe what they are being told if it is kept simple. An investigation into US policy in Afghanistan, America's longest war, showed that from the outset US officials conveyed to the American public a very different, far simpler narrative of how the war was progressing compared with what was actually happening on the ground. Suicide bombings in Kabul were presented as an indication that the Taliban were desperate and clearly losing the war. A rise in the number of American troop deaths was portrayed as the US Army 'taking the fight to the people'. Just like skirting those cones in a road, we are inclined to believe what we are told. So Euripides had it absolutely right, it helps to have a shrewd sense of what not to believe.

Superstition

22nd January 2012

I arrive at the frenetic market. It is a crowded muddle of people and vegetable stalls. A woman is standing on the back of a lorry, handing down massive bunches of green bananas to a throng of shoppers.

Everyone is preparing for Tet, the New Year celebrations which will start this evening. Huge yellow chrysanthemums are on sale everywhere. In the congestion of the market, people are edging their motorbikes through the crowd, transporting small trees strapped down on the backseat: blossoming plum trees and small mandarins laden with ripe fruit. Both trees are traditional at this biggest festival of the year. Last night I read that during the four days of Tet nothing is open for business, so I have decided to hunker down somewhere a little more comfortable. The Quang Binh Hotel is not quite as comfortable as I had hoped, but it is cheap, seemingly clean, and has internet.

The people in reception told me that there would be celebrations in the centre of town this evening, including a dragon dance and a countdown to the fireworks at midnight. So, at around ten o'clock I walk into town and eat at a stall near the river.

I smile and bow and point at various pots on the food stall. The woman smiles back with kindness in her eyes and gives me several small noodles dishes, served with salad, chillies, and a dipping sauce. I sit on a blue plastic chair at a blue plastic table. The crowds are thickening and there is noisy excitement in the air. People have brought drums and whistles and I can already smell the acrid smoke of firecrackers.

I pay for the meal and try to find a space near the water's edge, where I can sit and wait for the fireworks to start. The riverbank is already crowded, and people are staring at me with curiosity as I try to settle under a bush. I am not at all what they were expecting to see. The children are unable to resist repeatedly glancing over towards me, but I smile and soon they smile back.

But when the fireworks start, everyone reacts with cheers and laughter and much commentary. Loudspeakers blare out guttural music as an accompaniment to the glittery spectacle against the black night sky. I wonder how this small town has been able to afford such an impressive display.

It as well after half past twelve by the time it all comes to an end, and people start drifting home in the darkness. I walk back through the streets to my hotel and soon begin to see people emerging from their doors holding metal baskets and buckets, placing them on the road in front of their houses. At first I think they must be taking out their rubbish, but then I see that the people are lighting fires in these containers.

Smoke drifts down the street. I walk slowly past an old woman hunched over a metal canister and realize what she is doing, what they are all doing. Later, back in my hotel room, I read more about Tet. I learn that because it was the very first moments of the first day of the new year, the old woman, like everyone else, was feeding joss paper and hell notes, fake money, into her small fire, symbolically passing wealth down to her ancestors and ensuring herself good luck for the coming year. This practice isn't based on religion so much as a Chinese folk custom.

More front doors are being opened and more fires lit. There is smoke everywhere.

We humans are a superstitious lot. This is not pejorative. It is not just pigeons that develop nonsensical rituals in the expectation of a reward. Improbable events occur quite frequently and, perhaps not surprisingly, we are more likely to attribute meaning to them when they happen to us than when they happen to someone else. We are likely to infer that it was *our* thinking, *our* behaviour, or what we were wearing, or carrying etc., that caused it. Much like a pigeon. Human brains, above all, are insatiable meaning-makers and pattern-recognizers, always looking out for connections between events, particularly if those events happen to involve ourselves.

So, for example, research has shown that when something bad happens to us we are inclined to attribute the cause to events outside ourselves, but when the same bad thing happens to someone else we are more inclined to attribute it to something about the person themselves. Once again, just because we conclude something does not necessarily make it true.

People across the world continue to depend upon folklore and superstition to guide their behaviour. For at least the past couple of centuries people in parts of the West have believed that eating cheese before bedtime leads to bad dreams, but there is actually no evidence that this is true. Many people touch wood to give them luck. Friday the 13th is bad luck in many countries, but in Italy it is Friday 17th, and in Spanish-speaking countries it is Tuesday the 13th.

Like pigeons, almost everyone develops personal superstitions based on particular things that have happened in the past and which they continue to do, for luck, or sometimes for fear of tempting fate. Sportspeople carry the same charm they wore during their first big game, cancer patients often wear particular clothes before important meetings with their doctor and, allegedly, the late US senator and would-be president John McCain would carry 31 cents in his pocket at all times, and used to avoid salt shakers that were passed to him but not ones that he had picked up himself. Similarly, as we have said, people with obsessive-compulsive problems develop ritualised patterns of behaviour that must be followed to the letter, lest something awful happen later for which they will be held accountable. The main point is that all beliefs are based on assumptions, and very many of the assumptions we hold are just plain nonsense.

Superstition and taboo are endemic and are all around us. We attach value to an object that once belonged to someone famous, and we avoid owning things or living in places that once belonged to someone wicked and infamous. It may not be rational, but minds draw on information from the assumptive world, preferring not to go to the effort of looking for sound evidence, or having to drag their assumptions up into working-memory so that they can be analysed rationally by the controlled mind. Undoing an habitual assumption takes mental effort so is tiring.

When human beings began thinking in modern ways there was an enormous amount they did not know. There continues to be a great deal that humans do not know, but, taken as a whole, our species' ability to reason, gather evidence, and deploy our ingenuity has come an impressively long way, especially given how recently these model-making abilities came about in our evolutionary history. Even so, people continue to choke on the smoke of superstition the world over, and most people will admit to at least one ritualised behaviour or thought that they perform 'just for luck'. Italians think you are lucky if you hear a cat sneezing.

Religious Beliefs

Mount Kailash in western Tibet is the most holy mountain in the world, revered by Hindus and Buddhists alike. It is an impressive and very unusual-looking mountain, being fairly round and very steep. It also has a great big gash down the middle of its massive sheer rockface, as if someone had begun to cleave the mountain apart. It would be easy to create a plausible story that this mark could only have been made by something as powerful as a god. Not surprisingly therefore, many stories over the centuries have been elaborated about gods having been born there. Human stories, as we have noted, are excellent containers for the storage of ideas because many ideas can be connected and remembered within one story.

If we adopt a natural history perspective, in which human minds emerged from evolved brains and work more-or-less as we have described them, it becomes wholly understandable that modern minds would have thought up religious beliefs somewhere along the way. If modern meaning-making minds developed only 50,000 years ago, or thereabouts, it seems entirely plausible that by 20,000 years ago our ancient ancestors had developed sufficient language and models of the world to include belief systems regarding cause and effect. It is not implausible to imagine these early people discussing, in quite simple terms, how events and the things around them came to be. These embryonic beliefs and customs, whatever they were, would today be regarded as superstitions, taboos, and ultimately futile rituals.

Some of our ancient ancestors, such as the pharaoh Akhenaten who lived 3600 years ago, concluded, correctly as it turns out, that the Sun is the ultimate source of power on Earth. Of course, many people believed in other almost as plausible and equally mysterious aspects of Nature: the stars, the sky, the Moon, thunderstorms, wood nymphs, imaginary spirits, and so on. Astrology is still practised in one form or another in many parts of the world, yet there is not a scrap of evidence that the position of celestial bodies, such as planets and stars, has any influence whatsoever on human behaviour, let alone the characteristics of individual people. Yet, evidence is not remotely persuasive to those who believe.

People tend to be convinced of the veracity of the astrological predictions they have been given because of a well-understood psychological mechanism, called the Barnum Effect. The Barnum Effect is when we recognise something about ourselves from a bland, usually positive, description that also happens to fit with most people's image of themselves: *"You work hard but sometimes feel unappreciated. You itch to see new places and experience new things because you are naturally curious."* Horoscopes are like this, so vague as to render them meaningless.

Supporters of the so-called anti-vax movement, emboldened by their cult-like communities, continue to uphold their beliefs, despite these being rooted in a long-debunked study. They assert that the overwhelming evidence contradicting their stance is merely proof of a conspiracy to suppress the truth. Many 'alternative treatments' for cancer work on this same principle of apparent face validity but without any sound, replicable empirical evidence to support them. Political devotees often display the same in-group faith in their leaders, as do religious fanatics and fundamentalists.

Those early folk beliefs in spirits, ghosts, demons, devils and fairies often entailed helpful social rules that required a degree of *self*-regulation. For example, 'There will be no killing within the tribe because that would anger the spirits of Nature'. Such social rules in turn enabled more effective co-existence, even trust, and much later, the emergence of moral reasoning and later still, law. Similarly, rituals can have the effect of binding communities together, even if they have sometimes involved ruthless sacrifices. So early superstitious beliefs sometimes performed a useful social function. 'God-given' laws and customs have often served to restrain the impulses of the individual in favour of the community at large, helping people to regulate their drives and emotions.

From the earliest times, rulers have co-opted religious zealotry and power and redirected it towards their own ends. Just a hundred years ago most of the Japanese population revered their emperor as a living god and were therefore prepared to die for him. For centuries, European monarchs claimed the *divine* right of kings to rule, and were prepared to sacrifice their subjects in brutal 'holy wars'. These days most people understand that leaders are, for good or bad, just people not gods.

Religions may contain a fossilised conception of human nature, but they retain enormous social power, even in the 2020s, and having an official role in a religion in a poor country can confer real social advantages. In rural Laos and Nepal, for example, the best-fed people you will see are usually the Buddhist monks.

Religions can seem like colossal unassailable edifices of human belief, regarded by the faithful to embody the wishes of their particular god and the ultimate Truth. But in the end they are all products of human thought, handed down through generations by mere people. Religions are belief systems, much like those superstitions and taboos in our pre-history of 20,000 years ago. They developed from the prehistoric need to make sense of existence, death, and Nature, and the need to co-exist with other people according to shared guiding principles.

Roughly two and a half thousand years ago, around 500 BC, people began to consider different models of how society should be run and thought about, and the systems of moral order that they should adopt. Although many other models have since emerged, the influence of these original ideas are still very much with us today. They include Old Testament prophets such as Abraham, ancient Greek philosophers such as Plato and Aristotle, Confucian thought, Hinduism, and Buddhism. Only the Buddha preached non-attachment to things, even to gods, and only the Old Testament was promoting the big idea that, beyond this evidently material world around us, there exists a supreme being or supernatural power. This monotheistic belief is of course the basis of Judaism, Christianity and Islam. Hinduism, by contrast, believes in one and many gods.

If there is a Christian 'message' it is the recognition of a bond between all human beings. This universality proposes the noble aspiration to get along better with one another, to be kind and considerate even to strangers, and to try harder to see things from the other person's point of view. This is the foundation of compassion: love they neighbour, work towards agreement and mutual advantage rather than adversity, and do unto others as you would have them do to you. (Even allowing one's partner to be the person they happen to be, rather than someone that we ideally might want them to be).

This Christian ethic of social compassion is very much the secular humanist point of view too, albeit without the need for Jesus or God. But however noble its moral and ethical directives, they do not make the core beliefs of a religion any truer. Religions reinforce the faith of their followers by requiring them to make sacrifices in order to demonstrate their obedience: dietary and sexual restrictions, long pilgrimages, religious wars, fasting, and heaps of time spent in ritualised praying. Happily, self-flagellation seems to have largely fallen out of fashion, but terrorists still self-sacrifice in order to kill people from another faith or belief system.

Once you have committed effort or other resources towards something, the research shows that you are far more likely to continue to believe in it and, likely as not, you will become even more fervent in your beliefs. Such 'cognitive dissonance' has been thoroughly documented in psychology: "Of course the car I bought is the best one for the price. It is the one I bought after all. I'm not stupid". We believe what we would prefer to be true.

Religious beliefs are often regarded as harmless ancient wisdom, but just because something is old and has been revered for centuries only makes it interesting and worth understanding, but it does not make it true. Everybody in the world assumed the Earth was flat until the early Greeks showed it to be a sphere, yet the idea persisted. That may sound absurd until you realise that a lot of people these days still believe that humans are literally descended from Adam and Eve.

Gods in general have the great advantage of being invisible, all-powerful, all-knowing, and beyond comprehension. They can be whatever we need them to be. In Old Testament religions, God is depicted as male, a supreme divinity who is vastly powerful yet, paradoxically, requires us all to obey and worship him.

Most religions are associated with particular historical figures, and sometimes their mothers, while in Hinduism gods can include husbands, siblings, offspring etc. While some of these prophets may have been visionaries with interesting ideas about how people should behave, there is literally no reliable evidence to conclude that they were divine. Nonetheless, these human representatives and their gods, these symbols of eternity, are often depicted within inspirational stories and idealised as wise attachment figures of benign authority. Just being in their 'presence', whether in a church, a mosque, a temple, or a gurdwara, makes us feel contained and held, safe and connected, particularly when ordinary human relationships fail to provide this for us, or when the events of our lives appear to lack meaning.

Having a god in our life can provide a mental safe-haven in times of difficulty, a metaphorical secure base to which we can return as often as we need to, and re-establish a feeling of safe connection and imaginary guidance. It is no accident that the Christian church has adopted the familiar family terms of early attachment relationships: Holy Father, Holy Mother, Brother John, Sister Clara, and so on. Some research suggests that sudden religious conversions appear to be more common among adults who report having had an insecure relationship with their parents as children.

Confessing is something children must sometimes do in order to learn the moral principle of honesty, but on the whole, loving parents forgive the child and the child feels better for having confessed. Similarly, confessing to a priest helps people reflect on the consequences of their actions, and this of course can be helpful. It encourages self-regulation and self-reflection, taking stock, getting perspective. Religions therefore provide people with the comforting thought that their god is supporting them and keeping them morally wholesome.

Whichever heaven and whatever god we believe in almost always depends upon where we were born and into which religion we were instructed. Relatively few people migrate to another religion. Imagine for a moment that you had been brought up in Mongolia by strict orthodox Tengriist parents. The social world you grew up in, your family and friends, has collectively taught you that Tengriism is the right and only way to think about the big picture of where human beings come from, and what happens when we die. As a good Tengriist, you will have grown up to believe, devoutly, that your existence is sustained by the Eternal Blue Sky, a power far greater and more mysterious and unknowable than the material world of physics and biology, let alone human thought. And if everyone around you thinks it is so, why would you question it?

It is mentally less taxing and keeps life simpler if we believe in the prevailing religion around us, and go along with what we have been told to believe. For most people, survival is hard enough; why would we go to the time and trouble of challenging anything so monumental as the religious beliefs we have been taught? It is far easier to conform to the belief systems of our family and community than to question them, far simpler to pass around traffic cones than to question whether they are really necessary.

But that is not the whole story. Having been indoctrinated since childhood, a person's religious faith can feel fundamental to how they experience the world, like a huge overarching structure within their assumptive world. For many people it is the principal model, the main lens through which they see everything. So, understandably, they are not likely to want to dismantle it any time soon. For them the entire question of their existence has been taken care of by their religion.

Religions demand a leap of faith that atheists are not prepared to make. How can we surrender our minds to faith and superstition when they are the primary thing that distinguishes us from beasts? As the physicist Richard Feynman (1918-1988) is reputed to have said, "I would rather have questions that can't be answered than answers that can't be questioned."

The same is essentially true of every religion. The unknowable is obliterated by faith, leaving nothing to concern ourselves with. In other words, 'don't go there, don't question, just have faith.' After all, only the faithful go to heaven. If you don't know where you come from, it is much simpler to believe that there exist people (or even another life force) that really do know about these things. It is reassuring to believe that there is some bigger purpose and power, particularly if the god in question offers some hope of continued existence after we die.

Faith is reinforced by the pleasure of communion, being at one with other people. The feeling of communion is found in all religions and might be thought of as the act of sharing, or holding things in common, a deeply-felt participation that is sometimes helped along by singing, dancing and rituals (such as Christianity's Holy Communion). This of course can bind communities together in positive ways.

Just as Francis Bacon said, people prefer to believe what they prefer to be true. We find it reassuring to maintain even a tiny hope that there is a heaven to go to when we die, and that our minds go on existing, albeit in a different way. It is a very natural wish to survive, something that Nell (*in Chapter 1*) was unwilling to relinquish. This idea of continuing one's life in heaven is a largely Judeo-Christian-Islamic idea, though many cultures believe that some part of us (e.g. our soul) continues to live after our death. It can be very hard to let that hope go. Reincarnation is an equally implausible variant of the same wish. Imaginative certainly, but massively improbable. However, people buy lottery tickets, not with any expectation that they will win, but in the hope that they just might.

So-called sacred texts purport to explain our existence, but in reality they mystify it by reflecting obsolete concerns and outdated values. They may contain helpful moral guidance, but people the world over devoutly believe that *their* holy book is the final word and that everything else, and everyone else's books, are just so much commentary.

Perhaps, as a good Mongolian Tengriist, you believe that what you have been told is indeed The Truth, how things really are. But is this not just an accident of birth, and that what we end up believing is determined by the culture we happen to have been born into? Children absorb their local religion into their mental models because it is often an important part of the prevailing culture, and one can hardly blame a child for believing what they have been taught.

Morality is not some mystical insight that has been bestowed upon humanity by a god. Rather it derives from the fact that human beings in all cultures, regardless of which religion they practise, have agreed to some common moral principles. Broadly speaking, they all advocate that one should not cheat, kill, harm, disrespect or steal from other people. Instead, one should be honest, protect the vulnerable, respect other people, and (at least implicitly in most religions) avoid controlling or taking advantage of other people. But similarly, secular morality, such as laws and institutions, encourages people to care for those who are vulnerable, like the young, elderly, disabled and sick. It provides rational principles for a fair and well-functioning society, but on the understanding that following these moral imperatives does not require divine insight.

Unlike faith and superstitious beliefs, reason calls upon a higher power than mere human conjecture, accepted wisdom, or personal anecdote. It requires evidence, and sound *reason*able evidence at that. The central rule of science is that all experiments should be repeatable and verifiable by other people. Everyone is invited to repeat the experiment under the same conditions to see if they can replicate what was observed. This open transparency and honesty are the most important ethics in science. It encourages us to believe that if evidence is soundly derived we can feel more confident in the result. In fact, a belief in science and reason is the moral starting point for humanists the world over.

Certain ideas about causes and effects have been broadly verified by science and so perhaps it is '*reason*able' to hold them, even though they must always remain open to being disproved. The belief that life evolved on this planet and that humans are merely one life form, is one such belief but the evidence for it is so monumentally huge and compelling that it is a reasonable belief to hold. Religious beliefs, however, have not been verified in this way and there is no objective evidence that they are true, any of them, despite sometimes having some fine moral aspirations, such as love, care, charity and tolerance for one another.

There is no evidence, for example, that praying makes any difference whatsoever, other than enabling the person praying to feel better (probably from making their assumptions conscious and more coherent, and possibly feeling a bit righteous that they have prayed).

Yes, the world continues to choke on the smoke of superstition and religions. Some people will argue that religions make up the social fabric of our world, do relatively little harm, and are a force for good, even though they have clearly done enormous harm thus far. However, as Richard Dawkins has said, we can value the cultural artefacts that religion has inspired, but there is still the small matter of the truth.

On a good day, religious beliefs bring people together as a community, encouraging them to follow a loving and tolerant morality, and sometimes produces sublime art and music. Religious people and organisations often do valuable, kind and caring work for their fellow humans. The third pillar of Islam, *Zakat,* encourages us to be virtuous and give 2.5 per cent of our income to charity, and who is not moved by Bach's evident devotion when one listens to the transcendental beauty of the St Matthew Passion?

Even so, there is no reason to think that charitably contributing to the community or creating great works of beauty requires a divine calling. It is what human beings are able to do by virtue of their remarkable minds and altruistic intentions.

However, on a bad day, religion has led to massive bloodshed enacted by people who held arrogant convictions about the truth of their particular faith and beliefs. How many deaths in world history have been caused and justified by such blind religious faith and conceited certainty? Of course, there have been secular beliefs, historically quite recent, that are just as guilty of this type of hubris and violence, but religions have a far longer track record. Certainty and faith are the antithesis of scientific thinking.

The imaginative diversity of religious ideas across the world leads me to the inescapable conclusion that all religions are the end-result of model-making minds, and it is little wonder that such mass belief systems developed. In the short fifty-thousand-year history since modern minds came about, these large explanatory frameworks have inspired a great deal of beauty, but not a little horror. Religions quickly established elaborate historical precedents full of mystical imagery and symbolic ritual, but in the end all of them are based on human beliefs that have been handed down from one person to another, indoctrinated into children, and written in books that over time have become venerated as sacred texts and sacred beliefs.

If all this seems like secular fundamentalism, it nonetheless implies no disrespect for you and your beliefs, religious or not. We can discuss and persuade one another, but neither of us need insist that the other person agree with them because we share the species-unique ability to use language to disagree, to reason and argue without the need for physical violence. We can learn from one another and still disagree, and the evidence suggests that the more we have genuine contact with one another, the more likely we will tolerate, respect and trust one another.

Remarkably, there are some ideas that are even more fundamental than religious beliefs in terms of how people model the world. Our species has not yet reconciled itself to the fact that we are made up of two sexes. Women and men are obviously different, but in much the same way that two peas in a pod are different. Men and women have long struggled in their relationship with one another, but, again, if we take a natural history approach we can at least begin to discern the source of the difficulties.

Gender

Soon after I began working with people with cancer, I started meeting couples who were struggling. I particularly remember Ellen and Matt. They had two small children, and Ellen was going through chemotherapy. She told me of her exasperation that her husband was continuing to spend long hours at the office when she needed his help at home with the children. They could financially afford for him not to be working for a few weeks, but Matt insisted on maintaining his demanding work schedule. I invited him to our next session and, while attempting to avoid any trace of blame in my voice, I reflected out loud that he seemed to regard his work as very important to him.

"Of course the family is more important to me," he said, irritated by what he had correctly inferred from my comment. "I love my family. But what Ellen doesn't seem to understand is that in the real world someone still has to make a living and I'm that person. All this stuff," he said, waving his hand as if to indicate the conversation we were having, "is all very important of course, but I still have to live in the real world. I can't just walk off the job."

It dawned on me that many of the men I had met had been thinking in just this way. Their priorities were to do with their own personal aspirations and successes outside the home, from which much of their identity was derived, but these concerns had eclipsed the very real concerns of the people most important to them. For most mothers it was the reverse: their 'real world' was unquestionably the family and their relationships, with paid work usually coming a distant second. How is it that men and women have traditionally thought so differently about their priorities?

In order to better understand how men and women forge and develop relationships with one another, it helps to think about how gendered minds come about. The discussion that follows largely describes traditional heterosexual relationships because they remain the most common form of long-term relationship, but the principles discussed also apply to many other forms of relationship. But first, let us be clear about some terms.

In biology, **sex** is a biological fact. Mammals have two distinct sexes. At birth humans are either a female or male (here we are excluding the roughly one per cent of the population who are born intersex, people who have biological characteristics of both sexes). Foetuses are female by default, unless a gene on the Y chromosome is expressed, thus leading to the development of the male testicles, the testes. During foetal development the testes secrete testosterone and its derivative DHT and these two hormones lead to the masculinisation of the foetus.

Only women can give birth, and only men can provide the seed for the eggs in her ovaries. The behavioural drive towards that end, procreation, is expressed in the pleasure that men and women derive from the sexual act.

That is sex.

Gender is its cultural interpretation. In other words, gender is how masculinity and femininity are imagined and represented by individual people (their assumptions and mental models) and by society at large. When people talk about gender, they are talking about the different ways that people behave in accordance with, or in defiance of, any number of prevailing social beliefs about what is thought to be typically masculine or typically feminine. These beliefs, too often seen as binary (like sex) as opposed to variables, are passed on by the cultural traditions, customs and social expectations that surround a person as they develop.

We each construct our own images and mental models of gender by drawing on the media, institutions (e.g. religion), language, and the relationships we experience as we go through life. All of these are infused with cultural assumptions and social constructions about gender.

Femininity and masculinity have been described as two 'floating signifiers' because everyone has masculine and feminine qualities that find expression at different times and in different contexts. A person's gender is their identification with and expression of masculinity and femininity, and thus a person's gender is entirely unique to themselves. Most men identify with the masculine ideals associated with their particular culture, just as most women identify with the different types of femininity expressed in theirs, but men and women have long shared and borrowed one another's gender qualities, and in many different ways.

These days many people, not only lesbian, gay, bisexual, transsexual, and queer ones, reject the traditional binary notion of gender, where sex and gender are expected to align in specific ways. Instead, they recognise that gender identity is personal, fluid, and can be shaped by a variety of factors, including one's internal sense of self, cultural expectations, and sexual orientation. For some trans people, transitioning (socially, medically, or both) is a way to express and affirm their gender identity in a way that feels authentic to them. But that journey can also be very stressful.

The astonishing fact is that if you were an intelligent creature visiting from another planet, looking down on Earth, you would be forced to conclude that on this planet men display a great deal of contempt for women. In almost all recorded history, men have dominated and controlled the lives of women, and the social world has always represented men as the standard or norm, with women seen as deviations from this default.

The power of men is not even a guilty secret but openly taken for granted, because men maintain their power over women through state and religious institutions that are almost exclusively run by men, and through historical traditions that were made and recorded by men and which are now held to be sacrosanct. In the Islamic Sharia legal code, the testimony of two women is equal to that of one man. And this attitude is hardly unique to Sharia law but remains common in many of the world's other major religions. Timothy, Chapter 2, in the New Testament of the Christian Bible reminds us of the expected position of women:

12: But I suffer not a woman to teach, nor to usurp authority over the man, but to be in silence.

13: For Adam was first formed, then Eve.

St Paul's letter to the Ephesians states that *"The husband is the head of the wife... Just as the church is subject to Christ, so also wives ought to be, in everything, to their husbands"* (Ephesians 5.22-24 NRSV). Simply put, men have been written into history as having primacy.

The evidence for gender inequality and abuse is not hard to find. Before she died, BBC journalist Sue Lloyd-Roberts (1950-2015) documented some of it in her book *War on Women*. In some cultures, she noted, women are still considered property. In Saudi Arabia, women are often treated as if they are mentally defective, needing a male guardian to permit her to leave the house, seek an education, or even undergo medical treatment. Women were not permitted driving licences there until 2018.

It is hardly surprising that domestic violence towards women is so prevalent when some states condone it. Under Nigerian law, it is a husband's legal right to beat his wife "for the purpose of correcting" her, provided it does not cause her grievous bodily harm. UNICEF estimates that in 2024 across the world 230 million women had undergone female genital mutilation, a procedure in which the clitoris is cut away in order to prevent the woman from feeling any sexual pleasure; this is designed to make her more likely to be faithful and obedient. *230 million.*

Rape is endemic across the world but particularly widespread in India where the police often ignore it and very few perpetrators are brought to justice. Conquering armies have long raped the women of the vanquished side, but in the Democratic Republic of the Congo where gang rape is common, it has been estimated that 48 women are raped every hour. Lloyd-Roberts also described estimates of two or three honour killings (always women) taking place every day in Pakistan alone.

Finally, and this is truly chilling, it has been estimated that there are 100 million fewer women in Asia than would be expected, based on normal population statistics. The abortion of female foetuses and female infanticide are thought to account for most of this. What is the source of this contempt that so many men feel towards women, and what sustains this strain of horrific violence within masculinity?

If you were that space-traveller learning about Earth, your superior intelligence would soon lead you to notice that even in personal relationships men seem eager to take what they want from women but are often less inclined to consider, let alone accommodate the woman's needs. In most households across the world, women do most of the caring, cooking and cleaning, and men are mostly happy to be looked after. As a more intelligent being, you would almost certainly see the irony in this, in that most men depend on women a great deal throughout a large proportion of their lives, yet seem to show little recognition or gratitude for this support.

As you look down on Earth your brilliant spatial mind might speculate that men take women for granted because they have always been there, from the very start of their lives (their mother) right through to the end. Midwifery, nursing and end-of-life care services are almost exclusively female. As a space traveller you would find the unfairness of all this very puzzling in view of how interdependent men and women really are. Fish may not need bicycles, but both sexes clearly need one another.

It is not as if this widespread oppression of women always benefits men, despite men's many social advantages. The current state of relations between the sexes is associated with some dismal outcomes for men too. Men make up nearly 80% of suicides, 90% of the homeless population and 95% of the prison population. Men are more likely than women to be addicted to alcohol and other drugs, they have lower life expectancy than women, and they are significantly more likely to die at work and to die by violence. They are also far lonelier on average, and far less likely than women to seek help of any kind.

How can we account for this dismal state of gender affairs? You cannot theorise away biological sex differences as merely reflecting culture, any more than you can theorise away beliefs about gender roles as being biologically determined. Both forces must be at work. Only women are able to bear children, and only men's sperm can fertilise a woman to enable her to become pregnant. Yet power is in the hands of men in almost all societies across the world, and women today still have far fewer opportunities than men, despite there being no logical reason why this should be so... unless perhaps we look at cultural history from a wider natural history perspective.

However, this is not a story of historical inevitability. Look at what has happened in Western democracies over the last 100 years. They have gone from men having almost all the power to women increasingly become leaders, or at least having increasing control over what happens, albeit with still a long way to go. The result has been a feminisation of society and a general lessening of violence and conflict where gender equality has occurred most.

But first, what are the sex differences? Clearly, there are two obvious biological differences: men's larger size on average, and women's fundamental role in species reproduction. Darwin noted that evolutionary pressures are different for males and females when it comes to sexual selection. He observed that males compete with one another for resources, territory and dominance in order to attract mates, and females choose mates on the basis of the likelihood that the male will provide for them and their offspring, and that they have 'good' genes (i.e. they appear strong, dominant etc.). All this results in male-male competition and female choice over mate, with females providing most, if not all, the parental care; a pattern, incidentally, seen in 97% of mammals. Human males, in fact, show an unusually high level of investment in their offspring. Put another way, men have traditionally competed with one another for resources (dominance, status and wealth), and engaged in riskier behaviour, so that they can secure a mate, while women have traditionally competed with one another in their relationships in order to obtain the most genetically fit male and to secure the best prospects for their offspring.

Other than their reproductive equipment and the fact that on average men are roughly 15% larger than women, the two sexes are very similar on almost all physical and psychological variables studied. It is not even that male and female brains are notably different. They are almost identical. Despite decades of scientific research attempting to find reliable differences between the sexes, the few differences that have been discovered have either been trivial or somehow peripheral compared with the huge number of similarities that exist between the sexes. And, anyway, just because a sex difference is "statistically significant" only means that there is a *reliable* difference on average, not that that difference is necessarily large or important.

So we are essentially the same. The average differences *within* each sex are far larger than the average differences *between* the sexes. On almost every variable you look at there are women who can do better (or worse) than at least 95% of all men, and the same is true for men in relation to women. Boys are more likely than girls to engage in 'rough and tumble' play, and girls are more likely to play at being a parent. Men tend to be better at manipulating three-dimensional objects in their minds and are purportedly good at systematising the world around them, but women show more sensitivity to sounds and smells, have better verbal memory, and are better at accurately reading facial expressions and body language. Men are far more likely than women to be violent with one another, while women tend to have more confiding relationships than men.

But what about this tendency of men to be violent, particularly towards women? A United Nations study in 2013 found that men perpetrated 96% of homicides worldwide. Violence remains a nasty symptom of a particularly dysfunctional aspect of masculinity, but it has many social causes so it would be facile to attribute it to masculinity *per se*. However, a natural history perspective may be helpful here too.

As we have said, in our not-too-distant ancestral past, men were expected to hunt and compete for dominance within the social group in order to attract a mate and protect their kin. In fact, until very recently it has almost always been men who have been co-opted to fight wars on behalf of their tribe or country. In cold evolutionary terms, men are more expendable: the survival of females is more important to the propagation of the species because it only takes one man to provide the seed for many women, while one woman can bear only a limited number of babies. In other words, there has been a longstanding social expectation (presumably based on the survival advantage of men's greater average size) that if violence is necessary it will be men who will be required to provide it.

So violence holds an ancient place within traditional masculinity, though that certainly does not make it inevitable. Male aggression may have its origins in antiquity, but it cannot be casually dismissed as being biologically determined because it is plainly evident that not all men are violent, or wish to be. Modern societies no longer require men to be violent other than sometimes to fight wars, though thankfully this is becoming historically far less common. Modern agricultural practices no longer require the violent skills of hunting, even though some men still regard hunting as a mark of their masculinity.

Violence may come from a primitive mind but given the choice most people would prefer to live a life that is physically safe for everyone. Men are perfectly capable of spending an entire life without physically or emotionally harming other people, or at least not intending to. Men can be loving, kind, tender, open, generous, and honourable towards women and one another, and they can be selfless and devoted fathers to their young. Instead of spilling blood or promoting aggression as if this were a virtue, men are capable of using language to negotiate, collaborate, create, and communicate. Most men do not rape other people, and find the idea abhorrent, even if most middle-aged women report having experienced some form of unwanted sexual incursion at some point in their lives. 'Civilised' men are able to regulate and contain their urges.

Some men clearly find this hard to achieve, however, either because they have not yet learned to regulate their drives and emotions, or because they are conforming to gender norms and social conditions around them that have failed to promote more benign ways of communicating. As we have said, gender identification is heavily embedded in the culture that surrounds people as they go through life, so if you grow up with inner city macho gang culture, or have been drawn into some other violent subculture like a terrorist group, violence is more likely to be accepted and expected, and perhaps even killing someone can seem relatively normal and maybe even a badge of honour.

And while it is true that the orbitofrontal cortex, at the very front of the brain, plays a key role in impulse control (and where it has been damaged, impulsive aggressive outbursts and antisocial behaviour are more common), there is no particular reason to think that violent gang members or terrorists lack a functioning prefrontal cortex. Rather, it is the social conditions and cultural beliefs around them that have led them to behave in antisocial ways.

Girls usually grow up internalising a model of femininity from their mother (and other women they see) that emphasises selfless care, duty, and nurturance. She feels a natural continuity with her mother, knowing that there will be a future to their relationship and that she may still have a lot to learn from her. Gradually, though again not inevitably, she adopts the feminine role expectations from the social world around her. The struggle for mothers and daughters seems to be that their strong identification with one another, combined with their superior emotional intelligence and communication skills, often leads them to have highly intense and enmeshed relationships. But that is another story.

While boys and girls happily exist within their own playful world of games and sport, girls are also learning to relate to one another and compete for relationship status. While girls and boys are enjoying solving puzzles and having fun, girls are also developing an interest in people, relationships, and feelings. And while boys and girls are learning the language of doing and creating, girls are also learning a language of caring. They are developing their own relational models and a subtly different vocabulary for expressing themselves.

Toddlers grow up in a dreamy state of emerging consciousness and general wonderment, and it sometimes seems that boys and men are inclined to linger there. In reality, of course, there are as many variations and exceptions among boys as there are with girls. Like girls, baby boys are almost always cared for by a powerful woman, but as a boy you are different from your mother in a fundamental, binary way. She is a female adult, and you are male child. As this difference gradually dawns on you, it becomes a mystery as to what is expected of you. All you know is that you are different from the one person whom you know intimately.

So you look to your father, if there is one, and assume that you are supposed to be like him. But your father may be far less familiar to you. He is bristly, large, and with his deep voice he can sometimes be scary. You observe him and the boys and men around you to learn what is expected of you. As you grow up, you absorb expectations from the way that masculinity is signified within the social and cultural environment you happen to live in, and you grow up anxious whether you will be able to live up to the idealised images of masculinity around you – tough, strong, powerful, stoical, self-assured, independent, determined, respected.

For girls, there is a sense of continuity with their mothers, but for boys there is the anxiety of knowing that they will need to separate from their mother and assume these masculine qualities (or whatever the prevailing models of masculinity around them). No wonder men struggle with so much ambivalence about commitment in their relationships. As they grow up, boys gradually understand that one day they will be expected to **individuate** from, and manage without their mother.

Traditionally, and in most cultures today, masculinity or 'to be a man' means 'standing on your own two feet'. Boys learn that masculinity means being self-sufficient, an individual, separate from other people. Instead of depending on other people, they learn to depend on their physical strength or intellectual reason, and they tend to derive their self-worth through practical, tangible acts. So they reject the feminine parts of themselves in an attempt to live up to the vague, ambiguous expectations around them. They aspire to be independent and autonomous, and scramble to find their place within the pecking order, seeking to earn the respect of other men.

However, striving for this masculine ideal of autonomy and independence often comes at the cost of being unable to manage and engage in intimate relationships. It means keeping a detached and safe emotional distance from other people, and suppressing any vestiges of their own 'feminine side', such as any talk of their needs, emotions and relationships.

So, in becoming a masculine man, it is not only that boys are expected to push away their mother, they often feel compelled to renounce the feminine parts of themselves, qualities that they may have learned from their mother, such as the nurturance and tenderness that they once enjoyed with her when they were a child. In the process, boys learn to devalue what is feminine more generally, because they grow up despising the feminine traits within themselves. By stressing autonomy so much, traditional masculinity means that dependency is seen as dangerous and threatening for men. Femininity, by contrast, is more comfortable with seeing the world as an intricate web of relationships and inter-dependencies.

Young men fear being unmasked as a fraud, someone who has still not completely separated from his mother: a mama's boy, a sissy, a wimp, far from the idealised fantasies they may have woven about masculinity. Women don't have to prove their womanhood, but men often feel they are expected to demonstrate their manhood. Indeed, adult initiation rites and rituals in some cultures require the young man to endure pain, hardship and isolation so as to 'separate the men from the boys'.

If boys feel that they are expected to cast off their need for other people and any feminine parts of themselves, it still remains unclear what *is* expected of them. The confused and tortured form of masculinity that emerges is often a negative response to what men perceive to be 'weak' and feminine, rather than a positive statement about masculinity. It is far easier to present yourself to the world as tough and impenetrable than to allow others even a glimpse of your uncertainty or vulnerability.

The great cost, for both sexes, is that masculine boys often grow up to become careful and even fearful about what they say in relationships. Look around and you will find many more men who are lonely and isolated, especially as they age. If you cut yourself off emotionally, then there's a good chance you will feel alone. This may be why men often end up having few, if any, intimate male friends, and retain a wary suspicion about the power of other men. Male suicide rates are a reflection of this desperate emotional isolation.

So boys grow up to believe that happiness will primarily come from their own individual success and achievements in the 'real world', rather than through their relationships with others. He may compartmentalise his feelings, withdrawing into his own thoughts and fantasies, and his computer screen, but soon his withdrawal is compounded by his female partner's feisty questions about whatever he does manage to articulate.

It is in this repudiation of what is feminine within themselves that we can perhaps detect the source of some of men's fears and hostility towards women. When a woman asks a man to tell her what he is feeling, she is often met with what seems to her to be an obstinate silence. Having split off his feelings and his feminine side, it takes him longer to know what he is feeling, and he struggles to find the words with which to respond. The woman, frustrated by his lack of apparent engagement, presses on with more questions about what he thinks and feels about the situation.

Instead of being receptive and responsive to what she is asking, the man feels (to use American psychologist John Gottman's term) 'flooded' by her emotions and questions, and soon starts to feel that he is the victim of a hostile interrogation, particularly when she is again using that language that he cannot speak or understand. Her impatience and frustration at his emotional incoherence and poor communication skills thus carries the risk of reinforcing it.

Women tend to be better than men at articulating their feelings, but men often experience this skill as the woman being critical, judging and controlling, when this may not have been her intention. So men reciprocate by being controlling, bullying, or hostile. Unable to retaliate with words, he resorts to what power he still has: an intellectual defence perhaps, or anger, a threatening voice, or even violence. Or he simply leaves the room and disengages with what is being talked about.

Men are frequently more dependent on women than anyone would care to admit. He may be only too happy to be organised by women in the domestic arena (and unconsciously even willing to be parented and looked after by a 'bossy woman' just like his mother). However, male dependency and vulnerability can be an unspoken yet volatile incendiary within relationships. Women, understandably, may be more than a little ambivalent about their husband's dependency on her, because she can probably do without another child to look after. And she may even share some of his gender assumptions about manly self-sufficiency and masculine autonomy, and consequently she feels disappointed by his child-like dependency.

Increasingly, however, men are discovering the riches to be derived from a life that is fully engaged with family and other intimate relationships. They may have to learn a new vocabulary of emotions and relationships from the women in their life, especially their partners, though she may or may not have the time or patience to teach him something that she finds so easy and self-evident.

Human culture is anything but fixed and is continuously evolving, but in the realm of sexual politics change is happening in 'Slow Motion' to use the words of Australian-British author Lynne Segal. Historically, conventional gender roles have been the only ones on offer, but they are really no more inevitable than female genital mutilation, forced marriages or rape. The Enlightenment showed us that human beings can exercise choice by virtue of our extraordinary minds that are able to free us from the chains of our biological history. Other animals may engage in violence, rape and domination, but uniquely humans can deploy their prefrontal cortex, working-memory and language to transcend their primitive impulses and imagine a fairer, safer world for everyone.

Progress

I fear that this chapter may have left you despondent, disappointed perhaps that our modern clever minds are not so clever after all in view of the many catastrophic mistakes that humanity has made, and the many biases and blind spots that we all still suffer with. It is hard not to conclude that, for a species uniquely able to think and communicate, we are not very good at it a lot of the time. One only has to look at our recent social history to see that we still have a long way to go.

The greatest evolutionary advantage of our modern-brained way of thinking has been the ability to *reason*: to think creatively whilst being constrained by the laws of cause and effect, logic and evidence, and of course prior knowledge. The arts, and mental fantasy in general, are happily largely free from these constraints, but science takes thinking an important step further by formalising rules that have been designed to ensure the quality of the knowledge obtained – scientific methodology.

We humans may not always be perfect at deploying our capacity for reason, but by working together according to shared social rules, we have created the impressive technology and institutional systems that shape the social and material world around us, for better or worse. And we have finally begun to make sense of our place within the natural world, using evidence and reason, rather than dogma or received wisdom.

Human minds are unique within Nature due to our particularly cognitive form of intelligence and creativity. But this should not of course give us any cause for complacency or hubris. Controlled thinking demands both time and effort, so we often pass by the traffic cones, and go along with convention and conformity, side-stepping the effort and rigor required for thoughtful inquiry and reason. True knowledge – reliable and grounded in defeasible evidence – is costly, requiring substantial time, effort and resources to acquire, whereas mere opinions and ideas are abundant and cheap. Ignorance therefore remains the steepest hill to climb and misinformation the greatest threat to institutions that historically have curated human knowledge, or protected such truths as we have acquired as modern humans, such as universities, libraries, and the law.

Not only do we humans believe what we would prefer to be true, we are susceptible to simple slogans and aphorisms, rather than striving for a more complex understanding based on a wider source of information and ideas, a bigger context. Many of us still follow and obey leaders uncritically, believe implausible conspiracy theories, and conform to what the people around us are saying and doing rather than thinking for ourselves. Too many people are oppressed by their lack of a basic education and ability to think critically.

The world continues to be driven by greed, prejudice, deceit and power, with benefits going to a few at the expense of the many. There are shameful levels of inequality across the world, and the selfish dog-eat-dog, unfettered-capitalism version of 'freedom' is deeply uncivil and deeply unjust.

So, yes, there is a lot to feel disheartened by and an apparently insurmountable gap between how we currently coexist as a species and a fairer, more enlightened world that we know is within our grasp.

However... this bleak picture may itself be only accepted wisdom, for it too is just an assumption or a way of framing the evidence. Perhaps it would be more consilient to say that our species is only now gradually waking up to what is possible and what human thought is capable of. If we take a natural history approach, 50 thousand years only seems long because it has taken 99 per cent of that time for us to emerge from the quagmire of our ignorance and superstition, to fully deploy our extraordinary minds and intelligence.

Thankfully, most adult humans have developed sophisticated skills in self-regulation, and this is just as well because to function in adult society we are required to be able to resist a lot more than marshmallows. 'Civilised behaviour' is predicated on tolerance and respect for other people, playing by rules that are fair, and allowing others a chance to thrive too. People can enjoy fiercely competitive sport on the understanding that everyone is playing by shared rules, and that when conflict occurs, they will be able to deploy language and reason to avoid mutual damage and work toward a resolution that satisfies everyone involved.

Fortunately, having a modern human brain, with its extended working-memory, its big frontal lobes, and the capacity for language, enables us to resist our immediate physical drives and emotional impulses in the interests of collaboration with and respect for other people. From a young age we have learned to defer gratification, maintain our focus on longer-term goals, and thereby mentally control our biological urges. Potty training was just the start. With any luck, we learned to apply reason and self-control so that we could reap greater rewards later.

When the evidence is brought into the light, as Steven Pinker has done in his recent work, the data persuasively shows that humanity can feel optimistic about its future, provided we have not already made the planet uninhabitable, given how much of it is already irreparably damaged. In *The Better Angels of our Nature*, Pinker demonstrates, in characteristic forensic detail, that over recent centuries humanity has become less violent, particularly where there is civil order, lawfulness, better education, and lack of poverty. He attributes the global decline in violence to many factors: more stable societal structures, education and social morality, geographical and social mobility, and mass media, all of which teach tolerance and expose people to other world views and assumptions. But he also points to the emergence of *reason* as a unifying paradigm... as well as a gradual feminisation of society.

Much of this progress he puts down to the Enlightenment's emphasis over the past three hundred years on reason, science, and humanism. Humanity is finally starting to wake up to the fact that collective progress is possible when we use our unique capacity to think and reason for everyone's benefit, and when we control our more primitive drives and impulses in the service of the greater good.

In *Enlightenment Now*, Pinker goes on to list the many ways in which the human condition has vastly improved since the advent of this Enlightened thinking: health, subsistence, wealth, inequality, environment, peace, safety, democracy, equal rights, knowledge, quality of life, and happiness. His argument is that human progress has been largely the result of collaboration rather than adversity, humanistic altruism rather than selfish greed, and evidence, reason, and serious thought, rather than simple solutions based on dogma and superstition.

Human society comprises the symbolic storage of fifty thousand years of modern model-making minds. This cultural memory is reflected in the buildings, technology, art, customs and institutions that we have created as a species, but also in the cultural assumptions that we take for granted and all-too-rarely examine, such as religious and gender beliefs. It is the job of sociologists and anthropologists to shine a light on these prevailing assumptions. However, all of us internalise the cultural norms from the world we happen to have inhabited over the course of our lives, and each of us has the power to question them for ourselves.

●————————————●

Further Reading

Airenti G. (2016) Playing with expectations: a contextual view of humor development. *Frontiers in Psychology*, **7**: doi.org/10.3389/fpsyg.2016.01392

Aries E. (1996) *Men and Women in Interaction: Reconsidering the Differences.* New York: Oxford University Press

Baumeister R. (2010) *Is There Anything Good About Men? How cultures flourish by exploiting men.* Oxford: Oxford University Press

Berlin I. (1996) *The Sense of Reality: Studies in ideas and their history.* London: Pimlico

Brown G, Harris T. (1978) *Social Origins of Depression: A study of psychiatric disorder in women.* London: Tavistock.

Bryant G, Fessler D, Fusaroli R *et al.* (2016) Detecting affiliation in co-laughter across 24 societies. *Proceedings of the National Academy of Sciences*, 113, 4682-4687

Chodorow N. (1978) *The Reproduction of Mothering.* London: University of California Press

Clare A. (1988) *On Men – Masculinity in Crisis.* London: Chatto & Windus

Cohen S, Wills T. (1985) Stress, social support and the buffering hypothesis. *Psychological Bulletin*, 98, 310-357

Dennett DC. (2006) *Breaking the Spell: Religion as a natural phenomenon.* London: Penguin.

Dinnerstein D. (1976) *The Rocking of the Cradle: The Ruling of the World.* New York: Harper and Row

Effron D, Raj M. (2019) Misinformation and morality: encountering fake-news headlines makes them seem less unethical to publish and share. *Psychological Science*, 31, 75-87.

Falk R. (1989) Judgment of coincidences: Mine versus yours. *American Journal of Psychology*, 102, 477-493

Garrett N, Lazzaro S, Ariely D, Sharot T. (2016) The brain adapts to dishonesty. *Nature Neuroscience*, DOI: 10.1038/nn.4426

Gilligan C. (1982) *In a Different Voice: a psychological theory and women's development.* Cambridge, Mass.: Harvard University Press

Gottman J. (2011) *The Science of Trust: Emotional Attunement for Couples.* London: W. W. Norton

Granqvist P, Kirkpatrick L. (2004). Religious conversion and perceived childhood attachment: A meta-analysis. *International Journal for the Psychology of Religion*, 14, 223–250. Cited in Sochos A. (2015) Attachment – beyond interpersonal relationships. *The Psychologist*, 28, 986-988

Hamilton D, Rose T. (1980) Illusory correlation and the maintenance of stereotypic beliefs. *Journal of Personality and Social Psychology*, 39, 832-845

Harari, Y. (2015) *Sapiens: A Brief History of Humankind.* New York: Harper

Klein N. (2008) *The Shock Doctrine: The Rise of Disaster Capitalism.* London: Penguin

Kret M. (2015) Emotional expressions beyond facial muscle actions. A call for studying autonomic signals and their impact on social perception. *Frontiers in Psychology*, 6: doi.org/10.3389/fpsyg.2015.00711

Lehrer J. (2009). The frontal cortex, porn and mirror neurons. *ScienceBlogs*. http://scienceblogs.com/cortex/2009/08/24/porn-and-mirror-neurons

Lloyd-Roberts S. (2016) *The War on Women.* London: Simon & Schuster

Lucca K, Pospisil J, Sommerville J (2018) Fairness informs social decision making in infancy. *PLoS ONE*, 13(2): e0192848. doi.org/10.1371/journal.pone.0192848

Maltby J, Lewis C, Day L. (1999) Religious orientation and psychological well-being: The role of the frequency of personal prayer. *British Journal of Health Psychology*, 4, 363-378

McCarthy M. (2015) Sex differences in the brain. *The Scientist*, Oct 1, 7.

Mirowsky J, Ross C. (1989) *Social Causes of Psychological Distress*. New York: Aldine de Gruyter

Moynihan C. (1998) Theories in healthcare and research: theories of masculinity. *British Medical Journal*, 317, 1072-1075

Pinker S. (2012) *The Better Angels of Our Nature: A History of Violence and Humanity*. London: Penguin

Pinker S. (2018) *Enlightenment Now: The Case for Reason, Science, Humanism, and Progress*. London: Penguin

Searle J. (2010) *Making the Social World: The structure of human civilization*. Oxford: Oxford University Press

Seager M., Barry J. (2019) Positive Masculinity: Including Masculinity as a Valued Aspect of Humanity. In: Barry J., Kingerlee R., Seager M., Sullivan L. (eds) *The Palgrave Handbook of Male Psychology and Mental Health*. Palgrave Macmillan

Segal L. (2007) *Slow Motion: changing masculinities, changing men*. 3rd Edition. London: Palgrave Macmillan

Siedler V. (1989) *Rediscovering masculinity - Reason, Language and Sexuality*. London: Routledge

Wallston B, Alagna S, DeVellis B, DeVellis R. (1983) Social support and physical health. *Health Psychology*, 2, 367-391

Wargo E. (2008) The many lives of superstitions. *Observer* (Association for Psychological Science), 21, 16-24

Wolpert L. (2006). *Six Impossible Things before Breakfast*. London: Faber and Faber

Chapter 10

Life and Death

Waking up
Biophilia
Life and Death

Waking up

If there is one Nature-given thing that we all possess it is a sophisticated model-making mind. Having a mind feels like the most ordinary thing in the world because we each have one, so we tend to take it for granted, yet *everything* we experience depends on us having a mind that does the experiencing. Minds are extraordinary partly because they are such a recent and remarkable development within Nature, and partly because each one of us possesses a mind that is unique to ourselves and that only exists for the short time that we are alive. That is the way it is.

Science continues to pick over the details, but over the past century or two, and particularly the last fifty years, the natural history of the mind has come into clearer focus, even if our self-understanding as a species is still poorly joined up. Although the mind is invisible and changing all the time it has components that fit together and can be described; components like memory, that is stored in potentiated neural pathways, and consciousness, that combines information from our senses with memory stored from our past.

What makes human beings so unusual as a species is our astonishing talent to model the world in consciousness, record it in memory, and thereby reach into the future by predicting it – a mental trick that has made Homo sapiens the overwhelming superpower species on the planet. Other animals are trapped in the present moment, but human beings have large frontal lobes and minds that can reflect, remember, predict, imagine, and plan. Viruses and bacteria remain powerful adversaries, but human cognitive control and creativity have been in the ascendancy these past few centuries.

Our enormous *cognitive* survival advantage as a species appears to have developed astonishingly recently in the context of life on this planet. Just 50 millennia ago our minds began modelling the world in sophisticated new ways. Human ideas have been growing exponentially ever since. It would appear that our species is only very slowly waking up to its amazing potential largely because it is still choking on superstition and ignorance.

The moral responsibility that comes with possessing a mind is surely to use it in service of the common good rather than purely self-interest. And to be guided by rational evidence. Unlike other animals, human beings are able to temper their greed and feel compassion for strangers, but in the end everyone has to find their place along the moral continuum of altruism and selfishness, whether they think about it or not.

Behavioural Modernity may be recent in the big scheme of things, but our practical ingenuity and superior intelligence has come with a hefty price tag. Being able to model the world has led us down many blind alleys, and our failure to control our appetites continues to cause appalling human suffering and unconscionable inequalities across the globe. Ecological vandalism has messed up the ecosystem of our planet, causing environmental disasters, loss of biodiversity, and climate imbalances that threaten to destroy the natural world that we depend upon, make millions of people's lives unbearable, and cause thousands of other species to become extinct. Of the world's ten million species, one million are currently threatened with extinction, mostly as a result of the behaviour of just one species. Humans remain clumsy and ignorant, but mostly we are just greedy.

The price of clever modern minds is not only social and environmental but also personal. Our imaginative minds can summon unique trains of thought to solve complex problems and create works of art, but they can also cause people to suffer miserably from their feral thoughts and associated emotions.

René Descartes (1596-1650) more-or-less said 'I *do* exist because I am having this train of thought'. Impossible as it may seem, my life seems to be made up of many trains of thought and personal experiences, with everything roughly meshing together. Maybe I shouldn't exist, but here we are.

Human existence is characterized by the constant, forward-moving flow of time, whatever the physicists might say is really going on. In other words, our experiences, thoughts, and actions are fleeting and cannot be relived or undone. The human mind lacks a rewind function. Buddhism suggests that it is helpful to accept the impermanence of life, and that change is not only inevitable but intrinsic to every moment, shaping us in ways that continuously transform our sense of reality. Because everything happens just once in the way it does, every moment holds a unique, unrepeatable quality, making life both transient and precious.

Biophilia

As a species, we humans evolved our unusually long childhood so that we would have enough time to prepare for living within the complexities of human culture. In fact, the social and cultural world of modern life is so all-encompassing that it is in danger of blinding us to any other reality. It seems to envelope everything. We are drawn to the stimulation, yet we find ourselves needing to escape from it.

Look around. For most people, human culture is pretty well all they know and think about – non-stop excitement of their senses by human-made images, ideas and information: social media, music, sport, television, traffic, buildings, signs, other people, language, kitchens, cars, shops, schools, and in the news we hear of conflict, pain, and suffering. Not to mention the intensity or loneliness of our relational lives. The mind-brain is required to process a huge amount of information and, as we have seen, all this has mental and emotional consequences.

Walk down a busy city street with its crowds and traffic. It is mentally stressful because our brain has an incessant need to interpret or ignore whatever it perceives through its senses. To process all those signs, noises and faces is a drain on our mental resources. A literally exhausting amount of mind-brain information processing is going on all the time. It seems that human society is destined to become ever more complex and all-embracing, digitally intensified and AI-enhanced. The long journey since the dawn of Behavioural Modernity has led us modern humans to become suffocated by our technological ingenuity and almost entirely detached from our biological past.

Almost, but not quite...

We only have to remind ourselves that humans are just one very interesting and unusual bit of Nature, but a creature that is entirely dependent on the rest of Nature. This is the natural history perspective that I have tried to emphasise throughout this book. As members of an evolved species, we humans are not just drawn *from* Nature, we are drawn *to* Nature. We find it psychologically appealing, calming, and even healing.

Think about all the things we do to satisfy our need for a connection with Nature. It is not only small children who are fascinated by animals (animal names are some of the first words they learn), adults too are besotted with their pets. Everywhere you look you find humans captivated by the beauty and majesty of other animals, and people often feel a powerful connection with them too. Dogs, 'man's best friend', can always be relied upon to be happy to see us, more than can be said for some of our other relationships. The evidence indicates that dogs not only recognise the implications of some spoken words, they also recognise the emotional intonation of the owner's voice, so this really does qualify as an affectional bond or attachment. Cats also seem to love and need us, when in fact they are more likely just enjoying the warmth of our lap and the food we give them, but we don't care because we are ready to go on giving that apparent affection right back. Horse-lovers really do seem to have a weirdly intimate relationship with their horses.

At any rate, having a pet appears to be good for us. The evidence suggests that people who own a pet live longer. One study found that people who own a cat are 30% less likely to have a heart attack, a finding that may be down to repetitive stroking which is potentially stress-reducing, but equally it may be due to the feeling of having 'someone' to love and 'be loved' by. Such inter-species affection is strangely wonderful and even moving when you think about it.

Biophilia, this love of Nature, is not just about other animals of course. People bring flowers into their homes because they are beautiful, and because they manage to soften and warm the atmosphere at the same time. People enjoy tending their gardens if they are lucky enough to have one, though even an indoor plant or a pot on a windowsill will do.

Gardeners revel in cultivating and shaping the lives of plants within their earthy jurisdiction. They enjoy understanding how different species manage within different ecosystems, and what they as gardeners can do to enable their garden to flourish. Just by deadheading some marigolds, enjoying the reek of their woody scent, we feel a tiny part of our connection with Nature. Look at how we titillate our sense of smell with pleasant scents; odours can subtly enhance the ambience if they match our sensibilities at the time.

You don't have to be a naturalist or a gardener to appreciate the beautiful complexity of life on Earth. Just pick up a handful of earth and look at it in detail. Within a small plot of earth we see the persistence of 'weeds', the loosening of the earth by worms, and the voracious appetites of slugs, snails, weevils and larvae. Weevils, incidentally, are small beetles and there are thought to be 97,000 species of them.

Some gardeners even have the pleasure of eating food they have grown themselves. The very act of eating of course reflects both a biological drive and a corresponding source of exquisite sensory pleasure. Eating is almost certainly the most pervasive and simple pleasure known to humankind, but to eat vegetables that one has grown oneself is one of life's simple achievements and a uniquely human experience.

You may not wish to plunge your hands into soil, but there are few more relaxing and restorative pastimes than walking in the countryside. Here we get to breathe in the fresh air of Nature and immerse ourselves in its comfort, admire its beauty, and perhaps give way to contemplation. But time spent in Nature provides far more than just having the time to think. People experience joy in their relationship with Nature's intricacies, its constancy and its unpredictability. We get to listen to the calming sounds of birdsong, feel the Sun on our face, or the rain and the wind. We take pleasure from looking at billowing white clouds and eternal blue skies, vast landscapes of rolling hills and lush forests, mountain air and lakeside pastures.

Fifty-five per cent of humanity now live in cities, and somehow billions of minds manage to negotiate that complexity every day. The majority of people on the planet spend almost all of their time interacting with human culture, the world created by humans, rather than the natural world around them. But given a choice, most people prefer there to be trees on city streets and to be able to enjoy the temporary respite of a park. Cities clearly work best when they enable people to feel safe and comfortable, and when citizens are able to connect with Nature by having access to trees and parks for relaxation and reflection. As if to demonstrate this general idea, Japanese landscape researchers found that people were measurably more relaxed (psychophysiologically less stressed) when staring at a hedge or a vase of flowers, than when they were asked to stare at a concrete wall. And yes, they actually did this experiment.

When the sights, smells and sounds of Nature are all around us, the brash intensity and worries of our daily lives struggle to hold our attention and begin to recede and diminish. Nature opens up space, distance, and time. It helps us gain perspective. As such, 'wilderness therapy' is increasingly used to help troubled urban teenagers explore and reconnect to the natural world and discover their own resources, and without any need of a digital screen.

Stare across a seascape, smell the salty air, and listen to the ever-crashing shoreline. Watch the setting sun. Peer into a fire and observe the embers crackle and glow, just as millions of our hominid ancestors did for hundreds of thousands of years before us. Enjoy the smell of that burning wood, or the fragrance of wet grass. Eat a meal with your hands. Note the contours and angles of your body as you bathe. Relish the exquisite joy of sex when you can. Dance till you drop. We are all allowed to enjoy our senses while we are alive, for life will not go on forever and the party will one day end.

Because we are biological creatures our minds and brains simply feel more at ease when we are surrounded by Nature, or connected to it in some way, for it is truly the ultimate attachment figure, Mother Nature, so why not embrace her? Nature has a mother's enduring constancy and a power beyond imagination. Hurricanes, plagues and droughts remind us of its potential for wrath, violence, and its abandonment of our needs, yet it is also Nature that nurtures us with its abundance. Weeds soon grow up through the cracks of neglected paths, and given enough time a tree may one day emerge. Unlike human lives, Nature is effectively endless, or for as long as this planet still has water.

We are our bodies just as much as we are our minds, and we should look after them while we are alive, by getting enough exercise and eating wisely. Human bodies evolved to be agile athletic machines able to walk long distances. We are naturally nourished by a diet of vegetables, fruit and nuts, and only occasionally meat. Chimps and bonobos, our closest cousins in the wild, eat very little meat largely because it requires so much more energy and expense to acquire. And interestingly that remains true for us humans.

We are able to enjoy our bodies in so many obscure ways. For example, notice the simple pleasure of walking around naked. After all, naturists take off their clothes mainly because it feels good. There is certainly no harm giving it a try, though it is perhaps best if confined to your own home. Or have a massage, close your eyes, and tune into your muscles and nerve endings. Or give one to someone else as a gift.

Biophilia is this sensibility to Nature, and a distinct perspective on our lives. It reconnects us with the simple beauties of the natural world around us, like the quality of the air we breathe. Nature is the one sanctuary that all people share. Biophilia makes sense because, in an unconscious and visceral way, being in Nature feels... well, natural.

Simply living within human culture is intrinsically stressful. Brains cannot help but process all the complex information they are bombarded with. And in response to all that information, our minds cannot avoid activating all the taken-for-granted assumptions and emotional associations that we have developed over our lifetime to make sense of the information. The mental processing and physiological arousal that this entails is stressful and exhausting. Stimulation may be fun but it demands a lot of the mind.

By contrast, we find the natural world relaxing and restorative because our brains are already wired up through deep history to 'expect' the sensory experiences that we perceive. Accordingly, Nature can give us a feeling of pleasure, place, peace and perspective, and of course beauty.

In the end we live out our lives as biological creatures living on a planet with gnats, llamas, and trees, and many other wonderful lifeforms, under the thin atmosphere above our heads that keeps our lonely planet warm, moist and fertile. On a clear night, when the Moon is out, we can stare up at it and contemplate the majesty of the wider Nature that is all around us. This too is a simple pleasure. Consider the beauty of that Moon with its huge influence over life on our planet, the tides of the great oceans and the climate itself. No wonder there have been so many interesting beliefs about its power over us.

Nature is as close to a universal god as we can get – Life fed by the Sun. So obviously we need to nourish and protect it, and curb our greedy impulses to exploit and deplete it. Biophilia is an echo of our ancient natural origins, reminding us to love and care for our planetary home, and consider what other life forms are having to give up in order to satisfy our selfish appetites as a species. Like all other species we depend on Nature, are part of Nature, and our bodies will one day return to Nature.

●————————●

Life and Death

If the rest of Nature is anything to go by, then this is the one and only life that we will ever have. That is a fact of life and death. Once our lives are over we will no longer exist in any meaningful sense. Our physical bodies will decay until they become ash, dust, and earth, and our personhood will be lost forever, even if we manage to leave behind a few artefacts from our existence. The active mental life that personifies each one of us while we are alive is constantly being created and recreated in the pathways between the neurons in our brains. So once the body dies, the brain dies, and along with that, you and me. Every part of us.

Judaism and Christianity imagine us each possessing a soul imbued with immortality. That was a reassuring idea of course when people noticed that everything in Nature eventually dies. It is comforting to imagine that our mental existence and life energy does not end in our death but continues on in some other place. But unfortunately, the 'soul' is just another human idea, and one that leaves no trace for us to examine. It corresponds with nothing else in Nature, any more than angels or ghosts, and serves no purpose other than to provide people with a soothing 'spiritual' narrative. Had he lived now, William of Ockham would have omitted it.

In the end, we each have just one life in this world. We are biopsychosocial creatures with special brains, but when the body or the brain stops working the mind ceases to exist and is lost to oblivion. The eternal 'foreverness' of that idea can be hard to accept so you may prefer to turn away, but in the end all that most of us leave behind are our chattels, and some memories in the minds of the people who remember us.

Yet, for all my dry realism and disdain for the idea of a soul, I am happy to entertain the idea of a 'spirit', if used as a metaphor for how each person has an indefinable personal 'energy' about them, reflecting their particular personality and presence. The Chinese refer to this as *qi*, or *chi*. For me, a person's spirit is the composite of what they stand for, what they think, the way they behave and express themselves, their emotional aura, and how their presence affects other people. So, in this sense, a person's spirit may well carry on after they have died, embodied in the feelings and expressions of the people they have touched and affected during their lives, for good or bad. Human connection leaves an imprint in the minds of everyone involved, and this simple abstract truth can sometimes be a comfort to those left behind.

Whatever the outcome, my patients manage to find their way from one place to another, and for tiny moments during that journey I get to join them for an often intense one-hour appointment, one or two weeks apart. The greatest benefit for *me* in being a therapist, and being entrusted to listen to all those stories, has been to appreciate that almost everyone in their heart is harmless and likeable, or at least wishes to be. Most people have a lot of kindness within them. The few people I have met who struggle in this regard have usually been damaged by other people somewhere along the way. They too are trying to figure out how to make their lives work, what is expected of them and where they fit in, but like the rest of us they sometimes make assumptions that are unhelpful, ill-thought-through, or just plain wrong. And there is no manual for living a life.

Some patients are able to look back at the end of their lives and feel proud of the things they have achieved, but almost everyone learns that simple platitudes sometimes contain solemn truths: you take nothing with you when you die, but you can sometimes leave things behind. Almost regardless of where the trajectory of their illness takes them, most people come to deeply value the time that they have left in this world. They tell me that this new appreciation of life is an insight that they vow to cherish, a lesson they never want to forget. They tell me that any wealth they have acquired resides in the relationships they have had with other people, and not in the material 'stuff' that perhaps they once believed was so important to acquire.

It has been said many times that there is no 'meaning of life' other than the meaning we make of it while we are here alive. Nietzsche's answer to living a life was that "*if you have your own why, you will put up with almost any how.*" That may well be true, even if some of his other views were odious. Viktor Frankl (1905-1997) similarly believed that we should strive for purpose, not pleasure or power. Most people come to see that this is the one and only time they will be alive, and perhaps even realise that after they have gone they will soon be forgotten. If these are facts of Nature, then all the more reason to live life well, find a purpose, be kind to other people, be conscious of the richness of being alive during this short time that we are here in this world, value and enjoy Nature, treasure our relationships, express our love, and hopefully discover our own 'why', even in the simplest of moments.

Perhaps with some of these thoughts in mind, the people I meet in my consulting room mostly end up cordoning off their fears and regrets. They find a way to accept these facts of life and death and move on, choosing to savour and fully engage with their lives, no matter how long or short they turn out to be. We *spend* our lives and then they are gone. It is not worth squandering the time fearing death because whenever it happens it will be nothingness, like a deep uninterrupted sleep or total anaesthesia that goes on forever. No subjectivity, no consciousness, nothing.

So, it is surely far better to make sense of being alive now, for as long as we have, to experience the many joys of connection, love and friendship, creativity, curiosity, music and dancing, to the extent that we can. Now, while that may seem incredibly obvious, it is ideally not a lesson that you would wish to learn at the end of your life, as Nell did. It is more a lesson by which to live your life.

Youth and being in love are like potent drugs. We have to ween ourselves off youth as gracefully as possible, but love in its many forms can keep on growing with different people and in different ways until we die. These days my daughter Zoë is apt to remind me, quite rightly, to check my privilege. I am a Western white man who has spent his life living in relatively safe, rich countries. So, compared with most people in the world, and certainly historically, I have had an extraordinarily lucky and privileged life, one that I have come to enjoy and expect to be there, but one that I do my best never to take for granted.

But as I approach my old age and inevitable death I have come to value, just like Nell and my other patients, things that earlier in my life I had taken for granted: the changing seasons, the beauty and primacy of Nature, the value of relationships and love. Things just don't go on forever and nor do our lives.

Nowadays I see my life as a brief tiny spark in the aeons of time and the vast universe of space, and I see more beauty and consilience in that core belief than in all the fanciful inventions of religion. Simply understanding that, and the fact that our lives are merely a small part of Nature, seems far more plausible and parsimonious than all the gothic and mystical stories that have been woven over the past few millennia. There is something almost miraculous about being alive, and it is little wonder that so many interesting beliefs have come about to make sense of it. Unfortunately, however, miracles don't exist, but life can nonetheless be understood.

Mental life is just one particularly extraordinary part of Nature. This natural history perspective may be less mystical but all the more astounding for its evident truth. Whenever I try to contemplate the beautiful complexity that lies behind the apparent ordinariness of having a mind, or ponder the intriguing phenomenon of human consciousness, I feel a sense of numinous awe. I marvel at the fact that we have minds that allow us to be aware of ourselves being alive, and that they are able to do this by creating and reworking symbolic models that we record in the neural pathways of our brain.

And I find it astonishing to think about where our human consciousness, our moment-to-moment experience of being alive, sits within Nature, and how this came about. Our minds emerge as a speck of Nature within a brain that developed in the body of a species that evolved over a very long time, just one lifeform on this watery planet within a solar system that circles a star that is one among 250 billion stars within our galaxy, which is itself one of more than 200 billion galaxies in the known Universe that began 13.4 billion years ago in a Big Bang.

That thought may make our own place in the cosmos seem bleak, but it also highlights how astonishing it is that we each have a mind at all. Everything ends with death because that is simply how Nature works. Constant replenishment. We all must die, as books must end. A life, a mind, a death. It is only our human minds that worry about this.

Oblivion for eternity may sound scary, but we will never feel it or experience it, and in any event that is just the way it is, and we will all get through it whenever it comes to us. It just means that there is all the more reason to take off our coats now and engage with life as it is, all the more reason to be kind, respectful, and responsible towards our fellow human beings while we are here, so that we can end our lives feeling comfortable with the way we have lived them.

Well, anyway, compared with all the extraordinary things that can happen while we are alive, and even compared with the life of a gnat, death is just not that interesting.

Further Reading

Keniger L, Gaston K, Irvine K, Fuller R. (2013) What are the benefits of interacting with Nature? *International Journal of Environmental Research and Public Health*, 10, 913-935

Nakamura R, Fujii E. (1992). A comparative study of the characteristics of the electroencephalogram when observing a hedge and a concrete block fence. *Journal of the Japanese Institute of Landscape Architects*, 55, 139-144

Wilson EO. (1984) *Biophilia*. Cambridge: Harvard University Press

Wilson EO. (1998) *Consilience*. London: Abacus, Little Brown and Co

Glossary

Amygdala [p. 79] – a small structure in the brain's **limbic system**, critical for detecting and responding to threat, vital to processing emotion, especially fear and anger.

Assumption [p. 109] – a proposition or proposal about the world that is represented symbolically in the mind, and accepted as true. *See* **mental models.**

Assumptive world [p. 113] – the repository for all our **assumptions** and **mental models** and other forms of memory.

Attachment figure [p. 168] – someone whom we identify as the provider of safety and security. Primary attachment figures are usually mothers, but they can be fathers or other carers. *See also* **secure base.**

Automatic mind [p. 136] – mental processes and models used in habitual thoughts and routine behaviour that draws on unconscious procedural memory.

Behavioural Modernity [p. 41] – The past 50,000 years since human beings began using their brains to mentally model and predict the world in complex new ways. Also known as the Great Leap Forward, or the Cognitive Revolution. The genesis of modern minds and human culture.

Biophilia [p. 321] – the hypothesis that humans possess an innate tendency to seek connections with Nature.

Boundaries [p. 173] – limits on someone's (e.g. a child's) behaviour imposed by someone else (e.g. a parent). They provide containment and safety by reducing the uncertainty of a situation and limiting the range of behaviours within which one can operate.

Brain [p. 60] – also known as the **central nervous system**, the information coordinating centre for all sensation, perception, emotion, thought, movement and behaviour.

Cognitive drop-off [p. 50] – Absent mindedness, forgetting what we were doing or intending to do. Working memory fails to maintain a train of thought or mental representation because attention has shifted to new information.

Conformity [p. 279] – behaviours or beliefs that try to fit in with other people. For example, complying with accepted wisdom, the view of the majority, or the general view of people we know.

Conscious – information that we are aware of, as opposed to the **unconscious**, information that we know but are unaware of.

Consciousness – awareness of feeling oneself alive, existing in the present moment, experiencing oneself and the environment.

Controlled mind [p. 136] – mental processing that involves conscious, deliberate planning of action or thought. The controlled mind overrides the **automatic mind** when the automatic mind doesn't know what to do, or when something unexpected happens.

Dissociation [p. 197, 243] – a psychological defence mechanism in which a person disconnects from certain thoughts, feelings, memories, in order to be able to cope with overwhelming change or trauma.

Drives [p. 68] – brain and bodily processes that motivate biological organisms towards a goal, usually long-term. They tend towards pleasure, survival and safety, and away from pain and death.

Emotions [p. 68] – brain and bodily processes that react to the events we experience and work in the interests of our survival. Emotional reactions operate on a physiological, behavioural and cognitive level.

Explicit memory [p. 99] – memory that can be consciously and intentionally recalled, the type of memory that we are broadly familiar with.

Gender [p. 298] – how masculinity and femininity are imagined and represented by individual people and by society at large

Implicit memory/knowledge [p. 99] – memory that is acquired and used unconsciously. Includes know-how (physical, embodied memory) and procedural memory (routines of behaviour).

Individuate [p. 306] – when a child becomes his or her own separate person (as opposed to being entirely dependent on and enmeshed with another person, typically parents).

Lifeworld [p. 186] – Edmund Husserl's term for the background physical and social world around us.

Limbic system [p. 76] – an evolutionarily ancient part of the brain associated mainly with emotions and the formation of new memories

LUCA [p. 29] – Last Universal Common Ancestor. The organism from which all current life is descended. It existed about 3.5 billion years ago.

Mental adjustment to change [p. 190] – the psychological processes of adjusting mental models to new information or situations.

Mental model [p. 109] – a framework of ideas that represents an object or idea.

Mentalisation [p. 165] – the ability to imagine and ascribe thoughts and intentions to other people. The ability to form a **model** of other people's minds, thoughts and intentions.

Model – *See* **Mental model**

Modelling – the act of creating new mental models by thinking thoughts.

Modern minds – *See* **Behavioural Modernity**

Nervous system [p. 60] – the nerve fibres (**neurons**) in the **brain** and those that extend throughout the body. The system that allows us to have senses, feelings, thoughts, emotions, movements and behaviours.

Neural pathways [p. 64] – networks of connected **neurons**.

Neurons [p. 62] – cells in the nervous system responsible for carrying information between and around the **brain** and the body. (The basic unit of nervous processing).

Neuroplasticity [p. 65] – the ability of the **brain** to form and reorganise connections between **neurons** and **neural pathways**.

Neurotransmitter – A chemical, released by a neuron, that transmits signals across a synapse to another neuron, muscle cell, or gland cell, facilitating communication between these cells.

Play, symbolic [p. 162] – activity and communication in which one thing stands for another.

Pollocking [p. 276] – watching or looking at other people.

Qualia [p. 123] – the phenomenal quality of conscious experience e.g. the redness of red, the feeling of wetness. The feeling of what it is like to experience something.

Relational models [p. 172] – assumptions about relationships based on past relationships, especially from childhood. They provide a pattern or template that can sway a person's expectations about relationships later in life.

Repression [p. 243] – a psychological defence mechanism in which the mind unconsciously prevents distressing thoughts, feelings, and memories from being consciously remembered

Secure base [p. 168] – the person, people or place that a person, especially a child, relies upon for safety and security, and to whom they turn when feeling vulnerable.

Self-regulation – the control of drives and emotions by applying mental control.

Sex – (i) [p. 72] a core biological drive and primary genetic imperative to procreate the species, (ii) [p. 298] the two primary biological variants of almost all animals: male and female.

Selective attention – the ability to concentrate on particular things amidst other potentially distracting stimuli.

Social world – the entire human-made world, from geopolitics to individual relationships, all of which makes up human culture.

Synapse [p. 63] – the connection between two **neurons.**

Top-down processing [p. 142] – occurs when what is already known influences what is perceived. Bottom-up processing is when raw data has the greater influence on what we perceive.

Unconscious [p. 99] – knowledge of which we are unaware, implicit memory, as opposed to the **conscious** which is information that we are aware of.

Working-memory [p. 50] – a system of processes that enable the short-term storage and manipulation of thoughts and perceptions. A mental workspace, a bit like RAM in a computer.

Index

Bowlby, John, 171, 256, 257
braille, 61
brain modules, 70, 154, 163
breast, 26, 156, 159, 203, 228, 245
breast-feeding, 159
Brown and Harris study, 279
Buddhism, 183, 290
bullshit detector, 274

C

care, 71, 253, 275, 295, 301, 302
catastrophising, 237
cause and effect, 49, 50, 111, 204,
    219, 284, 295, 309
Chalkley, Jack, 258
change, 16, 20, 78, 178, 184, 189,
    192, 195, 196, 205, 207, 208, 215,
    242
cheat-detection, 44, 160, 271, 273,
    274
child-rearing, 44
Chimp Scale, 36
chimpanzees, 36, 49, 153, 225, 274,
    276, 323
Christianity, 290
Churchill, Winston, 191
citizens, 71, 281, 284, 322
classical conditioning, 101
claustrophobia, 58
clinical psychologists, 221
clinical supervision, 233
cognitive conservatism, 179
cognitive development, 151
cognitive dissonance, 291
cognitive distortions, 234, 239
cognitive drop-off, 50, 145, 179
cognitive revolution, 51
coherence, 117, 129, 139, 187, 199,
    242, 244
collaboration, 41, 45, 311, 312
colour vision, 38
compassion, 80, 87, 168, 257, 275
competition, 271, 280, 302
Completion Tendency, 192, 194, 197,
    243
complexity, 17, 29, 32, 66, 127, 219,
    258, 269, 284, 328
computational, 16, 51, 65, 133, 272

concentration, 102, 103, 106, 136,
    139
conceptual thought, 47
conditioned memory, 101, 145, 238
confabulation, 108
confidence, 71, 82, 169, 170, 178,
    201, 241
confiding support, 207, 279
conformity, 224, 280, 282, 293, 304,
    310
Confucianism, 290
connection, 70, 71, 87, 152, 159, 224,
    275, 292, 326
consciousness, 117, 123, 318
consilience, 327
consistency, 196, 242
conspiracy of silence, 202
contextualisation, 258
continuity, 117, 129, 139, 199
control, 188, 202, 208
controlled thinking, 131, **136**, 187,
    195, 282
conversation, 98
core assumptions, 192
cortisol, 82
counter-transference, 260
couple counselling, 253
covid-19, 114, 183
creativity, 134, 309, 318
Csíkszentmihályi, Mihaly, 81
cultural assumptions, 152, 227, 280,
    283, 312
cultural differences, 37, 275
cultural norms, 280

D

Damasio, Antonio, 85, 115
dancing, 80, 103, 208, 215, 293
Darwin, Charles, 29, 77, 109
Dawkins, Richard, 70, 295
deaf children, 164
defence mechanisms, 196, 243
delayed gratification, 174, 311
dementia, 108
denial, 243
depression, 86, 218, 242, 279
depth perception, 83
Descartes, René, 319

dichotomous thinking, 282
digestive system, 82
digital agility, 61
digital technology, 270
dignity, 202
dinosaurs, 34, 76
disgust, 77, 80, 83, 86
dissociation, 197, 198, 243
distress, 60, 215, 220
distress call, 156
diversity, 270
doctors, 201, 204, 281
dogma, 222, 312
domestic violence, 300
dominance, 272
dreams, 129, 135, **138**, 287
driving, 103
dualism, 5, 15
ducks, 47

E

Earth, 27, 29
eating disorders, 175
eavesdropping, 277
ecological niche, 132
education, 164, 284, 311
Ekman, Paul, 77
emotional analgesia, 219, 242
emotional associations, 96, 101, 105
emotional intelligence, 168, 305
emotion-regulation system, 87
emotions, 60, 69, **76**, 145, 158, 198, 215
empathy, 167, 273
endorphins, 87
Enlightenment, Age of the, 45, 308, 311
epigenetics, 151
ethology, 226
Euripides, 274, 284
evolution, 24, 29, 30, 34, 36, 39, 81, 123, 167, 186, 224, 268, 287, 302
evolutionary psychology, 223
existential, 203
existential awakening, 176
existential isolation, 204
expectations, 193, 206, 215, 233, 255, 271

explicit memory, 110, 114
Explicit memory, **99**
extinctions, 32, 33
eye-contact, 277
eyes, 26, 32, 37, 38, 104, 125, 130, 151, 154, 273, 276

F

facial expression, 276
Fairbairn, Ronald, 225
fairness, 274
falling asleep, 127
fame, 86
fantasy, 72, 74, 134, 256, 325
fashion, 84, 277
fear, 59, 82, 235, 243
fear of the unknown, 83, 188, 189, 208, 280
feelings, 84
femininity, 298, 305
feminisation, 311
Feynman, Richard, 293
fire, 39
flashbacks, 197
flatworms, 32
floating signifiers, 299
flow, 81
foraging, 40
formulation, 11, 258
Foucault, Michel, 217
free recall memory, 116
free will, 145
Freud, Sigmund, 100, 222, 224
frontal cortex, 66

G

galaxies, 27, 328
gay men, 74
gender, 298
generative modelling, 128
genes, 30, 33, 69, 72, 74, 151, 224, 302
Genesis, 43
genetic diversity, 33
Gilbert, Paul, 86
gnats, 21, 23, 25, 60, 324

goals, 60, 70, 84, 134, 143, 144, 174, 200, 242, 258
gods, 106, 288, 290, 291, 292
Gombrich, EH, 206
gossip, 278
Gottman, John, 308
Great Apes, 35
guilt, 73, 78, 80, 189, 218
gut feelings, 85, 138, 195, 274

H

habits, 136, 216, 271, 282
habituation, 104
Halo Effect, 141
hand axe, 40
hand-eye co-ordination, 38
hands, 37, 61
Harlow, Harry, 226
harmony, 189
hearing, 26, 62, 273
Hebb, Donald, 64
Hinduism, 290
history, 22, 106, 227, 296, 299, 302
Hominids, 36
Homo sapiens, 36, 39, 62
hope, 82, 201, 242, 294
hopelessness, 86, 236, 241
Horowitz, Michael, 192
humanism, 291, 311
humiliation, 84
humour, 206
hunting, 304
hunting and gathering, 40
Husserl, Edmund, 186

I

identity, 74, 166, 202, 297
illusions, 132, 142, 205
illusory correlation, 143
imagination, 16, 134, 162, 206
impermanence, 183
implicit memory, 99, 100, 116, 137, 140
imprinting, 169
impulse control, 66, 87, 176, 304
individuation, 306
inequalities, 75, 233, 310, 312, 318

information, 95, 98
information processing, 63, 65, 95, 320
injustice, 274
inner world, 14, 18, 94, 166
insight, 138, 190
insomnia, 219
instincts, 19, 42, 69, 82, 154, 169
intelligence, 111, 135, 138, 271, 309
intentionality, 133, 143
internal working models, 171
intuition, 85, 135, 138, 139
Islam, 290

J

James, William, 93, 104, 125
jokes, 205
joy, 77, **80**, 86, 215, 276, 322, 327
Judaism, 290
Jurassic period, 76

K

Kahneman, Daniel, 142
Kant, Immanuel, 13
Kierkegaard, Søren, 185
Klein, Melanie, 225
Klein, Naomi, 281
know-how, 67, 103, 157, 187
Konner, Melvin, 153, 160

L

language, 13, 41, 48, 133, 160, 162, 296, 304, 311
language development, 162
languages, 46
laughter, 273
laws, 76, 88, 152, 289
leaders, 162, 280, 284, 290, 310
LeDoux, Joseph, 79
lesbian women, 74
Lewin, Kurt, 186
life trajectory, 199
limbic system, 76, 80, 176
listening, 137
Locke, John, 151, 153

P

pain receptors, 62, 68
pair bonding, 177
paleobiologists, 76
panic attacks, 58, 78, 235, 243, 245, 246
parents, 71, 96, 151, 153, 154, 158, 161, 163, 165, 167, 172, 175, 201, 248, 281, 292
parsimony, 17, 133, 328
Pavlov, Ivan, 101
peek-a-boo, 158
perceptual system, 273
personal control, 202
personal growth, 204, 208
pets, 320
phenomenology, 13
phonological loop, 50
Piaget, Jean, 138, 150, 155, 191
pigeons, 237, 239
Pinker, Steven, 47, 311
pituitary gland, 154
planning, 139, 144, 242
Plato, 290
play, 47, 134, 157, **161**, 164, 166, 179
playing the piano, 67, 103
poetry, 215
pollocking, 276
pornography, 72
post-traumatic stress reactions, 197
potentiation, 64
power, 86, 299, 310
Power, Threat and Meaning framework, 232
praying, 207, 295
prejudice, 143, 233, 282, 310
pride, 80, 205
priming, 104
procedural memory, **103**, 136, 138, 187
propositional representation, 110
psyche, 15, 225
psychiatric interventions, 218
psychiatry, 217
psychodynamic theory, 110, 197, 214, 222, 225, 227, 259
psychological maturity, 177, 277, 284

psychological therapy, 207, 215, 222, 257
psychology, 12, 104, 111, **221**, 222, 223, 291
psychopaths, 168
purpose, 203

Q

qualia, 123, 131

R

race, 37
racism, 84
reason, 17, 134, 280, 287, 295, 296, 309, 311
reciprocal altruism, 72, 275
recognition memory, 116
reflexivity, 131, 208, 254, 261
reframing, 78
reincarnation, 294
relational models, **171**, 177, 201, 226, 248, 305
religion, 42, 73, 95, 203, 275
replication, 29
representation, 10, 43, 48, 110, 112, 125, 126, 130
repression, 198, 222, 224, 243
reptiles, 34
resource-seeking system, 86
Ridley, Matt, 43
risk, 176, 188, 239, 302
role-play games, 161
Romanian orphans, 151
routines, 103, 136, 216, 271, 283
ruminations, 203, 214, 239
Rutherford, Ernest, 12, 13, 17, 269

S

sadness, 80, 81, 218, 240
science, 18, 27, 47, 222, 295, 311, 317
scientists, 135
secondary emotions, 80
secure attachment, 253
secure base, 168, 169, 292

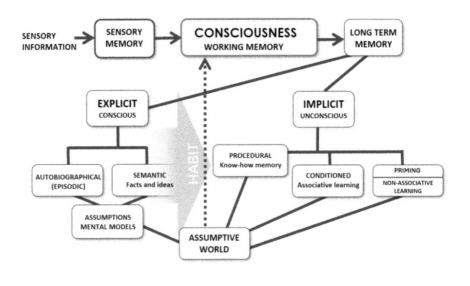

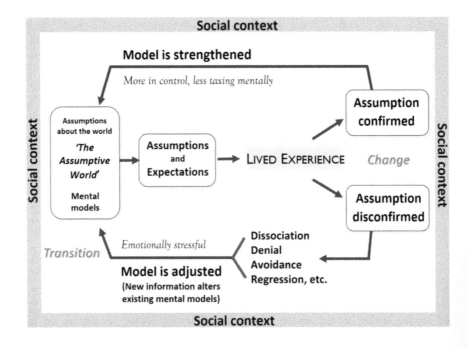

Getting any form of attention for a book like this is not easy.

If you enjoyed this book, please submit a review and recommend it to others. Asking for it at your local library may encourage them to stock it. If you didn't enjoy it, well... I'm sorry!

JB

Cancer in Context

"Sensitivity and knowledge
in perfect balance"

Irma Kurtz
Writer and Broadcaster

"Sensible, humane and
sophisticated"

Professor David Spiegel
Stanford University

"Generous doses of
compassion and sensitivity"

The Psychologist

"A reflective, informed and
empathic book"

Psycho-Oncology

About the Author

Dr James Brennan has been a clinical psychologist for over forty years, supporting a wide range of medically ill patients, especially those with cancer. He trained at the Institute of Psychiatry in London, and subsequently taught medical students and doctoral clinical psychology trainees for most of his career. While at the University of Bristol's Department of Palliative Medicine he authored influential journal papers and lectured internationally in the field of cancer and palliative care. His 2004 book *Cancer in Context* (Oxford University Press) received accolades in many academic and clinical journals and has been reprinted four times.

He lives and works in Bristol, UK

MODERNITY
PRESS

www.ingramcontent.com/pod-product-compliance
Ingram Content Group UK Ltd.
Pitfield, Milton Keynes, MK11 3LW, UK
UKHW021927170325
456376UK00003B/86